Great Masterpieces of World Art

Great Masterpieces of World Art

D. M. Field

Optimum Books

This edition published by Optimum Books 1979
Prepared by
The Hamlyn Publishing Group Limited
London   New York   Sydney   Toronto
Astronaut House, Hounslow Road
Feltham, Middlesex
England

ISBN 0 600 36363 5

Filmset by Photocomp Ltd, Birmingham, England

Printed in Italy

Contents

Primitive and Pre-Columbian Art

Man has been making pictures since a far distant time when much of the earth was still covered by ice. Prehistoric paintings, some of them amazingly well preserved, and fragments of pictures or carvings have been found in many parts, but the best known are the cave paintings of southern France and northern Spain. Twenty thousand years ago the earth was a grim place, very cold and dry, and man was a simple hunter, whose whole life revolved around the search for game. Fortunately, such animals as mammoth, bison, wild horses and various kinds of deer were plentiful, and those animals are the most characteristic subjects of Paleolithic (Old Stone Age) art. European examples are painted or engraved in the rock, sometimes both, though fragments of small carvings, in horn or stone, have also been found. Similar images have been found in northern Africa, in some parts of the western United States, in various Pacific islands, in Australia, and elsewhere, but the date is not always the same. Some, in fact, are comparatively modern, for art is governed not by time but by cultural development. Ever since Europeans set out on voyages of discovery in the 15th century, they have come across

other, simpler cultures, some of them long dead, others still flourishing. In western America, for example, they found people living in conditions similar to their own ancestors in Europe in the Old Stone Age, obtaining their food by hunting. A thousand miles to the south, they found settled communities of farmers, while in Mexico there was a civilization which in some respects (though not in others) was as advanced as their own. When the first European settlers went to Australia they found the Aborigines living in a Stone Age culture, and for a time the two cultures existed side by side. In Africa too, 19th-century explorers found people living the nomadic hunter's life of Stone Age Europe.

The first discoverers of primitive art were not very interested in it. They regarded it without question as inferior to the art of their own sophisticated civilization, and as of no greater artistic significance than the scrawls of a child. In the 19th century, attitudes were changing as man became more concerned with his own early history. Prehistoric paintings, the most direct messages our ancestors have left us, became relevant to the study of man and began to seem

artistically interesting in their own right. The first museums of primitive art were founded, and gradually people began to ask if primitive art was not as great an achievement as their own. The more unusual of its forms, especially the art of the Pacific islanders and of black Africa, became not only objects of admiration but also powerful influences on modern artists: Picasso, for example, was absorbed by African art, as many of his works demonstrate.

Interest in prehistoric and primitive art was sharply stimulated by the discovery, little more than one hundred years ago, of the cave and rock paintings of southern France and northern Spain. These paintings were mostly found deep inside the caves, farther from the entrance than the area where the cave dwellers lived and often in places hard to reach. These places were probably sanctuaries of a sort, and as the pictures are mostly of the type of animals that were hunted for food, they were probably meant to assist the hunt in

Opposite:
Animals drawn in charcoal and red ochre in the caves of Lascaux between 12,000 and 15,000 years ago.

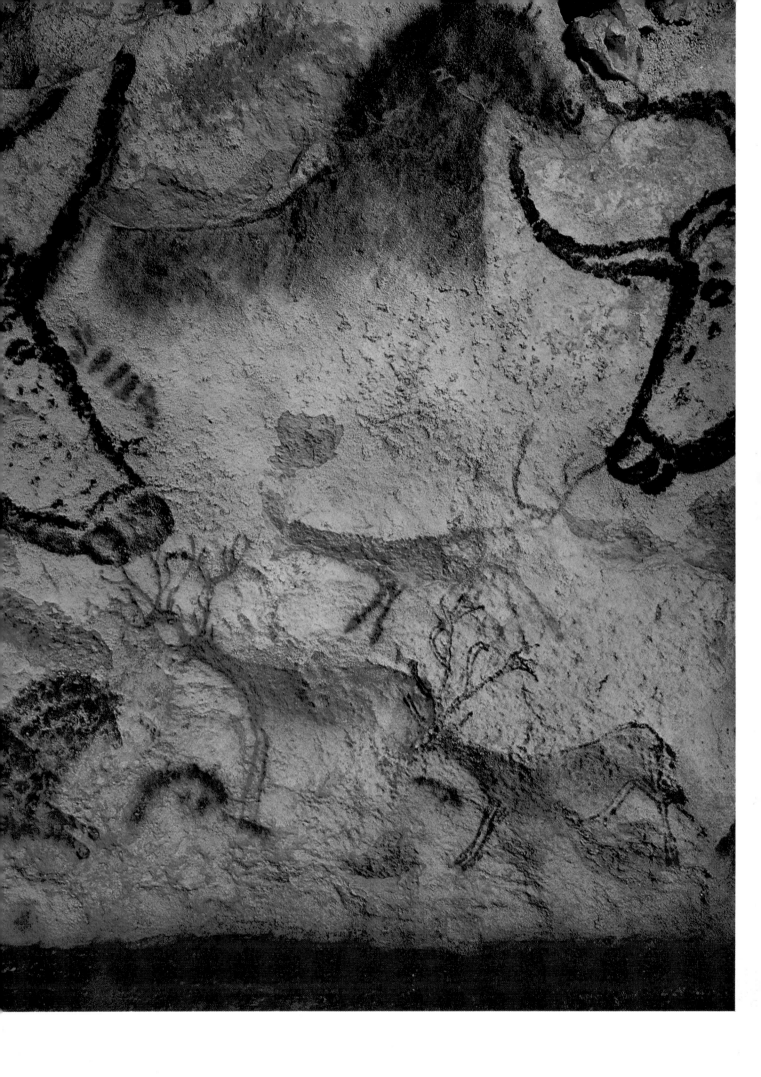

some more or less magical way. A representation of hunters killing a bison was probably meant to bring about that event, rather in the way that sticking a pin into a wax effigy is supposed to bring ill health or death to an enemy. The animals are represented in a vividly naturalistic, or realistic, manner, to make them appear as lifelike as possible.

In hunting scenes, it is noticeable that the animal hunted is portrayed in a much more realistic manner than the human hunters, who appear as stick-like figures that look as though they have been drawn by a small child. The artist, or artists, were intent on the animal – their food and livelihood – and not concerned with the men, who could therefore be indicated in a stylized or symbolic way. It may be, too, that it was considered unlucky to make a realistic representation of a human being, perhaps (as in parts of Africa) because he would thereby lose his soul or identity or because he would become a prey to his enemies in the same way that the hunted animal became the prey of its enemies by the very act of being represented.

The caves of Altamira, in Santander province in northern Spain, were discovered in 1868, but it was not until eleven years later that an observant girl of twelve noticed the animals painted on the walls and roof. The main cave is about 300 metres in length, and its most interesting feature is a single, vast painting some 15

Below:
The head of a musk ox (nose bottom left, horns centre top). This is an early image from Altamira, drawn with the fingers in wet clay.

8

Above:
The 'Venus of Laussel', one of the
earliest female nudes in art, carved
before 10,000 BC. The heavy breasts and
hips show that this was some kind of
fertility figure. Musée d'Aquitaine,
Bordeaux.

metres long. About twenty different species of animal are represented, some running, some falling wounded, some held at bay by hunters. Some individual animals are as much as two metres long, and are incised and painted in rich dull reds, yellows and browns. The rough forms and projections of the natural rock have been skilfully used to give a three-dimensional effect, almost as if the subjects were carved in relief.

The treasures of Lascaux, in the Dordogne, were discovered much more recently (in 1940), but in a similar accidental way. Some boys playing in the area lost their dog down a hole. To get the animal out again, they enlarged the hole, and thus uncovered the most remarkable of all sites of prehistoric art. In a series of galleries and chambers are paintings and engravings showing successive changes in style, but all of extraordinarily high quality. Later images are often superimposed on earlier ones. The animals are represented in a variety of colours, mostly reds, yellows and black. At one time they were open to public view, but like many other prehistoric caves, they have been closed in order to preserve the masterpieces inside them, which were in danger of deterioration.

Many rock paintings have also been found in eastern Spain. Here the style is rather different. They are often group compositions rather than single representations, and include deer, boars and horses painted in flat silhouette, with human figures more often obviously such. Less impressive than the great beasts of Altamira and Lascaux, the pictures are livelier, with many hunting scenes, and are mainly of a somewhat later date. (They are dated between 6000 and 2000 BC, as opposed to those of Lascaux and Altamira, which are dated to around 10,000 BC and 20,000 BC respectively.)

Some small Paleolithic sculptures have been found, of which the most famous is probably the 'Venus of Laussel' (page 9), which is one of the earliest, if not *the* earliest, representations of the sculptor's favourite subject, a nude woman. (The figure dates from around 15,000 to 10,000 BC.) She is not actually beautiful in any modern sense, but in the Stone Age, and among most primitive cultures, cosmetic beauty was of little interest compared with fertility. The large and ponderous breasts, the generously accommodating hips, which are emphasized by the artist's lack of interest in head or hands, suggest that this was indeed some kind of fertility object.

The end of the Ice Age (*c.* 10,000 BC) brought easier conditions for man but little development of his art. The intensely realistic art of Lascaux gradually disappeared, giving way to more stylized representations of animals and to forms of abstract art. In the Mesolithic, or Middle Stone Age, the most characteristic form of art was the painting of small rocks or pebbles with geometric patterns in red ochre. These enigmatic little objects undoubtedly had some social significance, and perhaps represented human beings, but their precise purpose remains a mystery.

The New Stone Age, beginning roughly 10,000 years ago, brought enormous, though gradual, changes. Man ceased to be a hunter roaming the land in search of game and sheltering in caves as he followed the herds. He became a farmer (around 2000 BC in Europe, much earlier in the Middle East), sowing and reaping crops, keeping domestic animals, and living in settled, permanent communities. His numbers increased, he learned to specialize, to make better tools from stone and pots from clay; he even had time, now and then, to forget the pressing tasks of everyday life and to relax. He wondered why the rain fell, why the sun shone, and in particular why no rain fell or no sun shone when they were needed to ripen the harvest. He came to the conclusion that supernatural agencies – gods or spirits – were at work. In place of the simple magic of his forbears, he gained a form of religion. This awareness of the spiritual nature of his world, the new interest in emotions and ideas instead of merely the immediate facts of nature, produced corresponding changes in his art, which became more abstract than the animals of Lascaux and was increasingly expressed in objects which represented the spiritual forces in the world around him.

He also became an architect, of a kind. He erected huge stones to mark burial grounds and, even more impressively, vast constructions of the type known as a *dolmen*, of which Stonehenge in England is the most famous example (though Stonehenge dates from the very end of the Neolithic period).

The most rewarding form of art surviving from the New Stone Age is pottery. Although it varies according to region, Stone Age pottery has many common characteristics. Its decoration is nearly always geometric, and the ware frequently imitates earlier types of container made of wood or reeds. Sometimes a spiral effect is retained from the way the pot was made (by hand) by coiling the clay – the potter's wheel had not yet been invented. In Egypt and the Near East, the home of the finest Neolithic pottery, there developed from early abstract patterns of lines elaborate designs which obviously have a representational character, although it is not always quite certain what the subjects are; they were probably connected with some kind of religious ritual. The beaker from Susa (opposite), made somewhere around 4000 BC, shows an intermediate stage of decoration between realistic and abstract. An ibex is still quite recognizable, though stylized. It is easy to imagine that the next stage would be a purely geometric design of a large double circle surmounting two triangles.

It is a curious and perhaps comforting fact, confirming the essential unity of the human race, that strikingly similar forms of art are produced by cultures at a similar stage of development in widely separated parts of the world, where there can be no serious question of the one influencing the other. The type of geometric designs characteristic of the Neolithic period can be found in pre-Columbian pottery, North American Indian textiles, Papuan totems, and African masks. Although we have tended on the whole to underestimate the mobility of prehistoric peoples, it is quite clear that there are some principles of form and decoration which are universal.

Left:
Beaker from Susa, 25 cm high, 4th
millennium BC. Musée du Louvre, Paris.

11

In modern Africa, examples of primitive art corresponding to the various periods of prehistoric art in Europe and elsewhere can be found. The Bushmen of the far south-west, when discovered in the 19th century, still lived the life of nomadic hunters, roving the sparse plains in search of game, with no permanent homes and the most rudimentary forms of social organization. They painted pictures of hunters and animals markedly similar in style to the prehistoric rock paintings of eastern Spain. Among the Negro peoples of West Africa, a later stage of development existed. The people there were farmers and fishermen, living in settled communities. Their religion, something like that of the early Romans, imbued everything – objects like trees, places like watering holes, as well as living creatures – with a soul or spirit. West African art was largely concerned with expressing these spiritual forces and powers, and endeavoured to represent the spiritual essence of things in concrete form, usually sculpture. These African figures have great power and impact and are often downright frightening – effects which could only be achieved through the intense conviction of the artist. For in this strange world of mysterious spirit forces there was no clear distinction between what was real and unreal, and the works of African sculpture were not intended merely as representations of a certain force or idea: they *were* that force. Carved figures and masks had a religious purpose: they were the resting places of spirits, of gods or ancestors, who could be called upon for assistance in times of difficulty.

Left:
West African carved camwood figure, about 1900. It was probably a 'good-luck' god and therefore an important feature of its village. The hands show European influence. Private collection.

Right:
Yoruba painted wooden head, about 28 cm high, from Nigeria. Museum of Primitive Art, New York.

In much of Africa life was affected, even dominated, by secret societies, in which a band of men (sometimes women) performed secret rites to bring about some desired end. These societies were not always, or not primarily, religious, though lines cannot be drawn between religious, social and economic concerns in 19th-century Africa as easily as they can in, for example, modern Europe. Their chief purpose in some parts was to superintend the elaborate initiation ceremonies which prefaced the admission of young men or women to adult membership of society. These ceremonies were conducted under the influence of ancestor or other spirits, represented in a more or less symbolic way by masks and carvings. The sculptors who made these objects went through a long apprenticeship, learning the traditional forms which could not be altered without incurring the anger of the leaders of the people. In this sense, African art was therefore highly conservative. However, not every village had its resident sculptor. Among the Yoruba in Nigeria, the fame of certain sculptors was known over a wide area. People would travel long distances in order to get masks or cult objects made by the hand of a famous master, and modern experts can detect the hand of certain African sculptors by their style just as we can distinguish between, say, a

Left:
The bronzes of Benin are perhaps the most famous and most sophisticated examples of African art. This head of a queen probably dates from the 16th century. British Museum, London.

Van Dyck and a Rembrandt. Such men became semi-priestly figures because of the powers they could create in their work; they used specially consecrated tools, and were regarded as channels of communication with the mysterious supernatural forces at work in the world.

Most African sculpture was of wood, often softwood, and as a result it has not lasted well. But from a very early date, other materials were also used. The famous Nok culture of eastern Nigeria produced heads and small figures in very skilfully worked terracotta; they are almost the earliest known works of African art – around 2,000 years old (some authorities claim a beginning of about 900 BC) – and among the most attractive. Even better known are the bronzes of Ife and Benin in western Nigeria, centres of rich and powerful kingdoms a thousand years ago. When Benin, for long in decline, was finally taken over by the British towards the end of the 19th century, large numbers of these bronzes suddenly appeared in Europe, and rapidly became collectors' items. Most people were astonished at their perfection and supposed this to be due to some outside influence (probably Portuguese, since the Portuguese had been

Above:
A painted wood carving of a bird by a sculptor of the Senufo people, West Africa. Staatliches Museum für Volkerkunde, Munich.

Left:
Terracotta head of the Nok culture, 2nd or 1st century BC. British Museum, London.

13

in contact with Benin early in the 16th century), thinking that the Africans were not capable of executing such perfect works of art without any external stimuli. The Portuguese hypothesis was soon exploded, although more recently it has been suggested that Benin bronzes are an elaboration of influences derived from classical Europe, at a time when there were close links between Europe and Africa.

The primitive art of Oceania – a convenient term for the vast area stretching from Indonesia to Easter Island and from Hawaii to Australia and New Zealand – assumes an enormous variety of forms, and is the manifestation of many rich and varied cultures. To generalize about so huge a region is difficult, but there are certain common cultural characteristics. The various peoples have different racial origins, the Polynesians being mainly Caucasoid, the Indonesians mainly Mongoloid, and are descended from a series of immigrant waves moving into the area from Asia. Most Oceanic cultures were comparatively unaffected by alien influences, and certainly less so than in Africa, but over the centuries there was a good deal of movement between the various islands (exactly how this movement took place is the subject of a good deal of argument today), resulting in a confusing interchange of cultural ideas and forms of art. Nevertheless, it is a little artificial to link the whole region through its common elements, which are actually few.

The people lived by fishing and farming, though the Australian Aborigines, for example, belonged to the earlier cultural stage of hunting and gathering food, and in spite of their maritime mobility, they lived basically in settled communities. Before Europeans entered the region in the 18th century, metal was unknown in most places, and tools were made of stone or shell, with wooden handles (some also used fish bone and even the teeth of rats). Art was no less important than in Africa, and similar motives lay behind much of it – ancestor worship and belief in spirits of various kinds. Sculpture was also the predominant art, though there was also painting, frequently on wood, and various artistic crafts such as basket making and pottery, which was especially significant in Melanesia (New Guinea, the Solomon islands and Fiji).

Several systems of classification have been put forward for Oceanic art, none of them really quite satisfactory, but it is possible to find specific styles common to certain parts of the huge region. In Micronesia (the many smallish islands north of New Guinea), decoration is mainly dictated by the way in which a particular object is made or the use for which it is intended; natural forms are simplified and stylized. The effect is sometimes very elegant, as in the figure in the Musée de l'Homme

(opposite), the elongated shape and clean, expressive lines of which rather resemble a portrait by Modigliani.

In Polynesia, which includes Hawaii and New Zealand and the islands in between, very elaborate surface decorations, more or less abstract but deriving from natural forms, are found on many objects. Other common features are the little devilish figure known as a *tiki*, carved in wood or stone, and the elaborately carved wooden club, which was a status symbol as well as a weapon. The Maoris of New Zealand, a proud and warlike people more advanced than some of their neighbours, carved human and animal heads on their houses and canoes; heavy and stylized, and not always easily recognizable, they somewhat resemble Mexi-

can and Central American forms. Ancestor figures were common, and chiefs sometimes wore small figures carved in jade like the kind shown in the photograph below which dates from about the time of European settlement; nevertheless, it was carved and finished without the aid of metal tools, a remarkable achievement, since jade is a very hard substance.

Below:
A jade pendant from New Zealand, with inlaid mother-of-pearl. This example dates only from the last century, but such ornaments, representing a stylized squatting figure, were traditional among the Maoris. The workmanship is remarkable in view of the fact that the jade, a very hard material, was carved without metal tools. Staatliches Museum für Volkerkunde, Munich.

Above:
Micronesian carved wooden figure from the island of Nukunono, north of Samoa. Musée de l'Homme, Paris.

Opposite:
One of the strange stone heads of Easter Island.

15

Below:
Offering bowl in the form of an ancestor
figure, from the Philippines. Museum
voor Land-en Volkenkunde,
Rotterdam.

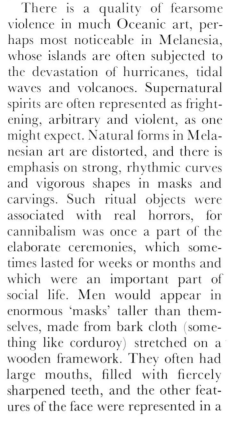

There is a quality of fearsome violence in much Oceanic art, perhaps most noticeable in Melanesia, whose islands are often subjected to the devastation of hurricanes, tidal waves and volcanoes. Supernatural spirits are often represented as frightening, arbitrary and violent, as one might expect. Natural forms in Melanesian art are distorted, and there is emphasis on strong, rhythmic curves and vigorous shapes in masks and carvings. Such ritual objects were associated with real horrors, for cannibalism was once a part of the elaborate ceremonies, which sometimes lasted for weeks or months and which were an important part of social life. Men would appear in enormous 'masks' taller than themselves, made from bark cloth (something like corduroy) stretched on a wooden framework. They often had large mouths, filled with fiercely sharpened teeth, and the other features of the face were represented in a

semi-abstract way, often resembling plant growths. In some areas, secret societies carried out their rites in exclusive buildings, barred to the laity, which were filled with cult objects.

Throughout Oceania, in Africa, and, in basically similar form, in South-East Asia and certain parts of North and South America, ancestor figures with knees bent in a kind of crouched position can be found. In Borneo, for example, the motif appears carved in relief, as figures in the round, and as a woven motif in textiles. The squatting figure is usually explained as symbolizing either the human foetus in the womb, or the position of a woman giving birth. Although these interpretations may seem far-fetched to non-specialists, there must be some fundamental explanation to account for the extraordinarily extensive spread of this characteristic, which probably first appeared in China. It possibly derives from the custom of burying a corpse in a crouched position, which was almost certainly a conscious attempt to return the body to the earth in the same position as it had been in the womb, to ensure that it should be safely reincarnated.

Squatting figures are also to be found in parts of Australia. The Australian Aborigines, when first discovered by Europeans, were at a very early stage of cultural development. They had simple tools (though some interesting weapons) and no pottery; they also had no real buildings and often lived in caves like the Europeans of the Stone Age. Their art had moved on past the naturalistic stage to symbolic stylization, and one of its most interesting forms was the so-called X-ray painting, in which an animal is shown in outline with a crude representation of its inner organs within. Similar paintings are found in many other parts of the world, for example in prehistoric rock paintings in Europe and in several areas of North America, though never in Africa. In Australia, most notably Arnhem Land, examples are found painted on bark (opposite), and it seems likely that they are comparatively recent, deriving from outside influence which some people suggest

Left:
A copy of an Aboriginal bark painting in Arnhem Land, and an example of the strangely ubiquitous 'skeleton' style.

Below:
A polar bear carved from walrus ivory by an Eskimo artist.

high degree of specialization, elaborate architecture, and so on.

In the far north, however, a genuine primitive culture was found among the Eskimos. Unlike most of the Pacific peoples and most Africans, the Eskimos belonged to a pre-agricultural, or to be more precise non-agricultural (since agriculture is scarcely possible in their homelands) society. The Eskimos lived mainly by fishing and hunting and were nomads, moving north or south according to the season. The relative scarcity of plant life also meant that there was little wood available – the most common material for the art of primitive cultures. Nevertheless, the Eskimos did make masks, as well as more strictly utilitarian objects such as bowls, out of driftwood. They had no metal of course: the polar explorer Robert Peary was criticized for carrying away a gigantic meteorite from Greenland on the grounds that he was depriving the Eskimos of their sole source of metal (rather a silly criticism, since the Eskimos had a far better source of metal in the *kadloonas* (whites) who followed in Peary's track). The chief materials for Eskimo carvings were bone and ivory (from walrus). Their ivory carvings of animals, in a strikingly naturalistic style, are particularly valued by collectors.

The American Indians, like the Eskimos, came originally from Asia. The immigration, beginning about 25,000 years ago, went on over a very long period of time, and involved many different peoples, often moving, it seems, in fairly small groups. They were nomadic hunters, who gradually moved south in search of better hunting, the stronger groups moving farthest south and driving others out. Some eventually reached the southernmost parts of South America.

may originally be Scandinavian. The early examples were usually quite realistic: a wallaby has a detectable spine, heart, and so on. But as time went on they grew increasingly less so, becoming eventually an abstract design with no obvious relation to the original animal.

Some Aboriginal bark paintings are rather frightening – a common characteristic of so much primitive art with its emphasis on the ominous spirit world – though they also have considerable charm. A very different effect is created by the enormous human figures found in other regions of Oceania and elsewhere. In the Marquesas, heavy carved stone or wooden human figures were made as tall as three metres, their heavy neckless heads giving them something

of the static, brooding quality of some pre-Columbian figures in Mexico. More famous are the giant statues of Easter Island, the farthest east of Polynesian islands, carved in volcanic stone and up to seven metres high. They astonished the first Europeans who saw them, and although it is now assumed that they were memorials to dead ancestors, they remain rather a mystery to this day.

Pre-Columbian art in the Americas included cultures that strictly speaking can not be classed as primitive. The precolonial peoples of Middle America (Central America and Mexico) and of parts of South America had a fairly sophisticated civilization, with established governments, institutionalized religions, a

Above:
A striking terracotta vessel in the form of a warrior, from the Mochica culture, Peru, 5th or 6th century AD. The Art Institute of Chicago, Chicago, Illinois.

Eventually they learned how to grow crops, developing many of the vegetables that we eat today. Some settled in village communities, while others lived a kind of dual existence as both hunters and farmers.

The art of the North American Indians has often been misunderstood, largely because our knowledge of them has tended to come from motion pictures and pulp novels, rather than from the works of anthropologists. There is a great difference between the simple art of the hunters of the north – Eskimos and certain Canadian and North-Western Indians – and the village-dwelling people of the south-west United States, although certain influences can be traced down from Alaska to Mexico. The X-ray style, for example, appears in Eskimo art, and also on the pottery of the Zuni Indians of New Mexico. One characteristic of North American Indian art is a preference for simple and useful forms, like the clay pipes which are no different in form from their modern equivalents. Unfortunately, few of the objects of North American art before the Europeans arrived have survived, largely because they were not made to last – or at least, that was not the primary intention of the craftsman. The Navaho, for example, used to make pictures on the ground, out of differently coloured sand. These served a useful purpose at the time, being connected with rites to cure sickness; but when the rites were over, the pictures were literally swept away.

The Pueblo Indians, so-called after their many-storeyed communal houses, made pottery with fine, abstract designs, rather similar to some of the pottery of the Peruvian highlands. Some elegant plates or bowls were buried along with corpses at funerals; a hole was knocked in the bottom first, apparently to make sure the bowl, like the person it accompanied, was 'dead'. But of all North American Indian pottery, probably the best known is that of the Hohokam people, who created delicate geometrical patterns on a brownish ground, sometimes in relief. Silver jewelry inlaid with turquoise, the main stand-by of all Indian 'souvenir' shops, is a comparatively recent tradition, not later than the 16th century. Of course, all such modern versions of 'primitive' art are debased, and in fact are not art at all. They might as well be, and no doubt they often are, produced by machines in factories.

The most advanced societies of the American Indians developed in Peru and Middle America. Ancient Peru included Ecuador and a large part of Chile – the empire of the Incas as it was when the Spaniards conquered it early in the 16th century. The people then had complex political, social and religious institutions, but lacked certain things which were developed at a much earlier stage in other parts of the world, such as writing and the wheel. Peruvian art included architecture and sculpture, although most of the examples to be seen in museums today are of textiles and pottery. The Incas also had marvellous works of art made from precious metals, which atracted the greedy eye of the European invader. In the mountainous parts – a large proportion of the country – stone was easily available, hence the prevalence of stone sculpture, as well as good clay, for making pottery. One of the earliest of these mountain cultures is known chiefly from the archaeological site at Chavín de Huantar, where the motif of a cat-like head with ferocious teeth appears in sculpture, pottery and even textiles; some sculptured figures bearing this head, which was sometimes attached to a bird-like or fish-like body, measured as much as two metres in height. The cat-like head obviously had some religious significance, though we do not know enough about these people to be more precise. It is found among other Peruvian cultures at different dates.

Some of the most interesting Peruvian pottery was made in the northern region between about 500 and 1000 AD. It was painted in bold reds, white and black, and was commonly used in funeral rites. The potters moulded their wares (as they did not have the wheel) in two halves, surmounted by a hollow handle. The Nazca pottery, of later date, shows a much greater variety of colours, up to a dozen sometimes being used in the decoration of one pot. A greater variety of shapes were also made, decorated with stylized animals, sometimes real, sometimes mythical, outlined in black. Similar designs can be seen in Nazca textiles.

Near Lake Titicaca in Bolivia the Tiahuanaco culture flourished around 500-900 AD. It had a distinctive art style, characterized by the motif of a stylized human figure, rather short and squat, with a heavy, square head. Vast figures were carved up to seven or eight metres high, great block-like objects which retain the shape of the square-sided column. Features of the Tiahuanaco style are found all over Peru.

The Incas began as a small people living in the neighbourhood of

Above:
A 'poncho' or cloak, from the Lake
Titicaca region, Bolivia. Musée de
l'Homme, Paris.

Above:
A figure of an Aztec god, carved in
volcanic stone. Reiss-Museum,
Mannheim.

Cuzco; by the early 15th century they had conquered most of their neighbours, achieving a dominance which they retained until the Spaniards arrived about a century later. The Incas were really interested more in power than in art, and although they were technically very adept, they introduced few new ideas; Inca art is largely an amalgam of earlier cultures. Apart from their formidable architecture, of which the ruins of Machu Picchu are the most famous example to be seen today, they excelled in textiles, employing a great variety of forms of weaving, with bright and complex patterns of stylized animals and human figures, arranged in a complicated but non-pictorial way which resembles the designs of Nazca pottery.

Moving further north, Mexico was also a region of high culture in the pre-Columbian period. People were living in settled communities at least four thousand years ago, existing on maize (sweet corn) in the rich valleys fertilized by the deposits of the mountain streams. This gave them the leisure not only for making works of art but for building the vast edifices, the most typical being pyramid-shaped, which are found throughout the region – all constructed without the aid of iron tools. Pre-Columbian architecture, like some Far Eastern architecture, was not a matter of building walls and a roof to enclose a space, as we automatically think of it, but rather of erecting enormous piles – symbols of power and grandeur – whose importance lay in their appearance as monuments.

Most Mexican cultures shared some common features. Besides the pyramids, which were often topped by small temples, they made elaborately carved human figures in stone, which were sometimes inlaid with semi-precious stones. Metals (mainly gold and silver) were used for jewelry, although there was no metal suitable for making tools, and potters made vessels in the shape of animals. Serpents were also a common decorative motif, especially among the Toltecs, who flourished about 800 to 1150 AD, and were highly regarded by their successors, the Aztecs, rulers of most of Mexico when Cortés arrived from Cuba on his expedition of conquest. The Aztec capital, Tenochtitlan, near the modern Mexico City, was as large and as splendid as many contemporary European cities. It was a kind of pre-Columbian Venice, built on a lake with many canals and terraces, temples and palaces, and even a court for a mysterious kind of ball game. The Aztecs, however, were a fierce people who lived by conquest and domination and whose religious life included the bloody sacrifice of hundreds of human beings to their relentless gods. This ferocious side to their culture gave their art, much of which was, like that of the Incas, derived from earlier peoples, its distinctive character. Statues of gods carved from volcanic rock appear strange and fearsome to us, yet how much more so must they have looked when in their original places in dark and gloomy temples. The serpent, symbol of the god-hero Quetzalcoatal, reappears among carvings decorating terraces, its teeth prominent and its unblinking eyes ringed with obsidian.

A more distinguished people, artistically speaking, were the Mayas. Their original homeland is unknown, but from about 600 BC, the earliest date for a known Maya archaeological site, they began to spread throughout southern Mexico and Central America. Their city centres, great works of architecture and sculpture, remain an inspiring monument to their culture. Besides these social-religious centres, they erected elaborately carved (again, without metal tools) stone *stelae*, vertical oblong slabs, to mark important dates when some religious ceremony took place. Some were about three metres high, with figures of priests, carved in relief, so swathed in ornamental dress and elaborate hats that they are hardly recognizable as human beings. These *stelae* are less common in the northern region, where intricately worked stone mosaics with geometric patterns are more often found. The Maya calendar was vital to their religious life, and exceedingly complicated; no one is sure now exactly how it worked. Long periods of time were represented by *glyphs*, stone forms consisting of human faces with different

Above:
Detail from the 'warriors fresco', Bonampak.

kinds of noses, chins, cheeks and headdresses. Shorter periods were reckoned by symbols representing five and one, and nought was conveyed by an open hand.

Maya culture experienced something of a renaissance around the 11th century when under Toltec influence, the most famous example being the great buildings of Chichen Itza, where some of the decoration of the temples had a fierce, uncompromising directness not found in the softer forms of early Maya sculpture. The great Temple of the Warriors gets its name from the extraordinary wall paintings found there, where the artists have conveyed a sense of distance by putting far-away objects at the top and near ones at the bottom. Like many other features of pre-Columbian art, the flat figures of the warriors and the non-pictorial composition are reminiscent of certain aspects of Oriental art.

Some scholars regard the Asian influence on American cultures as highly important, though there is much argument over how powerful it was and even over whether it existed at all. The arguments rest on no written evidence, but only on shared cultural features, such as the prevalence of the X-ray style and of certain purely decorative motifs which may have come from Asia across the Pacific. There are other similarities with Pacific peoples: Polynesian head-hunting becomes, in North America, the practice of scalping one's enemy. But what influence there was could only have been rare and spasmodic, since the distance is so great and America so remote from Asia, or even from the nearest Pacific islands. And if these common features are evidence of cultural contact, how is it that, for example, such useful ideas as the wheel remained unknown in America until the Europeans arrived?

The Ancient World

When considering the art of a society far removed from our own, we have to keep in mind that our ideas of what is 'good', 'beautiful', and so on may be, almost certainly are, quite different from those of the people who actually produced the art. Whether or not we fully comprehend the social, religious or other ideas that gave birth to the art, we can hardly see these ideas in the same light as did people of the time. Yet although our ignorance is often a bar to appreciating a particular piece of work, that does not necessarily prevent us admiring it, for we judge all works of art partly at least according to aesthetic criteria: when we say a picture is beautiful, we are making an aesthetic judgment. But as far as ancient societies are concerned, such judgments are, in a sense, irrelevant, because they were utterly foreign to the people of those societies. To say that an Egyptian pyramid or a Babylonian mosaic is 'beautiful' would have made no sense at all to the people who created them.

When man had learned to live a settled life, growing crops and keeping animals, building towns for a safer and more organized society, life became more complex. The search for an explanation for the inexplicable forces of nature led to the growth of religion; the need to organize community life led to the development of laws and government, usually a form of kingship.

The earliest advanced cultures of this kind grew up in the Middle East, roughly from Egypt to Persia, and in particular the river valleys – the Nile in Egypt and the Tigris and Euphrates in Mesopotamia, where the earliest civilizations have been discovered. The wandering hunters and herdsmen who came to these valleys learned how to exploit the rivers by irrigation and canals, and were able to grow crops more than sufficient for their own needs. A surplus of food created a stable society, and allowed trade with less fortunate neighbours. City states, with sophisticated political systems and considerable military power, came into being. In Egypt, the supreme ruler was known as the pharaoh. He was a very exalted figure, regarded by his subjects as divine, and controlled a wide area. Further to the east, no comparable empire appeared; Sumerian civilization in Mesopotamia consisted of city states, more or less independent, and the ruler, though a powerful, priestly figure, was not treated as a god.

From our great distance in time, the civilizations of the ancient Middle East appear similar, but they would not have done so to the people of the time, and the more they are studied, the clearer the differences become. Moreover, time's telescope minimizes the process of change, and we are apt to view the Sumerian or the Babylonian civilizations as less dynamic than they really were. Some periods may see greater changes than others of comparable duration, but no human society remains static for long.

While keeping these facts in mind, we may also legitimately look for characteristics which these ancient societies had in common. For a start, the widely separated societies of Egypt, Mesopotamia and Iran all developed writing, though in different forms, at roughly the same time. In the arts, though styles and methods varied greatly, the motives that produced the art were similar. Egypt, geographically separate and more self-contained, remained thoroughly and exclusively 'Egyptian' in its art and culture for an amazingly long period of time, but the region further east had a more disturbed history, with many different peoples appearing on the scene at various times,

bringing with them new ideas, new types of government, and new forms of art. Though that was sometimes enriching, the frequency of war and other social upheavals was an inhibiting factor not present in Egypt, and perhaps explains why, to most modern eyes, the arts of Egypt reached a higher level of accomplishment than did those of other ancient civilizations.

However, the earliest ancient civilization developed not in Egypt but in Mesopotamia, a region roughly corresponding to modern Iraq. The Sumerians arrived there around 3500 BC, merging with the local inhabitants and ultimately founding a strong, theocratic society based on large-scale agriculture with extensive irrigation works. At Uruk, called Erech in the Bible, they built temples of bricks made from mud, and a great ziggurat which was the base for a temple. On the walls they made striking geometric patterns with pieces of terracotta set in the plaster. Their stone sculpture included hunting scenes in relief as well as heads and nude figures in the round. The alabaster vase (opposite), which dates from about 3000 BC, is a remarkably sophisticated shape, with its flaring top and recessed base. It was found in one of the temples of Uruk and was used in religious rites: the scenes depicted in low relief are of crops and animals being offered to the goddess of fertility who, in the topmost band, receives them outside her temple. The stately arrangement of the figures reflects the Sumerians' love of good order and conveys a sense of calm assurance. A work still more impressive to modern eyes is the head of a woman from Uruk in marble, which may once have been part of a full-length figure. The elegant sensitivity of this face can scarcely be excelled in the art of any period.

Above:
Early Sumerian vase in alabaster, about 3000 BC. Iraq Museum, Baghdad.

Right:
Female head in marble, Uruk, about 3000 BC. Iraq Museum, Baghdad.

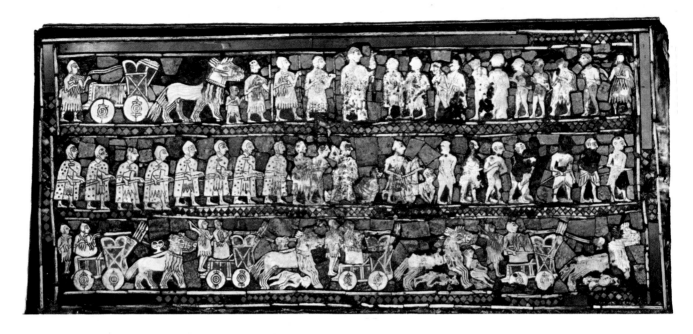

Above:
This panel, made of shell, limestone and lapis lazuli set in a bitumen base, was found in a Sumerian tomb and dates from about 2500 BC. It illustrates royal victories in war: in the top row, the king receives prisoners of war; in the middle row are soldiers and captives; and in the bottom row are chariots and bodies of the dead. British Museum, London.

Left:
Alabaster statue, about 3200-3000 BC, of the superintendent of the temple at Mari, on the Euphrates river. Musée du Louvre, Paris.

Not long after these works were made a decline set in probably due to some contemporary crisis – perhaps the Flood of Sumerian mythology, which is markedly similar to the story of the Flood in the Book of Genesis. In this transitional period, the self-assurance of earlier work disappears: sculpture becomes more dynamic, with scenes of men wrestling with beasts. Then, about 2700 BC, a new era began, known as the Early Dynastic period, with more temple building. The temples were no longer built on massive and lofty platforms, but at ground level, more in the manner of·French Gothic cathedrals, not really bringing religion closer to the people as the central shrine was kept carefully isolated. The most common subject of sculpture is a human figure in an attitude of prayer, though usually standing, not kneeling. These figures were placed in the temples to provide a permanent con-

Above:
This panel, placed back to back with the panel opposite, shows scenes of peace: top row, a banquet; second row, animals arriving for slaughter; bottom row, men with donkeys carrying goods. British Museum, London.

Below:
This famous relief in copper-plated wood shows the Sumerian lion-headed eagle spreading his protecting wings over two stags. It probably stood over the entrance to a temple. British Museum, London.

gregation of worshippers, and would seldom, if ever, have been seen by ordinary people. Such statues, with their large staring eyes (fixed on the god), have been found over a wide range of sites in Mesopotamia, with certain differences in style according to location.

By about 2500 BC the Sumerians seem to have regained their self-confidence, and this is shown in sculpture which becomes both more realistic and more massive. At Mari on the Euphrates, outside Sumeria proper, human figures are more lively, with something of the old stately calm, while at Ur, excavated tombs have revealed marvellously wrought pieces of metalwork, though the finest example of Sumerian metalwork is the relief in copper (above), three metres wide, which shows the lion-headed eagle of Sumerian mythology giving his protection to a pair of stags. It was probably made to stand over the door of a temple.

About 2350 BC a new dynasty came to power in Mesopotamia, with its capital at Akkad, giving its name to the Akkadian period (2350-2150 BC)

which saw Sumerian art reach its highest peak. The main characteristics of the period are a broader view of life, more interest in everyday affairs and less fearful obedience to superstition. Sculpture is again the outstanding art form, though surviving examples are few. Figures are still often monumental, but have gained a liveliness of expression absent during the Early Dynastic period; there is more detail, and more awareness of movement. The most famous example is the bronze head (opposite) from Nineveh (possibly a portrait of Sargon, founder of the Akkadian dynasty) which is now in a museum in Baghdad. The head is noble and wise, though not without a touch of avarice, and displays the complicated hairstyle typical of Sumeria. Relief carvings of the Akkadian period show a new awareness of composition, and an example in red sandstone, now in the Louvre, includes a conventionalized landscape.

New invasions from Iran broke up the Akkadian civilization, though in southern Mesopotamia the newcomers never gained control. In that area, now beleaguered after the comparative peace of the Akkadian period, artists reverted to the style of the Early Dynastic period, a striking example of stress making people reactionary. Further invasions of Mesopotamia brought an end to the Sumerian culture, though traditions continued under the newcomers in the period known as Neo-Sumerian. Ziggurats reappeared in architecture, and the main subjects of sculpture were again silent worshippers in the temple.

Various Semitic dynasties appeared in Sumeria in the second millennium BC, the dominant power being Babylonia. By about 1500 BC, the Babylonians had taken over what had been Sumerian civilization, but attacks by a relatively primitive people from Syria, the Amorites, caused a long period of sparse artistic production. There are few architectural remains from this period, and sculpture adhered to Neo-Sumerian traditions, though with certain significant innovations. Human figures are less lively, but have more gracefulness about them, particularly in details of dress, and show a greater consciousness of the qualities of light. The commonest relics, however, are terracotta figures of human beings and animals, made in moulds, not in themselves of outstanding artistic interest.

A period of greater creativity began with the conquest of Babylonia by

Above:
The Ziggurat at Ur, about the 21st century BC. It owes its remarkable state of preservation to its facing of brick.

Left:
Boundary stone of the Dassite period, about 1100 BC, with a royal figure in low relief. British Museum, London.

the Kassites, which brought a revival to the old city of Uruk. The Kassites, it appears, were reponsible for introducing the rounded stone slabs called *kudurrus* on which figures and writing were inscribed. They were probably boundary stones, the figures represented being responsible, it was hoped, for protecting the border against enemies.

Roughly contemporary with the Kassites were the Assyrians in northern Mesopotamia. They instituted certain architectural changes, although they preserved the traditional form of the ziggurat, which they seem to have regarded as indispensable in temple construction. Their relief sculpture is notable for its depiction of narrative, rare in ancient art although examples are known from Hittite cities farther west. The later Assyrian period saw some great building projects, associated with individual rulers of special power, which included rock carving in relief on a massive scale. One of the best known examples is the famous lion hunt (below) from Nimrud, now in the British Museum, which shows the king, Assurnasirpal, shooting a lion with bow and arrow from his chariot. The scene of a king killing a lion was not merely an Assyrian 'sporting print', but had symbolic significance. The relief carvings at Nimrud are of striking quality, and some scholars have spent a good deal of time trying to discover where this remarkable development came from, though without reaching firm conclusions. What is undisputed is that the Nimrud reliefs represent a dramatic step forward in the art of ancient Mesopotamia. Somewhat similar scenes decorating palace walls were made during later reigns. At Nineveh, for

Below:
An Assyrian relief showing a lion hunt, 9th century BC. The lion hunt was a common motif and symbolized the victory of good over evil. British Museum, London.

27

Above:
Decoration in glazed bricks made ancient Babylon a brilliant place in the days of Nebuchadnezzar II (604-562 BC). Vorderasiatisches Museum, Berlin.

instance, the figures are depicted in a well-defined landscape, and although groups of people – slaves, soldiers, etc. – often appear identical, like cut-out figures, a more human touch of individual detail, absent from the more formal religious scenes, becomes increasingly apparent. Walls were also decorated with painted pictures, though unfortunately these have survived even less well than the carvings. Similar subjects – court scenes and battles especially – were depicted.

Assyrian art was a court art, and it

virtually disappeared with the fall of the Assyrian empire. In Babylonia, old traditions continued despite the influx of more successful but culturally less advanced people, like the Aramaeans. During the reign of Nebuchadnezzar II the streets of Babylon were decorated with bright glazed tiles bearing the images of animals (opposite), real and mythical, in a stylized form. This type of decoration was not new – it was known in Kassite times – but it had not previously been adopted on such a big scale. The method used was to model the animal (a lion in this case), in a single flat slab of wet clay. The slab was then cut up into bricks, which were glazed and fired, and then reassembled on the wall. Very large areas were covered, and the impression when first seen must have been breath-taking, although they are not really in the first rank as works of art.

The ancient civilizations of the Middle East that flourished from the fourth millenium BC onwards did not, of course, only exist in Mesopotamia. In Palestine, there was a walled city at Jericho in 6000 BC, where a tower remains that is over six metres high. Among the finds made by archaeologists are semi-precious stones from other parts of the Middle East, showing that the people of the city must have been engaged in trade (probably selling salt from the Dead Sea among other products), and some small terracotta figures that display considerable grasp of the sculptor's craft. A stranger find has been of human skulls which, for some obscure religious purpose, were coated with plaster in which the features of the face were remodelled, with cowrie shells inset for the eyes. They have an eerie appearance.

In Anatolia, a region corresponding to modern Turkey, buildings have been found which date from about the same time. At Çatal Hüyük (now in southern Turkey), the walls of temples are decorated with paintings and reliefs, often of bulls' heads, a common motif in ancient art. The earliest paintings are of geometrical patterns, but later ones show human figures, hunting scenes, and dancing.

Above:
Mother Goddess in clay from Çatal Hüyük, Anatolia, early 6th millennium BC, about 88 mm high. Archaeological Museum, Ankara.

They are the earliest known wall paintings in the Middle East. Another familiar theme which makes an early appearance at Çatal Hüyük is the carved female figure known as the Mother Goddess, her heavy breast and hip suggesting fertility. The figures were in stone or terracotta, and although they have now almost all disappeared without trace, they were probably painted in some cases. The Mother Goddess cult was to last considerably longer than Christianity has so far, and in fact did not disappear until early Christian times.

In general, much of the most important evidence from archaeological excavations of early sites is in the form of pottery. The art of making vessels out of clay, hardened by a fire, is an old one. It was common throughout the ancient world about 8000 years ago, and it is possible that Anatolia was the place where it originated. The earliest known pottery comes from Hacilar (southwest Turkey), though it was also being produced in the Zagros mountains of Iran about the same time: it may have been invented in more than one place. The Hacilar pottery of the sixth millennium includes wide-bodied jars with abstract patterns, frequently spirals, in white on a red ground, or vice-versa. More elaborate forms were adopted by Iranian potters in the fifth millennium, with designs based on animals reduced to near-abstract patterns. Pottery seems to have spread from east to west, and proves that there was a good deal of contact across a wide area in the ancient world.

From the later part of the fourth millennium, Sumeria was in the lead, culturally speaking, and all the arts of the region took their example from her, although different parts contributed original ideas of their own; the pottery of Susa (Iran), for example, has marked differences both in shape and decoration from Mesopotamian wares. Some interesting terracotta figures from Elam (western Iran) in the third millennium show a strong divergence from Sumerian style, and betray a preoccupation with the grotesque, characteristic of much early Iranian art. Iranian as well as Mesopotamian influences are detectable in the great civilizations of the Indus Valley, in Pakistan – for example, in the use of unbaked bricks for building (originally due to a shortage of the more obvious building materials, stone and timber).

Anatolia is a particularly interesting area for archaeologists because it was the region through which civilization was transmitted from the east to the west. In greater or lesser degree, all the Bronze- and Iron-Age cultures of Europe may be traced indirectly to Anatolia, via the Aegean. Our picture of Anatolia from the third millennium is, however, confused, and the three best-investigated sites, including those at Troy and Alaca Hüyük, display marked cultural differences. At Alaca Hüyük, royal families were buried in tombs along with their private possessions, including jewelry and gold metalwork of surprisingly high quality. At another site, stylized female figures in marble suggest a link with the culture of the Cyclades (see Chapter Three), and Crete too probably owed a cultural debt to this region. Migrants moving westward from Anatolia took with them their knowledge of metalwork and pottery as they travelled in search of good farming land, and their influence gradually extended throughout the whole of Mediterranean Europe.

During the second millennium, the Hittites settled in Anatolia. At the time of its widest extent, the Hittite empire reached well into Syria, and beyond the Euphrates at Carchemish, posing a challenge even to Egypt. (The Hittites of the Old Testament were a later people, mainly remnants of former colonies in Syria which persisted after the breakdown of the parent state in Anatolia.) Their origins are still something of a mystery. Assyrian merchants in Asia Minor reported that numerous principalities were held around 2000 BC by rulers all trying to expand their territory at the expense of their neighbours. It is not certain that these were 'Hittites' in the later sense of the name, though the Old Kingdom of the Hittites was established soon after that time, and by 1750 BC it was spreading into Syria. There was then a setback, the result of political ambitions at court, and the Old Kingdom disappeared about 1650 BC. Two centuries later Hittite power revived, and by the 14th century BC the Hittite empire was menacing Egypt; around 1300 BC the pharoah Rameses II was forced to make a treaty of peace with the 'great king of the Hittites' in which he formally acknowledged Hittite possession of Syria.

The Hittites did not impose their own exclusive culture upon the people they conquered. Many of their ideas and practices were taken over from the original inhabitants. Excavations at Hattusas, the Hittite capital, and elsewhere, have not yet made clear the historical circumstances of the establishment of the Old Kingdom, nor fully explained Hittite art.

By 2000 BC in many places in Anatolia, the forerunner of the type of pottery known as Cappadocian ware was being produced. The vessels are mostly slim and tapering, with long spouts, a rich reddish brown in colour and sometimes decorated with geometric patterns and animals. A different type of pottery entirely existed in the south of Anatolia, which suggests that the Hittites had not yet

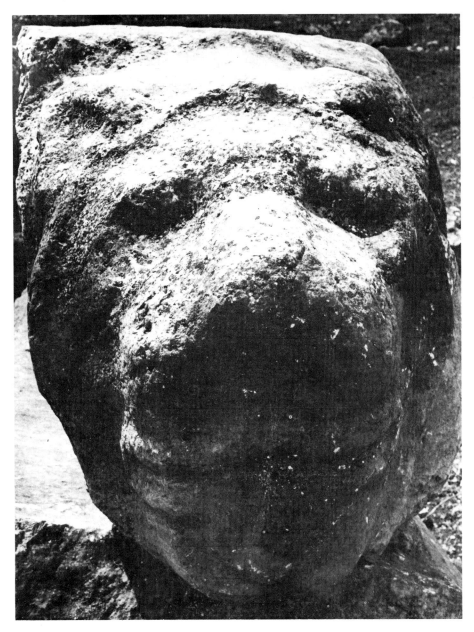

Above:
The head of one of the lions of the Hittite Lion Gate, Hattusas, 14th century BC.

Opposite:
Figure from the Warrior Gate, Hattusas. The torso is shown frontally, the head and legs are in profile. Archaeological Museum, Ankara.

were built of monumental stone blocks, and the carvings were intended to protect them against enemies. The figure shown in the photograph (opposite) is a typical guardian of this sort. He is a war god, wearing a helmet and armed with an axe (in his right hand) and sword (slung at his waist). The figure is carved in low relief and in profile, but his chest faces forwards. This is a common convention in ancient Middle Eastern art, and most familiar to us from Egyptian examples. It creates some problems for the sculptor, however. In this case, both the sword and the axe are curved, although there is no doubt that they would have been straight in reality, to compensate for the change from a frontal to a profile view. If the sculptor had made the axe handle straight, it would have looked as though the warrior was carrying it more or less vertically in front of his body, whereas the true position is like that of the baton in the grip of a relay runner.

The lion (left) is one of a pair standing on either side of a gate at Hattusas, dating from the 14th century BC, which guarded the road approaching from the south-west and was one of several gates in a wall which surrounded the city. The wall is no less than six and a half kilometres long. The lion is carved out of a single block of stone weighing several tons. People who have seen these Hittite figures speak of them 'leaping out of the rock' at them. They are perhaps the most impressive works of Hittite art, and although possible influences from both Mesopotamia and Egypt can be pointed to, they are really something new in sculpture, and show a remarkable ability to exploit the potentials of the raw material on a large scale.

Mesopotamian culture was, in general, in decline in the second millennium partly as the result of the insurgence of various peoples from the mountains. However in the second half of the millennium there was a cultural revival in the Iranian plateau, particularly around Susa. One building discovered quite recently is an enormous five-stage ziggurat. One of the most extraordinary works of art discovered in this area

established their cultural dominance throughout the country. In fact, comparatively little has been discovered from the early Hittite period; it is not until the establishment of the empire that continuous lines of artistic development can be traced, and even then they are not very clear, partly because comparatively few sites have so far been excavated.

The Hittites were great builders and sculptors. But to them architecture and sculpture were not two separate arts as they are to us. They were perhaps the first people (they have had many successors) who treated sculpture as an integral part of architecture, or vice-versa. The sculpture of Hittite temples and palaces is not so much decoration as a part of the buildings. The walls of their cities

Above:
A golden bowl from Ugarit (Ras
Shamra), made by the *repoussé* method
by Syrian craftsmen probably influenced
by Egypt. National Museum, Aleppo.

is a statue of an Elamite queen in
cast bronze (left), roughly life-size,
and now in the Louvre. Unfortunately the head is missing, but enough
remains to show that the Elamite
metalworkers of (probably) the 13th
century BC were masters of their craft.
The figure was cast in two stages; an
outer shell about 25 mm thick was
made first, and then filled with molten metal. The statue is also evidence
of another development in Elamite
art, found also in wall reliefs, of using
script as both explanation and
decoration. The queen's skirt tells us
her name and threatens anyone who
dares to steal or damage the statue
with a deadly curse.

Syrian art in this period, although
it was directly derived from Mesopotamia, was often superior to it in terms
of craftsmanship. However, Syrian
architectural developments showed
some new features and, especially in
the palace of Yarim-Lim, shows some
similarities with the better-known
palaces of Minoan Crete. Most Syrian
sculpture of this period remains somewhat primitive in conception and
execution, though there are notable
exceptions such as the head alleged to
represent Yarim-Lim (above), who
lived in the 18th century BC. It is not
difficult to detect the old traditions of
the Sumerian sculptors still maintained in this confident and accomplished piece, though other Syrian
heads of about this time show more of
an Egyptian influence.

Right:
Syrian *stele* of a weather god, nearly
5 metres high, 14th century BC. Musée
du Louvre, Paris.

Below:
Bronze ornament from Luristan, 10th or
9th century BC. Archaeological
Museum, Teheran.

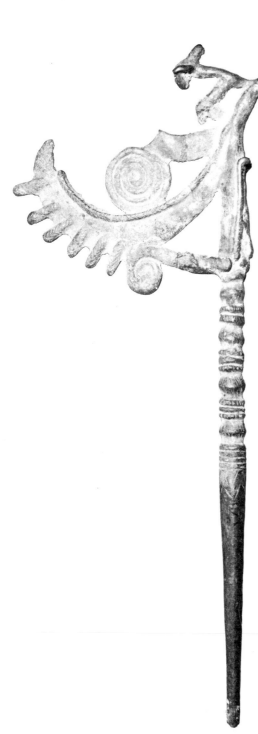

34

Another typical Syrian development in this period was a *stele* (a stone post or slab something like a gravestone, carved in relief and usually marking some event of importance) of a type apparently made mainly for decorative purposes, like that of the weather god (opposite), who was a particularly important deity in ancient Syria. The Egyptian influence is obvious here, in the lean, broad-shouldered figure, and in the way he holds his right arm aloft like many a pharaoh pictured vanquishing his foes. What marks this figure straight away as Syrian, however, is his horned helmet; the lightning issuing from his spear betrays his identity as god of storms.

Among the smaller arts of Syria about 1200 BC was the carving of ivories, not a new development in itself, but given an impetus by the Syrian love of ornament. Syrian culture in general, however, received a sharp setback about this time as the result of invasion by a new and still mysterious people, known to the Egyptians as the 'People of the Sea'. Hittite culture disappeared more or less completely, and the Egyptians were forced to retreat almost to the Nile. The destruction of these influences had some compensations, especially in North Syria, where new and independent princes appeared and encouraged fine artists and sculptors. Among the most famous works of the period around 1000 BC is the sculpture of Carchemish in which figures of gods and warriors are depicted in relief.

In Iran, the revival of the late second millennium had petered out, but a new and important art arose about 1000 BC in Luristan. These works were small objects in bronze. They have been found, in quite large numbers, in tombs, and although some appear to be mainly decorative, the majority are either harness fittings or similar objects, or weapons. They were the family 'heirlooms' of a nomadic people who, by the nature of their way of life, possessed no large objects nor, indeed, any buildings except their tombs. The Luristan

Below:
This little ivory, only 10 cm high, of a lion attacking a youth, is of Phoenician workmanship, and was found in the palace at Nimrud. British Museum, London.

bronzes are free in form, even fantastic, and some of the more common decorative features are grotesque animals of various kinds, a style found throughout much of central and eastern Asia.

In the 6th century BC the great Persian empire came to hold sway over the whole of the region described here, but this did not, as might have been expected, result in the final and splendid apotheosis of all the ancient Middle Eastern cultural traditions because, by that time, a rather different culture had arisen and the centre of civilization had moved west – to Athens.

That civilization should have developed early in the valley of the Nile is not surprising because of the existence of the river itself. Egypt, said the classical historian Herodotus, is 'the gift of the Nile'. Even simple methods of agriculture were highly productive in a region where the soil, apart from being watered by the river (though irrigation was necessary), was fertilized by the annual flooding which deposited a layer of rich silt on the

land. When the earth grew drier after the ending of the last Ice Age, and North Africa became more desert-like, the hunters of the region, if they were to survive, had no choice but to settle near the Nile and learn how to make use of it. There were two main settlements, one in the delta region in the north (Lower Egypt) and the other along the river farther south (Upper Egypt). The Nile provided the necessary link between them. Although both regions were included in the ancient Egyptian kingdom, certain differences between them always remained, more apparent at some times than others, and at different times one or other of the two Egypts was dominant.

Although short of wood, except palmwood which is of limited use as a structural material, the region was amply provided with stone in the cliffs along the valley, from which the greatest monuments of Egyptian civilization were built. There was also clay, which was generally used for building ordinary houses, and papyrus reeds, which could be cemented with clay for walls as well as for roofs.

Above:
Relief of figures bearing tribute, flanking the grand staircase to the audience hall of the Persian king Darius I (518-460 BC).

Opposite:
Painted limestone statues of the Fourth Dynasty high priest Rahotep and his wife Nofret. The Egyptians always gave men a darker skin than women, a convention also found in many other places. Egyptian Museum, Cairo.

Egyptian civilization lasted a remarkably long time (roughly 3,000 years) and remained remarkably self-contained throughout its existence, though that is not to say, of course, that it was completely unaffected by developments in other parts of the world. Moreover, although there were many changes in fashion, style and method, Egyptian art stuck so closely to its own traditions that, over three millennia, it retained the same fundamental character. That alone makes Egyptian culture unique: no other country shows such long-standing loyalty to established forms.

The long era of ancient Egypt can be conveniently split up into four

periods. The first, following a period of preparation which culminated in the unification of Egypt, sometimes called the Predynastic Period, is known as the Old Kingdom, and lasted from the late fourth millennium to the middle of the third millennium. There followed a period of strife which ended with the establishment of the Middle Kingdom, about 2100 BC. About 400 years later the Middle Kingdom collapsed and, after another more or less anarchic interlude, the New Kingdom was founded in about 1570 BC. It is sometimes called the Empire, for this was the period when Egyptian power extended farthest, into Nubia in the south and Mesopotamia in the northeast; this was also the time of the Israelites' bondage in Egypt, the subject of such stirring tales in the Old Testament. After another period of weakness, there was a revival in the Late Period, sometimes called the Saite Period after the capital at Sais on the Nile delta, in the 7th and 6th centuries BC.

The continuity of Egyptian art reflects, naturally, a continuity of social and religious customs, and relatively stable government. The central figure in Egypt was the pharaoh, the ruler who besides being head of state was also a god, the equal of any creature in heaven or earth. He was thus a far more powerful ruler than most other kings of the ancient Middle East, though in practice his absolute authority depended on the priests and the nobles, who sometimes controlled him utterly. Most official positions, as in other early civilizations, became hereditary (like the office of the Pharaoh himself), and their incumbents tended to grow more powerful with time.

The reason we know, comparatively speaking, so much about the civilization of ancient Egypt is an indirect result of Egyptian religion. The Egyptians were strong believers in a life after death, in a much more materialistic sense than in the Christian religion: the body itself would live again. For that reason, it had to be preserved, and the Egyptians went to tremendous efforts to make their tombs safe – with the result that some survived in more or less their original conditions for thousands of years. The tomb was, literally, a house of the dead, and it was equipped to support life after death, even to make it enjoyable. Originally, food was brought to the tomb by surviving relatives, but this soon gave way to representations of food being prepared and, later on, to scenes of all the activities of life, especially those likely to bring comfort to the departed. Tombs became veritable picture books of Egyptian life. Moreover, in case the body, despite all efforts to safeguard it, was damaged or destroyed, it was customary to place in the tomb replicas – statues – of the dead person to act as alternative resting places for the 'ghost'.

Egyptian civilization came into being with what seems to be rather surprising speed. Scholars suppose there was a Mesopotamian catalyst in the Predynastic Period; there is not much hard evidence to support this belief, but it does seem to be a likely idea, especially now that it has been definitely established that Mesopotamian civilization is older than Egyptian.

A wall painting in a tomb at Hierakonpolis (below) shows some typical motifs of art at the end of the Predynastic Period which were to reappear again and again: boats, hunting scenes, battles and lions. However, this is a very rudimentary form of painting, a collection of subjects with no thought of space or composition. The battle scenes may record the struggle to unite Upper and Lower Egypt.

The earliest monumental sculpture dates from the First and Second Dynasties, about 3000 BC, and demonstrates the importance that the figure of the pharaoh had already attained. The same monumental quality, without the physical dimensions, appears in smaller statues of, for example, the pharaoh Zoser of the Third Dynasty, in whose reign Imhotep, regarded as the first architect in history, built the step pyramid at Saqqara. This was the forerunner of the well-known pyramids of Giza, which were built during the Fourth Dynasty (2600-2480 BC). The pyramids were the result of long years of experiment; Imhotep's stepped pyramid was developed from the older Egyptian tomb called a *mastaba*, and the simple, four-sided pyramid was

Right:
Wall painting from Hierakonopolis, from the Egyptian Predynastic period, about 3200 BC, showing boating and hunting scenes. Egyptian Museum, Cairo.

Opposite:
This painted wooden funerary stele shows a dead woman worshipping the Egyptian sun god, who holds his traditional crook and flail. Museo Egizio, Turin.

Above:
Statue of King Chephren in dark green diorite, slightly more than life size, about 2560 BC. Egyptian Museum, Cairo.

Right:
The dwarf Seneb and his family, painted limestone, about 33 cm high. This is one of the most remarkable and realistic sculptures of the Old Kingdom. Egyptian Museum, Cairo.

Opposite:
The enormous head of the mysterious Sphinx of Chephren (about 4 metres wide) which has stood guard over the tombs of the pharaohs since about 2500 BC.

the point of perfection. Many still stand, symbolizing, by their exquisitely simple form, the enduring nature of Egyptian art. The agonies of the slaves who built the pyramids are felt no longer.

The statues of pharaohs, seated on their box-like thrones, have a basic similarity; though more expressive than earlier figures, they appear rigid, though certainly conveying a sense of power. They obey formal conventions already well established. The statue of Chephren, belonging to the Fourth Dynasty, found at Giza, is one of the best examples (above left). It is made from a form of greenstone called diorite and shows many of the conventional aspects of such works – headdress, 'royal' beard, right hand

clenched, left hand resting on thigh. Invisible in this picture is the falcon standing behind the king's head and protecting him with his wings: this is the royal god Horus who imbues him with his power. Often more interesting than this type of statue, made very much to rule, though of the best craftsmanship, are lesser works not intended solely to convey the idea of the divine pharaoh, remote and immutable. A very different impression for example is conveyed by the limestone figures of the dwarf Seneb and his family (above), dating from the Sixth Dynasty (about 2300-2200 BC), which is a fairly realistic and human family group. It came from Seneb's tomb, a *mastaba* at Giza, and his burial place alone shows that the

dwarf was a highly placed person at
court. Few ordinary citizens rated so
grand a burial chamber.

The walls of Old Kingdom tombs
are covered with relief carving and
inscriptions, often describing the
great deeds of the deceased. They are
invariably painted and, since they are
carved in low relief, there was really
little difference between sculpture
and painting. However, some pure
paintings from the Old Kingdom
have survived, including the geese
(above), which are actually part of a
group of six such birds who waddle
across the plaster wall of a tomb in a
strikingly realistic manner, despite
the characteristic stiff, two-
dimensional quality of the work.
Egyptian painting is a matter of
strong outline and flat colour tones;
there are no shadows.

There is something of a decline
apparent in the art of the Old Kingdom between the Fourth and the
Sixth Dynasties. The Sixth Dynasty
culminated about 2200 BC in a period
of internal disorder which lasted four
or five generations. The central unity

collapsed, and the very few records of the time speak of the misery and deprivation of the people. This so-called First Intermediate Period was that of the Seventh to Tenth Dynasties, where the power of the pharaoh was considerably weakened. About 2080 BC centralized authority was restored by a new line of princes from Thebes, in Upper Egypt, but nothing was ever quite the same again. Egypt regained much of its lost power and prosperity, but a certain confidence – confidence in the unchanging social and political order – was gone. This naturally showed itself in art. Royal statues become less 'ideal', more realistic; there is no solid, central idea, and although there is no sharp break with the traditions of the Old Kingdom – to which people looked back with admiration – the concept of the pharaoh as god gives way to the pharaoh as king, wise and brave, but perceptibly human. The chief works of the Middle Kingdom come from the Twelfth Dynasty (19th century BC). Sculpture shows a new awareness of the dramatic properties of light, as in the sphinx from Tanis (opposite), a figure one metre high in black granite, which was one of four discovered there. The sphinx was a familiar creature in the mythology of ancient civilizations, renowned for its wisdom. Sculptures of sphinxes in Egypt, of which the best known is the enormous granite example at Giza dating from the Fourth Dynasty, were often made with the face of the contemporary ruler. As a rule they also had the typical royal headdress, although the Tanis sphinx (portraying Amenemhet III) is equipped with a lion's mane.

After the end of the Twelfth Dynasty, another period of chaos began, the Second Intermediate Period. Lower Egypt was invaded by people from Syria and Palestine, perhaps including Hebrews, who set up their own pharaohs in the delta while Upper Egypt apparently remained under Egyptian princes from Thebes. The invaders brought with them new weapons, horses and chariots, but eventually the Egyptians made better use of them and drove the invaders out. With the establishment of the New Kingdom in

the 16th century BC, Egypt entered on its period of great imperial expansion.

In the reign of Queen Hatshepsut, there were new developments in art, perhaps partly at least due to influence from Asia Minor. In her magnificent temple (above) appear the famous scenes of the expedition to the Land of Punt, which sailed down the Red Sea to north-east Africa. The scenes have a freedom and liveliness not seen before in Egyptian art, with monkeys roaming about the ships, and incidentally provide us with excellent information about the nature of ships and shipping in this period. The sculpture of the time shows a rhythmic, graceful charm, as in the granite relief of the queen herself (right).

The most interesting developments in the art of the New Kingdom were in painting, of which examples exist in illustrated papyri, on sarcophagi (coffins), and on the walls of the tombs, which were cut deep into natural rock, sometimes to a distance of 200 metres. Painting was freed from its subservience to relief carving and entered into its own. In the royal tombs, it is governed by strict rules of orthodoxy, but in those of lesser people the artist had more scope for imagination and invention. It is among these works that

Above:
The temple of Queen Hatshepsut at Thebes.

Below:
Queen Hatshepsut, represented as a man, with the god Amon, Eighteenth Dynasty, New Kingdom (about 1501-1480 BC). Karnak.

Above:
Head of a girl. An example of the fine
painting done in Thebes under the New
Kingdom. Tomb of Menna, Sheikh-
abd-el-Qrnah, Western Thebes.

44

the most attractive – to us – examples of Egyptian art are to be found, with landscapes (previously ignored), and lively scenes of boating and hunting. The charming head of a girl (opposite) comes from a scene showing a fishing expedition.

In the reign of Amenhotep IV in the Eighteenth Dynasty (1575-1308 BC), there was a major change in Egyptian life, which underwent a minor revolution. In brief, Amenhotep swept away the tangled worship of many gods that was Egypt's religion and replaced it with the worship of one god, Aton, the sun god. He changed his own name, which had associations with the Theban god Amon, to Akhenaton, 'instrument of Aton', and moved his capital from Thebes to Tel el-Amarna. This revolution affected all aspects of Egyptian life, including art. In the Amarna Period, as it is called (after the capital city), monumental sculpture forsook the calm dignity of tradition and took on a sinewy expressionist quality. The giant figure of Amenhotep IV (below) from Karnak (now in the Cairo Museum) has a sardonic characterization which approaches caricature, although it also preserves traditional forms – the royal headdress and (false) beard, the crook and the flail held in each hand, etc. Complete breaks with the past are inconceivable in art, or in any other human activity, all the more so in ancient Egypt; and after all, the artists were the same men, or workers in the same tradition, as in the previous reign. (Akhenaton's chief sculptor at Amarna was the son of the chief sculptor of his father and predecessor.) The official portraits of the reign are magnificent and, despite changes in some features of official style, they are firmly in the old tradition. Perhaps the most famous, and surely the most often reproduced portrait in all of Egyptian art, is the painted stone head of Akhenaton's queen, the beautiful Nefertiti, now in Berlin. Yet the real novelty of portraits of the Amarna period is that they are realistic: they attempt to reproduce the actual physical appearance of the

Left:
Amenhotep IV, renamed Akhenaton, carved sandstone, more than twice life size, Eighteenth Dynasty, about 1375 BC. Egyptian Museum, Cairo.

Below:
Queen Nefertiti in painted limestone, from Tel el-Amarna, about 1370 BC. Ägyptishes Museum, Berlin–Charlottenburg.

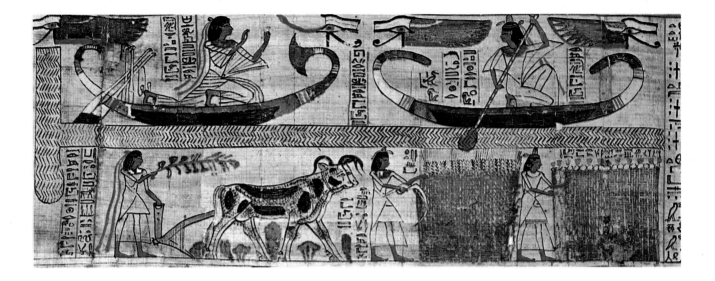

Above:
Detail from a papyrus roll of the Twentieth Dynasty, showing boats on the river and, below, scenes of ploughing and harvesting. Museo Egizio, Turin.

Below:
Relief showing Rameses III hunting, about 1190 BC. Medinet Habu Western Thebes.

subject, whereas earlier official sculpture depicted the office of the man (for example as pharaoh) rather than his essence.

Akhenaton was succeeded by the youthful Tutankhamen, without doubt the most familiar of all the pharaohs to us. This is due not to his importance as a ruler which, as he died quite young, was very slight, but to the simple fact that his tomb was discovered by modern archaeologists untouched. All the other tombs of the pharaohs had been partially looted or otherwise damaged at some time during the long centuries that divided ancient Egypt from the modern era. The discovery of Tutankhamen's tomb is one of the most exciting stories in all archaeology, and recent exhibitions of his relics, on loan from the Cairo Museum, have atracted record-breaking crowds in the western world. The mummified body of the king was enclosed in a coffin of solid gold. That in turn was contained in a second coffin made of gilded wood inlaid with coloured glass and precious stones, which was protected by yet a third coffin.

Akhenaton's revolution did not long outlast him. Tutankhamen moved the capital back to Thebes, and during the following reign, the whole heritage of Akhenaton was set aside. There was even an attempt to erase all memory of the radical pharaoh, somewhat in the way that now unfavoured persons are removed from history books in the Soviet Union, and Egyptian art returned to the customs of the earlier part of the Eighteenth Dynasty.

The last great artistic period of the New Kingdom took place under the pharaohs of the early Nineteenth Dynasty, Rameses I, Seti I, and Rameses II, whose combined reigns lasted from 1308-1224 BC. Official sculpture shows a conscious return to the earlier grandiose tradition that preceded Akhenaton, although there are traces of the Amarna style to be seen in, for instance, the individualistic treatment of features of the face. This was another period of great building. Rameses II enlarged and rebuilt temples and erected gigantic statues of himself, while ancient Thebes is still dominated by the mighty reliefs of Rameses's victories in war. These reliefs, though harking back to the tradition of Queen Hatshepsut, owe some of their vitality to the experiments of the Amarna Period and perhaps also to the Hittites, whose influence was still strong in Syria, where Seti's and Rameses's conquests had taken place.

During the Twentieth Dynasty, Egypt came under attack from various peoples, who included the 'People of the Sea' and the ancestors of the Greeks. Rameses III, last of the great warrior pharaohs, defeated the invaders in land and sea battles which are commemorated in huge sculp-tured reliefs in Thebes, but though Egypt herself was saved, the provinces of Syria and Palestine had been lost for good. Moreover, by relying still on its own resources and rejecting outside influence, Egypt in a way caused its own downfall. The Mediterranean region was entering the Iron Age, but Egypt, the greatest of Bronze Age civilizations, did not follow, for though well supplied with copper, from which bronze is made, it had no large resources of iron. After the death of Rameses III, Upper and Lower Egypt again became divided and were ruled by separate families. No worthwhile art was produced for about three hundred years, when a slight cultural revival occurred, first under Nubian rule, then under the Saite (Twenty-Sixth) Dynasty (664-525 BC); but it took the form mainly of nostalgic efforts to recreate the glories of the past. The Saite Period ended with the conquest of Egypt by the Persians in 525 BC. The old cultural traditions lingered on in one way or another, but with the Persian conquest and the rise of Greek civilization, the long day of Egypt was finally over.

Below:
Pillars with giant stone figures from the Temple of Rameses III.

Above:
Head in black granite of a Nubian king
who lived in the 7th century BC. It
would once have been part of a full-
length statue. Egyptian Museum, Cairo.

48

Classical Art

Classical art is the art of the ancient Greeks and Romans. It begins about four thousand years ago and ends with the triumph of the Christian Church in the 4th century AD, although during that long period there were long stretches which, from the point of view of artistic creation, were relatively insignificant. The ancient Greeks stand at the beginning of our civilization, and their ideas and discoveries, to a large if barely conscious extent, govern our own feelings about art. It was the Greeks who discovered the means of representing man and nature in what seems to us the natural way. Nevertheless, the Greek attitude to art was not the same as ours, and it is important to keep in mind the ideas and motives of the artists and to appreciate that what, through long familiarity, seems obvious to us, may have been a revolutionary discovery in the context of the time.

The Greeks made no distinction between the artist and the craftsman; the artist was a useful, professional craftsman, like a blacksmith or a carpenter, whose proficiency was attained through long training and apprenticeship. However, it would be absurd to say that someone like the sculptor Pheidias was regarded as no more than a particularly skilled blacksmith. The very nature of his craft made him something greater than that. The purpose of art was to show the perfection of man and the gods – a moral purpose – and to illustrate the superiority of Greek civilization over that of the 'barbarians'. The achievement of 5th century BC sculpture in perfection of ideal form came as close as conceivable to realizing these aims, and therefore led inevitably to changes of emphasis in the succeeding era, in particular to a greater variety in themes and techniques. In the later, Hellenistic period (from the 4th century BC onwards), the art of the past was deeply respected, and indeed collected in a way not dissimilar to our own day, with rulers and rich men amassing great collections of Greek art and incidentally encouraging copies of earlier works (often the only evidence we have of them). The adoption of Greek art by the Romans gave it a universality it would not have otherwise achieved. In the first century AD the Roman empire stretched the length of Europe (and into western Asia and North Africa), and throughout that empire the Greek artistic tradition was spread; new buildings, statues and paintings were made in the Greek manner, often by Greek artists. The Romans, however, were not merely slavish copiers, even when they thought of themselves as little else, and as we shall see they made many contributions of their own to the classical tradition.

It is worth briefly sketching the development of classical civilization from its first flourishing in a Mediterranean island down to the period when it was subsumed in or rejected by Christian and Byzantine art.

The earliest centre of Greek art was Bronze Age Crete, the Crete of King Minos and the Minotaur. This extraordinary culture was only discovered early in the present century, through the work of European archaeologists, and in many respects it remains exotic and mysterious. The chief economic reason for its dramatic rise was the discovery and use of metals, spreading from Asia Minor to Crete some time before 2000 BC. The Minoans made fine objects in gold and built cities and palaces, decorating the walls with lively and colourful painting. The best known palace is the one at Knossos.

By about 1600 BC the first Greek-

speaking people had arrived on the mainland of Greece from the north and became dominant too. They are called the Mycenaeans, after one of their cities which was excavated in the 19th century by Heinrich Schliemann, who also discovered Troy. Their painting and sculpture were derived from that of the older civilization in Crete, though their cities were very different because the Myceneans, unlike the Minoans, had to build strong fortifications to keep out their enemies. By about 1400 BC, following some disaster in Crete the exact nature of which is a matter of argument, Minoan civilization collapsed, and the Mycenaeans became dominant in Crete also. But after about two hundred years, Mycenaean civilization also collapsed and was followed by a longer period of comparative obscurity, the 'Dark Ages' of Greece of which we know little apart from what can be deduced from the later Greek epics.

The Mycenaeans appear to have been overcome by another wave of invading migrants, the Dorians. Little apart from pottery survives from the early Doric period (c. 1100-800 BC), although Mycenaean traditions were not forgotten. Gradually, the Greeks formed communities of the type we know as the city state. Each little state commanded a greater or lesser area of the surrounding country, and power lay in the hands of an aristocratic ruling class. By the 8th century, these communities were becoming strong and prosperous through trade, and the Greeks were spreading to other parts of the Mediterranean world. They came into close contact with other, older cultures, including that of Egypt; sculpture and painting had reappeared largely due to Egyptian influence: the large statues of the 7th

century are clearly the result of what the Greeks had seen in Egypt. Thus the first period of Greek art, known as the geometric period because of the abstract, geometric patterns employed in the decoration of pottery, that started around 1000 BC, gave way to the second, 'orientalizing' period during the 8th century BC.

In this period, important political changes took place. The commercial prosperity of Greece had given rise to a new class of merchants, rich farmers and others, who were powerful economically but not politically. They reacted against government by an aristocratic élite, and during the 6th century BC most of the city-states came under the rule of a 'tyrant', in the Greek sense of the term which does not have quite the sinister overtones that ours does. These men, even more than the aristocrats whom they replaced, were often great patrons of the arts, since the arts existed partly at least to glorify them and give support to the established order. Rule by tyrants, however, was not popular, and by the 5th century democracy (where each man had a part to play in the state) was adopted by Athens and other city-states. Athens played a significant part in resisting the Persian invasion, which increased her influence and helped make her the undisputed leader of Greece. The successful war against the Persians also saw the emergence of new artistic

traditions, the expression of Greek self-confidence and the achievement of a limited but unique perfection of form in sculpture and architecture.

But the period of prosperity and confidence was short-lived. The Greeks quarrelled among themselves and the long Peloponnesian War (431-404 BC) resulted in the decline of Athens. Art became less universal, less the triumphant statement of perfect form: figures of the gods became less Olympian and more like ordinary people. The art of portraiture made its appearance, and economic decline caused a dissipation of state art, with artists becoming more independent of the state, often travelling from place to place. The new centre of Greek civilization in the 4th century was the kingdom of Macedon and, under the rule of Alexander the Great (356-323 BC), Greek influence was extended throughout the wide area of Alexander's conquests. Following the death of Alexander, new kingdoms arose, more or less Hellenic (Greek) in tradition, in the provinces that he had conquered. In this new cosmopolitan world, Greek art ceased to be the expression of religion and the state, and became more the product of private patrons and hence more secular and more personal, with much greater variety in themes, techniques and emotions.

Meanwhile, the power of Rome had been growing. Already, the

Romans had been in intimate contact
with Greek traditions, partly indirectly through their forerunners,
the Etruscans, and partly through the
Greek colonies in Italy. Rome's defeat of Carthage in the 2nd century BC
brought direct contact with the Hellenized kingdoms in the east and
south. The Romans, to their credit,
recognized the qualities of Greek
civilization, though not always in a
way with which the Greeks would
have concurred and not always
mirroring modern reactions to classical Greek art. But for three hundred
years classical traditions were spread
among people who had no previous
knowledge of them, and took root so
strongly that they survived the largely
hostile influence of Christianity
which, however much it might de-
plore pagan art, nevertheless took
continuing inspiration from it.

Early examples of Cretan art include
pottery apparently based on Anatolian prototypes and carved ivories
reminiscent of Egyptian art. There
are also simplified human figures in
stone (page 50) made in the islands of
the Cyclades. The beginnings of a
more strictly Cretan style of decoration can be seen in ornamental bands

which repeat a certain motif, or merely a wavy line, on pottery.

The palace at Knossos and other great buildings were constructed soon after 2000 BC. This Bronze Age civilization, called Minoan after the legendary King Minos, constantly rebuilt or altered its buildings, and what was discovered by Sir Arthur Evans at Knossos and by other archaeologists at other sites is comparatively recent construction, dating from the late 17th century BC. Even so, the buildings as reconstructed do not appear particularly 'Greek' – except, perhaps, for the free-standing columns (in concrete instead of wood) themselves. It is to this later period that surviving Minoan sculpture and painting also belongs. The technique of wall painting was learned from Egypt, though Minoan paintings have little in common with those of Egypt. Some, though not all, are true frescoes – the picture being painted on the plaster of the wall before it dries. They are in strong colours, reds, yellows and blues, and the scale varies considerably. Some fairly simple conventions are used: for example, men are red, women are white. The technique is hard outline and flat tone, and human figures are frequently represented in that common, though awkward, combination of head and legs in profile (sometimes with two left, or right feet) and torso frontal. Perhaps their most remarkable feature is their liveliness; Minoan artists were not afraid, in spite of their limitations, of trying to depict violent action, and they managed it with extraordinary success. Background details are sometimes rendered in a way that can only be called impressionist. In short, Minoan art is a remarkable mixture of the comparatively primitive and the sophisticated.

The same qualities of vigour and movement appear in other arts. The gold cup (page 51) now in the National Museum of Athens shows a bull tossing a hunter (contests between bulls and human beings was a major preoccupation of Minoan art) with striking realism. This magnificent piece was found on the Greek mainland but has been indisputably proved to be Cretan of about the 15th century BC. The relief ornament was done by the *repoussé* method, in which the metal is hammered from the back into soft material such as leather. An even more famous Minoan bull is the *rhyton* (a vessel in the form of an animal's head) of black steatite (opposite), with eyes of inlaid rock crystal and gilded horns, found at Knossos (and somewhat restored since then).

Another piece of sculpture found at Knossos and characteristic of the time is the small figure of a woman (below) in contemporary dress, which exposed the breasts, handling two snakes. This figure is generally known as the 'Snake Goddess', though her precise status is uncertain. Just as the bull was a symbol of manly strength, the snake represented fertility in other places besides Crete. It is also fairly

Below:
Earthenware 'snake goddess' from Crete, about 1600 BC. National Archaeological Museum, Athens.

certain that the Mother Goddess was central to Minoan religion. Sir Arthur Evans discovered on the engraved stone seals of the Early Minoan Period numerous representations of a female figure who seems to be the subject of worship. She is sometimes shown with a male figure, who is usually smaller, a common way of suggesting inferiority. Later statuettes of aristocratic court ladies may also have represented the Mother Goddess, whom Evans identified with Rhea, mother of Zeus, though she would probably have had other identities, like later Greek gods. Evans also suggested that the lady with the snake may represent the goddess in her aspect of goddess of the Underworld, though most modern scholars would doubt this.

In the 15th century BC there were certain changes in style in Cretan art. There was a movement away from naturalism: paintings took on a more formal, stiff appearance, suggesting Egyptian influence, and the attempt at realistic depiction of the world of nature was abandoned in favour of a more conventional form of decora-

tion. Possibly these changes were the result of Mycenaean invasion from mainland Greece.

Mycenaean culture, developing later than Minoan, is known mainly from the excavations of Schliemann and his successors at Mycenae and Tiryns. At Mycenae, Schliemann removed over a ton of gold objects from the shaft graves of (it is assumed) the Mycenaean kings of the 16th century BC, including the gold mask (above) laid over the face of a dead king, whom Schliemann romantically associated with Agamemnon, the leader of the 'Achaeans' (Greeks) during the siege of Troy. The close similarity of these precious objects – weapons, jewelry, vessels of various kinds – to Minoan work made some people suppose that they were the booty taken in raids against Crete. Many do seem to have been the work of Cretan craftsmen, but they were made to Mycenaean order: the themes illustrated (hunting scenes are common) reflect Mycenaean tastes, and the attitude of the Mycenaeans towards the Minoans as far as art was con-

cerned was probably deferential in the way that, in a later age, the Romans were to respect the Greeks. At Tiryns, traditionally the birthplace of Herakles, is found the first Greek example of the close alliance between sculpture and architecture which was to be a notable feature of Greek art. The 'Lion Gate' at Mycenae (opposite) has an enormous stone lintel surmounted by a heraldic device in massive relief showing two lions flanking a column (the column symbolizing the citadel which the lions are guarding). Again, the workmanship appears to be Minoan, but the whole conception is Mycenaean: there was no sculpture on this scale in Crete.

Historians tend to describe any period for which they have little information as a 'Dark Age', but just as the Dark Ages of early medieval Europe seem less 'dark' as more research is completed, so the Dark Ages of Greece are steadily appearing, through the work of the archaeologists, not so shadowy as was once thought. Around 1100 BC the Mycenaean civilization came to a fairly abrupt halt, as a result of the invasions of the Dorians, users of iron whose advent marked the end of the Bronze Age and led to the development of the Greek city states some four centuries later. Such an interval is appropriate, in a sense, for there can be no dispute about the fact that the world of the Minoans and the Mycenaeans was very different from that of classical Greece. The Minoans were not Greek, though their language, for some years indecipherable, has

Below:
A vase decorated in proto-geometric style, from 11th-century BC Athens. British Museum, London.

turned out to be an early version of Greek (otherwise, perhaps, it would never have been deciphered). The briefest glance at Minoan art shows clearly how 'un-Greek' were its creators. The Minoans were inspired by nature, and their art imitated nature, on the whole realistically. Their palaces, though grand, were rambling affairs, not built according to any rigidly conceived plan. Nothing could be less like the Greek sense of order and correct form, with buildings conforming to a strict sense of symmetry. However, the Mycenaeans provide a direct link between the disparate worlds of Minoan Crete and classical Greece. Their art may have been largely Minoan, but their architecture foreshadows the classical plan. The Greeks of Homer's time clearly and rightly regarded the Mycenaeans as their ancestors.

The land which the Dorians entered was a rugged land; life was tougher than it was in the fertile valley of the Nile, and perhaps the very toughness of life encouraged the Greek resourcefulness, energy, and willingness to experiment. The legends passed down to us from Homer were known throughout the Greek world and fostered a sense of fraternal unity and superiority to the barbarians (non-Greeks) though not enough to prevent constant wars and quarrels between the city states until these were seriously threatened by the Persian attack. The smallness of the city state, however, permitted a true form of democracy in which every citizen had a voice in the government. Individual citizens felt pride in themselves, and in their work; potters took pleasure in their own creations, as many inscriptions attest.

The land provided the materials necessary for the development of architecture and sculpture. There was no lack of timber (the Greek forests have since disappeared owing to the depredations of goats), there was plenty of rough limestone, and above all there was fine marble, like that of Paros, which was hard enough to last for centuries and yet amenable to the sculptor's chisel.

Sculpture during the so-called Dark Ages was limited to small works in terracotta or bronze, and by the 8th

century had taken on a style similar to the geometric pottery of the preceding two or three centuries. The little (10 cm high) bronze group of a man and a centaur (below) is an example of this style. It is interesting to note that at this date (mid-8th century) the centaur is represented as a complete man with the hindquarters of a horse attached; later, the creature would evolve into a horse with the head and torso of a man. The group possibly illustrates one of the stories about Herakles. The hero was carrying off Deianira, whom he had won in a fight with a rival, when they came to a flooded river where the centaur Nessus offered to assist by carrying Deianira over on his back. No sooner was she mounted than he ran off with her, whereupon Herakles shot him

with an arrow. As Nessus lay dying he advised Deianira to take some of his blood and smear it on Herakles's shirt if he ever were unfaithful to her. On a later occasion, exasperated with the hero's infidelity, she did so, whereupon the poisonous blood of the centaur burned Herakles's flesh from his bones, fulfilling the prophecy that he should die at the hands of an enemy already dead. The triangular shape of heads and bodies in this group is typical of the geometric style of sculpture.

Below:
An archaic figure in bronze, only 10 cm high, of a man and a centaur, 8th century BC. Metropolitan Museum of Art, New York, Gift of J. Pierpont Morgan, 1917.

By the time this bronze was made, the increasingly prosperous Greek city states were already establishing colonies in the Aegean and across the Adriatic, and trade was bringing them into closer contact with other cultures – Egyptian, Anatolian and Phoenician. These foreign artistic influences were incorporated into Greek art and skilfully adapted to Greek tradition. They are seen in the more natural depiction of human figures and animals on pottery. Potters at Corinth developed the black-figure style, in which the figures are painted in dark silhouette on the reddish body of the vessel, sometimes with engraved lines and the addition of other colours for added emphasis. This was to be the dominant style in Greek pottery until the 6th century BC. The Athenian amphora (a two-handled, wide-bodied wine jug) in the British Museum (opposite) dates from about 530 BC. The scene depicted is an incident from the Trojan War (though one not described by Homer), in which Penthesilea, queen of the Amazons and ally of the Trojans, is killed by Achilles, who was said to have fallen in love with her in the moment he slew her.

This amphora is a fairly late example of the black-figure style. Within a few years, it had given way to red-figure painting, in which the old technique was turned around: instead of painting the figures in black on the body of the clay, the body was painted black and the figures left in the natural colour. At first this may seem no more than a whimsical reversal, but in fact it offered several important advantages to the vase painter. In black-figure, details within the figure had to be engraved, so that the red colour of the clay showed through the black, but in black-figure this rather cumbersome method of delineation was no longer necessary, as internal lines could be painted. The artist achieved greater flexibility, especially in depicting movement and in suggesting three dimensions, for black-figure paintings are generally in flat profile, while in red-figure, the turn of a limb or the fall of a cloak can be more easily suggested. To appreciate this greater realism, compare the amphora discussed above with the depiction of the same scene by a red-figure painter (page 59) seventy or eighty years later. The considerable distortion that is the result of a flat photograph of a concave surface (the inside of a cup) does not destroy the impression of a remarkable advance in realism nor the powerful human feeling of the later picture, which incidentally, like the black-figure amphora, is the work of a particularly fine painter. Not easily detectable in the photograph is the use of other colours – red, blue and gilt – in the red-figure cup.

There were other techniques in vase painting, especially the use of a white slip (an overall coating of creamy clay) on which the design was painted in outline and filled with a variety of colours; while black-figure and red-figure are sometimes found on opposite sides of the same vessel, though the older technique gradually disappeared.

The growing prosperity of the Greek city states in the 8th century permitted the building of temples and the creation of monumental sculpture. No doubt examples seen in Egypt and the East were responsible for the latter, and possibly the earliest examples were in wood. Nevertheless, the precise origins of this immensely important development are somewhat mysterious; there seem to have been no examples before the 7th century, when the geometric style had been almost totally abandoned in the search for the ideal human form, though traces remain in the wasp waists and wide shoulders of male figures and other details that recall Egyptian art. These traces too were soon to disappear.

Greek sculpture of the 7th century is sometimes called 'Daedalic' after the man who in legend was said to have been the first sculptor. (Daedalus was said to have been an Athenian who, as a kind of resident engineer to King Minos in Crete, created the Labyrinth in which the Minotaur was imprisoned; he also invented wings with which he and his son, Icarus, escaped from Crete, with the tragic result that Icarus flew too near the sun, which melted the glue and sent him to his death in the sea below.)

Architecture is not part of the subject of this book, but its vital importance in Greek culture, and the fact that it provided the stimulus and opportunity for the development of other arts, especially sculpture, must be remembered. The establishment of the Doric order in the 7th century BC gave rise to new types of sculpture and painting, notably in the decoration of the entablature of temples. Some examples of painted terracotta metopes (the squarish spaces divided by triglyphs which together make up the horizontal decorative band below the pediment) have been found from a late 7th century BC temple; the technique is similar to that of the vase painters. But the earliest example of sculpture used to fill the triangular space of the pediment comes from a temple of Artemis (Diana) in Corfu. In the centre is the figure of a Gorgon (a terrifying female with snakes for hair) and she is flanked by two lion-like beasts, with her sons crammed into the corners at either end. The problem of filling a space which gradually slopes away into a sharp corner was to be overcome rather more successfully in later temples, but it always remained a problem. The Corfu pediment survives only in a fragmentary state, and there is comparatively little monumental sculpture of this type until the 5th century, when Greek art entered its heroic period. There is, however, plenty of other 7th-century sculpture and painted pottery, showing that oriental influence had virtually disappeared and that Greek art had found its own course of development. Artists were searching for new ideas and gradually conquering the problems of representational art, attaining a lucid nobility of form unparalleled before and seldom equalled since.

A major impetus behind this development was the Greek religion. The poems of Homer made the gods of Olympia vivid personalities; Apollo, Artemis, Ares and the rest, including Zeus, are not abstract conceptions, they are individuals and often all too human – quite different, for instance, from the animal-headed gods of Egypt. But although they appear in human form, they are, of course, more

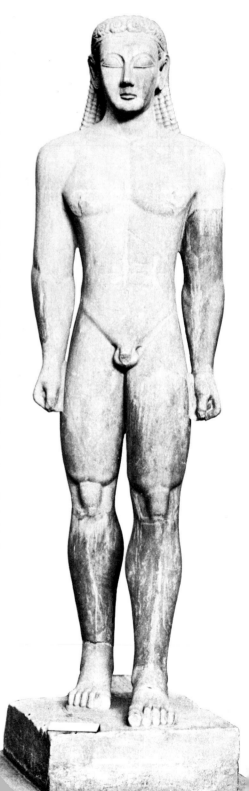

60

than human, not only more powerful but more perfect physically. When the Greeks made statues of their gods, therefore, they had to make statues that were realistic – no conventionalized version would do in view of the intense individuality the gods had achieved through folklore – yet at the same time they had to be rendered in forms more perfect than any to be found on earth; they had to be at once human and superhuman. The sculptors eventually reached an ideal form by starting out from a basis of realistic knowledge and gradually eliminating incidental or accidental features. This ideal was not achieved quickly. Up to the end of the Archaic Period of Greek art, which can be equated with the victory over the invading Persians in 480 BC, experiment was continual, as artists slowly worked out the potential of the human form and acquired the ability to make the stone, under the persuasion of their chisels, give up the image within. Their goal was always greater realism, and one unusual and important feature of their progress was their readiness to abandon tradition when they saw its shortcomings. The simplest way to observe the extraordinary progress made is to compare, for example, the statue of a youth from Attica (opposite), representative of many similar figures, which dates from about 600 BC, with the statue by Polykleitos known as the Diadoumenos (right). It is a striking contrast. The earlier figure, sometimes said to be, like most figures of handsome young men not otherwise identified, a statue of Apollo, is a stiff formalized derivation from Egypt. The sculptor was clearly dominated to a large extent by his material. It is easy to imagine him confronting the original block of stone, drawing an outline on the facing surface, and chipping away from that until he had, first a rough relief, then eventually the finished figure – still, however, loudly proclaiming the lifeless block of stone from which it came. The rather rudimentary rendering of detail and the way in which the hands are still attached to the sides (despite the fact that the figure is striding forwards) suggests that the sculptor was fearful of spoiling his work by carving away

too much. Nevertheless, this figure shows some notable differences from what we may regard as its Egyptian prototype. There is no supporting slab or throne; the figure is nude, which suggests that the Greeks were already concerned primarily with the human body as their subject, and there is some attempt at anatomical detail.

A major advance in sculpture in the 6th century was the discovery of the technique of hollow-casting large bronze figures. Unfortunately, because bronze may usefully be melted down and used for other purposes, very few large bronzes have survived

from antiquity. We tend to think of Greek sculptors working mainly in stone; on the contrary, bronze was the favourite material of the great 5th-century sculptors. The solitary example of a life-size bronze figure of the Archaic Period closely resembles contemporary marble figures, and may well have been cast from a stone model.

Below:
The statue of Diadoumenos by Polykleitos, Athens, 5th century BC. National Archaeological Museum, Athens.

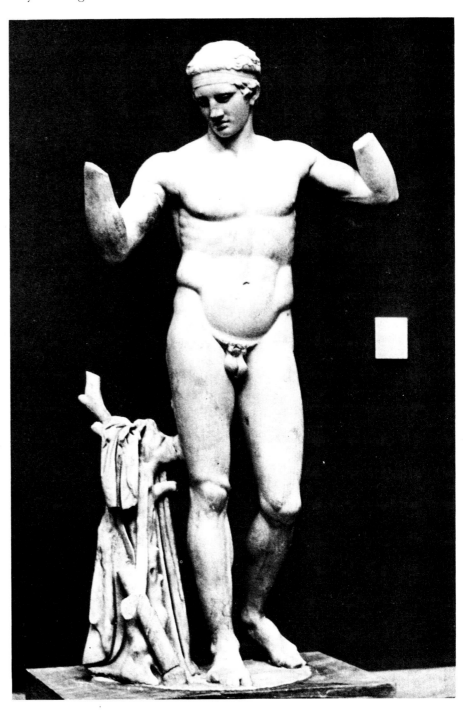

Above:
Perseus and the Medusa, from the Archaic period of Greek art, 6th century BC. Museo Nazionale, Palermo.

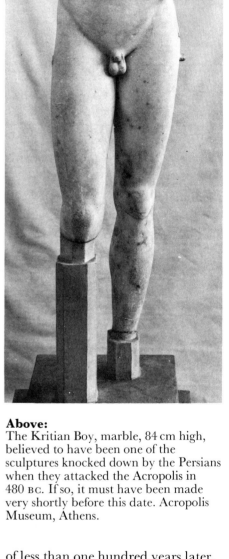

Above:
The Kritian Boy, marble, 84 cm high, believed to have been one of the sculptures knocked down by the Persians when they attacked the Acropolis in 480 BC. If so, it must have been made very shortly before this date. Acropolis Museum, Athens.

The 6th century also offers examples of sculptures from pediments showing how much progress was being made in overcoming the difficulties of the pedimental shape. A fragment from the Acropolis made use of a three-headed monster whose tail trailed away into the narrow angle, and in a battle scene on the pediment of the Temple of Aphaia at Aegina (actually dating from the early 5th century), the sculptor has managed to fill the space convincingly with human figures all on the same scale by adopting a series of poses for the figures which require progressively less vertical space – standing, falling, crouching, kneeling, lying. A more truly archaic work is the group (above) from the metopes of a temple in Sicily (where many Greeks settled). It shows the hero Perseus cutting off the head of the gorgon Medusa, which he had to do without looking directly at her since a single glance would turn a man into stone. Thanks to the gods, however, he was well-equipped for the task: Athena, here represented on the left, gave him a brightly polished shield in which he could watch the image of Medusa without the dire results of a direct look; Hermes gave him winged sandals and a sickle to chop off the head; Hades, god of the Underworld, in an unusually generous mood, gave him a helmet which made him invisible. Thus armed he completed the assignment, despite the warnings of Medusa's children Pegasus, the winged horse, whom she is seen caressing, and Chrysaor the warrior. This sculptured group is decidedly old-fashioned for its period (it dates from the second half of the 6th century BC), even allowing for a cultural time lag between mainland Greece and the Greek colonies. It is certainly a far cry from the Greek art of less than one hundred years later.

At the beginning of the 5th century BC the Greek world lay in the shadow of the Persian empire to the east. The Persians had taken the Greek cities of Asia Minor and intended to conquer mainland Greece also. In 490 BC King Darius sent a powerful force across the Aegean Sea to Euboea and Attica. The Athenians, with little support from the rest of Greece, met

the Persian forces on the Plain of
Marathon and, though vastly out-
numbered, won a great victory. (The
messenger who carried the news home
to Athens started the tradition of the
marathon race which is still run in the
modern Olympic Games.) The battle
was important not only for its military
effects but even more for the pride and
confidence it instilled in the Athenians and in Greece generally. However, the resources of the Persian
empire still vastly exceeded those of
Greece, and in 480 Darius's son
Xerxes led across the Hellespont an
army larger than any previously seen
in Greece. A number of Greek states
submitted, but others, led by Athens,
were determined to resist. One force,
under Leonidas of Sparta, heroically
held the Pass of Thermopylae against
overwhelming numbers until defeated by an act of treachery. At sea,
the Persian fleet was brought to battle
at Salamis and resoundingly defeated
by the Athenian Themistocles.
Xerxes was compelled to withdraw,
and in the following year the force
that he had left behind was defeated
at Plataea. The might of Persia had

been hurled back by what on the face
of things had seemed an insignificant
bunch of opponents.

The Greek states now entered on
their greatest period. Their feelings of
superiority over non-Greeks had been
powerfully reinforced; they were
prosperous and confident; the arts
flourished. Indeed, art went through
what is sometimes called a revolution
at the time of the Persian wars;
victory acted as a catalyst though
hardly as a cause (as is sometimes
said) in this artistic revolution. We
have seen already how sculptors were
gradually relinquishing the Archaic
tradition in favour of greater realism
and flexibility; this was a gradual
movement, and the 'revolution' consisted in the – apparently sudden –
abandonment of the old type of
statue, the upright, front-facing figure
familiar through many centuries of
ancient art. From the evidence that
survives (and we must keep in mind
that only a small proportion of Greek
sculpture has survived), this decisive
step seems to have been taken between the two Persian expeditions of
480 and 490 BC. It had certainly been
taken by the time of The Kritian Boy
(opposite), which we know dates from
shortly before 480 BC. This figure was
found on the Acropolis at Athens
among the rubble left after the Per-

sian attack on the city. It has been
described by Kenneth Clark as the
'first beautiful nude in art'. The stiff,
four-square pose has gone completely; this figure is relaxed and
natural, one leg slightly forward so
that the hip is higher on one side, the
head slightly turned. The meaningless smug grin, which was usually a
feature of the earlier type, has gone,
and is replaced by a thoughtful gaze.
The search for an ideal of human
beauty has taken a tremendous step
forward since the time of the youth
from Attica (page 60).

In the years after 480, when the
Persian threat had been repulsed but
while hostilities continued, the great
temple of Zeus was built at Olympia.
The pediments, 30 metres wide, at
both the east and west ends of the
temple, were filled with sculpture
magnificent in conception and
powerful in feeling. The two scenes
are in deliberate contrast. At the east
is a quiet, almost motionless scene
showing the preparations for the
chariot race between Pelops and
Oinomaus (Pelops had to win the race
in order to gain the hand of Oinomaus's daughter; he cheated by
tampering with Oinomaus's chariot,
which crashed killing its driver). At
the west all is furious action – the
battle between the Lapiths and the

Centaurs (an episode in the career of Theseus, symbolizing the Athenian victory over the barbaric Persians) is shown. The metopes, six at each end, portray the Twelve Labours of Herakles. The head of Apollo (right) is from the central figure of the west pediment: it radiates calm self-assurance, without conceit. Incidentally these sculptures were only recovered in bits and pieces, and much is still missing; but the scenes have been ably reconstructed. The assembled remnants are displayed in the Olympia Museum.

Of the bronze sculptures of the time, very little remains. The Athenian sculptor, Myron, at his peak in this period, was famed for the realism of his bronzes. His bronze heifer, which stood on the Acropolis, is said to have attracted appreciative moos from passing cows. His most famous work, today at any rate, was his discus thrower, which we know only from copies. Judging by the number of these, it was equally popular in Myron's time. He seems to have been especially interested in athletic figures which he caught in moments of violent physical movement. This athlete (below) is modelled at the moment when the backward swing of the discus has reached its limit and the forward swing is about to begin; he is caught, beautifully poised, in a moment of stillness. This preoccupation with producing a perfect athletic action was to be largely abandoned by the next generation of sculptors in favour of an ideal figure in a relaxed, motionless pose, a style which was foreshadowed by the figures on the east pediment of the Temple of Olympian Zeus.

By a great stroke of luck, one superlative bronze figure (page 65) has survived from this period. It was recovered from the protection of the sea, which saved it from being melted down, as recently as 1928, and was at first thought to represent Zeus, father of the gods, in the act of throwing one of his thunderbolts. Modern opinion, however, holds that it is more likely Poseidon hurling his trident, although the unruly sea god is here sleeker and calmer than he usually appears in Greek art. The figure dates from the 460s BC, but the name of the

Above:
The head of Apollo, from the sculpture on the pediment of the Temple of Zeus at Olympia. First half of the 5th century BC. Archaeological Museum, Olympia.

Left:
Myron's famous discus thrower, Athens, mid 5th century BC. This is a Roman copy of the original. Museo Nazionale Romano, Rome.

Opposite:
Fragments of the extraordinary sculpture that once decorated the east pediment of the Parthenon at Athens. British Museum, London.

64

sculptor is still not known.

After the Persian wars, Athens and her allies, not including Sparta, formed the Delian League for mutual defence. The members of the League were supposed to supply ships or taxes to pay for them, but in time Athens became the sole supplier of ships while the other cities simply provided the money. The allies became steadily subordinated to Athenian policy, and the League looked more and more like an Athenian empire. Members were not permitted to withdraw; if they attempted it, they were forced into line. In Athens there were two parties, an aristocratic party and a democratic party, who were divided not only over constitutional issues but over policy towards Persia and to-wards Sparta, Athens's chief rival for leadership in Greece. Cimon, the leader of the aristocratic party, was expelled for his dove-like attitude to Sparta, and an expansionist policy was adopted by the dominant democratic party, whose leader, until his death in 429 BC, was Pericles.

The age of Pericles witnessed the peak of Athens's glory. The Athenians devoted the funds originally subscribed for defence against Persia to rebuilding the Acropolis, where some of the most magnificent and famous of the buildings of ancient Greece soon arose – the Parthenon, temple of the patron goddess, Athena, the Propylaea, the great gateway to the sacred enclosure, and the Erectheum, among others. The greatest artists of the time were Polykleitos, who brought the athletic statue to perfection, and Pheidias, friend and associate of Pericles, who is said to have been the director of the construction programme. Of Polykleitos's work we have only later copies. Of Pheidias's work we have nothing at all, but it is reasonable to suppose that he designed the sculpture of the Parthenon, and may even have made at least some of it with his own hands.

Most of the sculpture from the Parthenon is in the British Museum, brought there in the 19th century by Lord Elgin and thus known as the 'Elgin Marbles' (the Greeks have periodically suggested they should be returned). Besides the pediments and the metopes, a sculptured frieze ran around the upper part of the wall of the *cella* (the main chamber), a feature of the Ionic Order which was soon to supersede the Doric. The pedimental sculptures celebrate Athena; on the east her birth (she sprang, according to Hesiod, fully armed from the head of Zeus), and on the west her competition with Poseidon to decide who should be the patron of Athens (Athena won by her gift of an olive tree, which was more valuable than the salt-water spring

Above:
An incident from the Battle of the Lapiths and the Centaurs, from the metopes of the Pathenon. British Museum, London.

provided by Poseidon). The scenes on the metopes were all designed to symbolize the victories of the Athenians and included the battles between Lapiths and Centaurs, the gods and Titans, Greeks and Trojans, and so on. The frieze showed the procession of the Great Panathenaia, a festival held every four years when the people of Athens presented a new robe to the image of Athena. Inside the temple stood Pheidias's image of Athena in gold and ivory; all such images have, not surprisingly, vanished, but the female head that is in the Archaeological Museum at Bologna is believed to be a Roman copy of a bronze figure of Athena by Pheidias which stood on the Acropolis in about 440 BC. The sculpture of the Parthenon, or what is left of it, demonstrates the fully developed Greek sculptural ideals, blending

together in an almost awesome way naturalism with ideal form, and exploiting all the possibilities offered by the human body. The sculptor was limited to certain types of subject: youths or mature men in their prime, young women or matrons before the marks of age appear. Children and old people were not portrayed, since the artist was concerned with an idealized physique – the human body as it might be, perfect in proportions, not as it actually is. His treatment was generalized: all trace of personal idiosyncrasy is absent, as it would detract from the broad purpose of creating an intellectual analysis of the human figure. In Periclean sculpture, naturalism transcends reality. 'They look like human beings', said a 19th-century sculptor, 'but where do you find such models?'

The sheer quantity of the sculpture of the Parthenon would have meant that it was impossible for one man to make it all. Undoubtedly many hands were involved, and in fact it is possible to see, for example, in the metopes, which are somewhat better preserved

than the pediment figures, differences of style and ability. The Lapith fighting with the Centaur (left) is a masterly example, in which the sculptor has daringly and successfully sacrificed realism for the sake of design (the cloak is unlikely to have fallen in such convenient folds in reality), and it is tempting to suppose that this might have been the work of Pheidias himself, whereas certain other figures have a slightly awkward angularity which suggests a comparative novice.

The frieze, by its great length, presented unusual problems to the designer. It was about 130 metres long but only one metre high, and the subject is an almost endless procession of people. Imagination held boredom at bay: the figures are clothed or nude, in a variety of poses, some mounted, some on foot; there are chariots, animals for sacrifices, youths carrying water jars, the occasional god – altogether a splendidly varied company. But a greater difficulty existed. The location of the frieze close to the ceiling meant that light would reach it mainly from below. If the figures were carved in normal relief, the shadows cast by the lower parts would obscure the upper parts. To overcome this, the planes of relief slope outward towards the top, so that the upper parts project relatively farther out than the lower parts – a brilliant solution to a difficult technical problem.

The Parthenon is perhaps the greatest building of the Doric Order. The nearby Erechtheum is a very different building, and represents the peak of the Ionic Order – less powerful, more elegant. Perhaps the most remarkable feature of this building is the Porch of the Maidens, in which the superstructure is supported not by columns but by caryatids (female figures acting as columns). Such a device might well have looked ridiculous on a large scale, but the porch is a small one, the figures are graceful but substantial, and the architect made the entablature lighter by omitting the usual frieze. (One of the figures, incidentally, is a concrete model from a cast of the original, which is among the Elgin Marbles in the British Museum.)

Polykleitos was the most academic of the 5th-century sculptors. He wrote a book explaining the principles on which his most famous work was based – the athlete carrying a lance, known to us from many copies – (it was even more popular with the Romans than Myron's discus thrower). Polykleitos abandoned the violent action which Myron and others had preferred and opted for the figure at rest; he was criticized in his own time for monotony by those less impressed with intellectual conceptions of art and the rules of mathematical proportion.

Painters in 5th-century BC Athens were no less famous than sculptors, but little remains of their work except that which exists on pottery. In vase painting we can follow the same developments as in sculpture: the gradual abandonment of Archaic traditions and the growing command of figures at rest or in movement, all the awkwardness removed and drawn with a marvellous economy of line. The man who perhaps has most in common with the ideas of the sculptors is known as the Achilles painter; he specialized in single figures with the same idealized form as the painters. He is famous for his paintings on *lekythoi*, a type of vase made to be placed in tombs. Painted on a white ground (right), these quiet scenes suited the deceptive simplicity of his style.

The dominance of Athens in the Age of Pericles aroused jealousy and resentment, especially in Sparta, but Athens had become dependent on her imperialist policy for her economic survival. In dispute with Athens, other cities appealed to Sparta for help, and in 431 the Peloponnesian War began. It lasted off and on for twenty-seven years and almost all the cities of Greece were involved. Weakened by plague and by the death of Pericles, Athens was ill-led and vulnerable. In 413 BC the Athenian expedition to Sicily, which had drained the city of her men and

Right:
A slip-painted funerary vase in white by a superb artist whom we know only as the 'Achilles Painter', Athens, about 440 BC. British Museum, London.

money, was utterly defeated (an episode memorably described by Thucydides, greatest of all military historians). In 404 BC the walls of Athens were destroyed, and the city accepted defeat. The heroic age was over; Athens never again dominated Greece and such projects as Pericles's rebuilding of the Acropolis could not be considered. Athenian leadership in art and literature was not destroyed along with the city walls, and the state continued to be the chief patron of art, but the whole artistic atmosphere changed. The great sculptors and painters of the 4th century BC were no longer devoted to the ideals of the state and state religion, but frequently sought work abroad, for private patrons, and thus gained a freedom to experiment that was absent in the highly integrated cultural community of Periclean Athens. There is plenty of evidence of technical mas-

tery, but the grandeur and nobility has gone.

Sculptors like Scopas and Praxiteles were the equals in genius of Pheidias and Polykleitos, but their art was different. Scopas reverted to the earlier interest in violent action and emotion; his Dancing Maenad (left) was a popular work (maenads were the ecstatic followers of Dionysos). Praxiteles seems to have preferred marble to bronze; his best-known surviving work is the statue of Hermes (below) now in the Olympia Museum. More delicate and refined and less muscularly athletic than the works of his predecessors, Praxiteles's Hermes represents the peak of the Greek passion for physical beauty. Praxiteles was also the first to use the female nude as a subject for sculpture; previously, female figures had been almost invariably – and in contrast to male figures – portrayed clothed. In the 4th century, Aphrodite replaces Apollo as the favourite subject of sculptors, though all figures of gods and goddesses are distinctly more human than the grandly detached figures of the 5th century. The group in which Aphrodite threatens an amorous Pan with her slipper (page 72) is downright playful.

Another new development was portraiture. Realistic portraits are few before the 4th century because of the preoccupation with the ideal form; now we see far more attempts at characterization of individuals, including children and old men. Lysippus, a younger contemporary of Praxiteles who is regarded as the

Above:
The Dancing Maenad of Scopas. This is a Roman copy. Skulpturen Sammlung, Dresden.

Right:
Praxiteles's famous statue of Hermes with the infant Dionysus, about 330 BC. Archaeological Museum, Olympia.

Opposite:
This magnificent crater (a large-mouthed vessel), nearly 6 metres high, is decorated in red-figure with incidents from the fall of Troy. Astyanax, son of Hector, is being thrown from the battlements by Neoptolemus, while below Aphrodite intervenes between Menelaus and Helen, with the defeated King Priam lying on the ground. Museo Nazionale di Villa Giulia, Rome.

69

progenitor of a taller, slimmer type of
male figure in Greek sculpture, executed at least one bust of Alexander
the Great, to whom he was official
artist in his later years.

Developments in painting in the
4th century BC were even more dramatic than in sculpture, but unfortunately we have no first-hand evidence
of them. Not only have the paintings
themselves all disappeared long since,
but there is comparatively little high-
quality vase painting from which,
since it appears that these were often
copied from wall paintings, we might
derive an idea of current trends – the
development of 'illusionist' (creating
an impression of three dimensions)
painting. Previously, painting consisted mainly in filling in outlines with
flat colours, or drawing in colours.
Now, artists were learning how to
create shape and form in colour.

Towards the end of the 5th century BC
an Athenian artist named Apollo-
dorus is said to have modelled his
figures in painting by the use of
varying shades of colour; it is he,

therefore, who should get the credit for creating illusionism.

The most notable example of the new development in painting can only be seen in a mosaic – the famous mosaic from Pompeii of Alexander in battle against the Persians (opposite, detail). Mosaics are more durable than paintings, although in fact this mosaic is a 1st-century BC copy (although believed to be a faithful one) of a 4th-century work (it is now in the National Museum, Naples). The colours are limited to various tones of red and brown (plus black and white), and the work shows a sophisticated use of foreshortening, perspective, and highlights – note, for instance, Alexander's head, also the way in which the tree, primarily through the use of colour tone, is clearly recessed from the horse's head.

Under Alexander the Great of Macedon the Greek world was transformed and expanded. Greek cities and colonies were founded, and peopled largely by Greek soldiers, with a life patterned on that of Greece though influenced by the oriental surroundings. The Greek language became the common vehicle for trade, government, law and literature. The history of Greek civilization was now dictated not by the old city states but by the much larger kingdoms founded by Alexander and his successors. The period from Alexander down to, roughly, the birth of Christ is called the Hellenistic Period (*Hellas* is 'Greece') because a large part of the world, stretching as far east as India, was 'hellenized'.

It is difficult to generalize about Hellenistic art, largely because the geographical area involved is so large and conditions so different in its various regions. Although very little painting has survived, there is an almost embarrassing quantity of sculpture, though much of it is Roman copies of Hellenistic originals. Styles vary from region to region, or city to city, and the most diligent studies of generations of art historians have not really clarified the situation sufficiently to speak of distinct

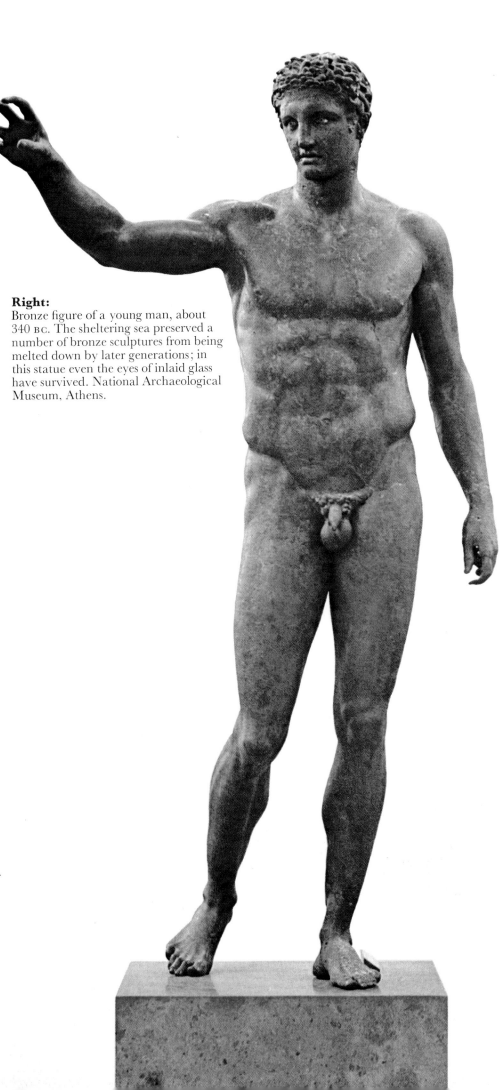

Right:
Bronze figure of a young man, about 340 BC. The sheltering sea preserved a number of bronze sculptures from being melted down by later generations; in this statue even the eyes of inlaid glass have survived. National Archaeological Museum, Athens.

'schools' or 'styles' in the various centres. We may have a good idea of the style of Alexandria, or of Pergamon, but as we know little or nothing about some other places, it is impossible to be certain that those styles were unique to the centres with which they are associated.

It is possible, however, to draw certain distinctions between the art of the Hellenistic world and that of its source, classical Greece. The artist as servant of the community, working all his life to propagate and exalt the ideals of the state, has disappeared. Instead, we find artists moving about, serving as 'court' artists rather than 'state' artists, no less respected, perhaps than their Athenian predecessors, but primarily engaged in satisfying the artistic tastes of their patrons. Art becomes divorced from the total social context, less a matter of social exhortation, of propaganda even (though propaganda on a very exalted plane), and more one of aesthetic satisfaction and amusement – as in the group of Aphrodite, Pan and Eros (below), made for a Syrian merchant on the island of Delos in about 100 BC, the purpose of which was purely decorative.

There are no great names among Hellenistic sculptors to compare with Praxiteles or Lysippus, partly because they could follow, perhaps equal, the examples of their predecessors but could not exceed them. A great work like the Venus de Milo (below), found on the island of Melos in 1820, differs only from the work of Praxiteles in the rather more complicated pose of the figure; there was really no advance to be made in this area. Attempts to develop new poses, to catch the human figure in more exaggerated movements, were on the whole not particularly successful; they seem mannered, and the sculptor's striving for new effects is too obvious. Some figures are more thor-

Opposite:
A glass jug of the 3rd century BC. Highly advanced techniques of glass-making, not excelled until very recent times (and still in some aspects not fully understood) developed in late Hellenic and Roman times. British Museum, London.

Below:
The Venus de Milo, *c.* 100 BC. Musée du Louvre, Paris.

Above:
An amusing group in marble made for a rich Syrian merchant about 100 BC, very far from the spirit of Athenian art three centuries earlier. National Archaeological Museum, Athens.

has an overwhelming effect; but all too often such technical mastery degenerated into mere clever tricks. This criticism has even been made of the famous group of Laocoon and his sons (left) which, when it was discovered in Rome in 1506, had such an impact on Michelangelo. (Laocoon was a Trojan sceptic who doubted the Greek story that if their wooden horse were pulled into Troy the city would become invincible; a serpent thereupon emerged from the sea and strangled him and his sons, an omen which persuaded the Trojans to admit the wooden horse.)

The Laocoon group is an example of the Hellenistic trend towards greater realism. Symptoms of this can be seen in the increase in realistic portraiture, in portraits of more or less physically unattractive people such as dwarfs and hunchbacks, and in depictions of violent actions – a child strangling a goose, a Gaulish chieftain killing his wife and himself, besides the more common battle and hunting scenes.

Such groups illustrate one very important aspect of Hellenistic art – a greater closeness to the affairs of everyday life. The art of classical Greece was confined to a narrow tradition; had its range been wider it would surely not have attained greatness. Hellenistic art falls short of that. It resembles less a single towering peak than a range of attractive and varied hills; the view is often charming, but seldom grand or noble. Yet the descent from Olympian peaks to the foothills of ordinary life was not only inevitable but desirable; for the first time, men saw that art has a part to play in the ordinary.

Undoubtedly Hellenistic painting, if it existed in anything except occasional fragments, would strengthen this impression, and provide more evidence of the advances in technique shown by the Alexander mosaic (page 70). We cannot make judgments without evidence, however, and almost the only painting that survives comes from the later period and is classed as Roman rather than Hellenistic. Nevertheless, it is based on Hellenistic work that no longer exists.

By the second century BC, the houses of rich men were usually lavishly decorated: furniture was

Above:
The Laocoon group, reconstructed. It was the work of three sculptors, and made a powerful impression on Michelangelo when it was found in Rome in 1506. Museo Vaticano.

Left:
This charming 'conversation piece' in terracotta, about 20 cm high, illustrates a fondness for domestic themes characteristic of the Hellenistic period. British Museum, London.

oughly realistic than those of classical Greece, suggesting the use of an individual model. In the later Hellenistic Period, when Roman influence was becoming predominant, schools of sculptors specialized in copies of Greek sculpture in which they sometimes combined the features of different periods in the same work. There were, however, a few single-figure sculptures which can be numbered among the great achievements in the history of art, such as the famous Winged Victory of Samothrace, in which the disposition of the figure and the folds of the clothing convey a sense of instant movement. Standing, as it now does, on its eminence in the Louvre, this work (which possibly gains from its present headless state)

more elaborate, the floors were covered with mosaics and the walls with paintings. By the 1st century BC, illusionistic wall painting had reached a high degree of achievement, and included still-lifes, portraits, landscapes (hardly to be seen, except as the odd rudimentary tree or rock, in earlier times), scenes from everyday life, as well as the more traditional mythological subjects. One rather popular theme was architectural – a view of receding pillars, doors, and so on – and this surely derived from the tradition of scene-painting in the Greek theatres. An extraordinary realism was sometimes attained in mosaics, as in the doves drinking from a bowl (right) which comes from the elegant villa of the Emperor Hadrian at Tivoli. Best-known, partly because best preserved, among 1st-century BC murals are the examples from Pompeii, a city frozen in time by the accident of a volcanic eruption. In the Villa of the Mysteries there is a broad painted frieze (below right) showing the initiation of a young woman into the hedonistic mysteries of the cult of Dionysus, including a scene of flagellation. Until quite recently the authorities refused to admit women tourists to see these paintings, whose background of deep red is perhaps calculated to encourage a feeling of rather sinful goings-on. But their chief interest is the skilful modelling achieved by colour tones, and the movement and expression of the figures. Other surviving wall paintings attempt much more ambitious illusionism, with elaborate landscapes and dramatic architectural perspectives. One notable mosaic, known only from a copy in some disrepair, displays on the floor the after-effects of a banquet – pieces of food cast aside by careless eaters, and so on. There are really very few genres of painting which cannot be traced back to the classical world.

Greek art influenced other countries before the days of Alexander the Great, and in many places we can see the influence of the Greeks in local traditions, sometimes providing the stimulus for representational art where none existed before. Of the people who were heavily influenced

Above:
Mosaic of doves drinking from a bowl, which probably came from the villa of the Hellenophile Emperor Hadrian, 2nd century BC. Museo Capitolino, Rome.

Below:
The frescoes from the Villa of the Mysteries in Pompeii are thought to show initiation rites connected with the cult of Bacchus (the Greek Dionysus).

by Greek artistic ideas and yet maintained a certain separateness, perhaps the most interesting are the Etruscans, who were also in their turn an important influence on the Romans, transmitting to them certain ideas that were Greek in origin. Some mystery surrounds the Etruscans, whose land, Etruria, was roughly equivalent to an enlarged Tuscany, reaching to the River Tiber. They may have been aboriginal inhabitants of Italy; it is more likely that they were immigrants from Asia Minor who first reached Italy as raiders but eventually, at some time before 800 BC, became conquerors and settlers. For three centuries or more, their league of cities, united by the rather grim Etruscan religion, represented the dominant power in central Italy at least. The Tarquins, legendary kings of early Rome, were Etruscans. We know the Etruscans, however, only through their art and through the later writings of Roman historians; their language, of which comparatively few inscriptions survive, has not yet been fully translated. They were clearly receptive to foreign artistic influences, though what is most interesting about their art is its native element, which remains strong even when Greek or other influence is evident. They were fond of depicting the world of nature, a characteristic which they certainly did not get from the Greeks.

Etruscan sculpture was well advanced by the 7th century BC. They were particularly adept at modelling in terracotta, a skill which according to tradition was introduced by Corinthians; the best examples from this period appear to be the work of foreign craftsmen. The Etruscans were less well supplied with fine marble than the Greeks (the famous quarries of Carrara were not opened until Roman times), so large sculpture was mainly in bronze, of which little has survived, though they also made large figures in terracotta. The most famous of all Etruscan sculptures is a life-size figure of Apollo (opposite) in painted terracotta, which once formed part of a group on a temple room showing Herakles stealing a sacred hind from Apollo's shrine at Delphi. It was made about 500 BC, when Etruscan power was at its height (though very soon to go into decline). Although the Greek influence is clear, this is a thoroughly Etruscan piece, belonging to the so-called 'school of Veii'. The subject shows that the Etruscans had assimilated Greek religion, and the anthropomorphic gods of the Greeks had become merged with Etruscan deities. But the whole spirit of the Etruscan Apollo is very un-Greek: this is not a remote, aloof figure; on the contrary, it radiates a rather sinister power, and the feeling of menace is not a whit abated by the grin on the face of the god as he advances upon the larcenous hero.

When the Romans displaced the Etruscans in the 3rd century BC there

Below:
A hydria (water jar), probably painted by a Greek artist in the Etruscan town of Caere in the late 6th century BC, showing the blinding of Polyphemus by Odysseus and his men. Museo Nazionale di Villa Giulia, Rome.

Left:
The Apollo of Veii (an Etruscan town near Caere), about 500 BC. Museo Nazionale di Villa Giulia, Rome.

Below:
Mithras slaying the bull, a common motif in Mithraic temples. This sculpture of the 2nd century AD shows the god in Greek clothes and is the work of an Athenian sculptor. Museo delle Navi Romane, Ostia Antica.

was no sharp break in artistic traditions. Etruscan art merged into Roman art. By the 2nd century, Rome's growing influence was becoming extended over the whole Hellenized world; in the following century Rome not only influenced but ruled that world, to which it added the western provinces of Spain and Gaul. Even Britain had experienced Roman power, though it was not yet under Roman rule. In the generation after Julius Caesar, his heirs quarrelled over the inheritance; with the defeat of Mark Antony by Octavian (soon to be the Emperor Augustus) in 31 BC, the Roman Empire was established.

Rome had, of course, long been in contact with Greek culture; there were Greek cities in southern Italy at an early date and since the 3rd century BC Rome had been in direct touch with the cities of Greece herself.

77

Above:
Bronze bust of a bearded Roman citizen, 2nd century BC. The eyes are of inlaid enamel. Museo Capitolino, Rome.

Above:
Bronze bust of a Roman citizen, about 160 AD, British Museum, London.

Below:
Relief from the Arch of Titus, AD 81, showing the Emperor's triumph over the Jews.

Rome was filled with Greek works of art which had been removed from captured cities by victorious Roman generals. The influence of the Greek cities in Italy and of the works of art collected by Romans, combined with the Etruscan background, made sure of a continuing Greek influence. Romans with the means to do so collected Greek art avidly, which encouraged the rise of schools of artists specializing in the reproduction of Greek works and also provided a living for the many Greek artists hired by individual Roman patrons. These artists were not, as a rule, hired to reproduce known works, but to execute new ones, perhaps portraits of their patrons, or works inspired by Roman rather than Greek traditions. Thus although they naturally worked in a Greek, or Hellenistic, style, the works they produced were specifically Roman in subject-matter and to some extent in artistic traditions. The Romans already had, for example, their own tradition of portraiture. To this and to the skills of Greek artists we

owe such works as the bronze bust of a bearded man (above left) dating from the 2nd century BC. Although the identity of the subject is not known, it has been suggested that it is intended to be L. Junius Brutus, founder of the Roman Republic. Its expressiveness also betrays Etruscan influence. In the same tradition are the comparatively numerous figures of more or less 'noble' Romans in their togas – law-makers, generals, and so on – which were made alongside the traditional Greek nudes celebrating the beauty of human physique. A vital feature of Roman religion was the concern with ancestors, of whom wax masks were made, which were kept in houses and used in funeral rituals.

Roman relief sculpture also depends on the threefold influence of Roman, Etruscan and Greek tradition. The Romans were fond of commemorating historical events in paintings or relief sculpture, and there is evidence that this was also an Etruscan custom. As early as 168 BC the Roman general Aemilius Paullus commissioned a sculptured frieze for a column celebrating his victory over the king of Macedon in that year, and this may not be the first example.

The foundation of the empire brought some changes. The state became the chief patron of the arts, and when Augustus embarked on his great building programme, turning Rome, as he said, from brick into marble (and also building many provincial cities), artists were employed to glorify the state and its achievements. So far as we know the artists were still mainly Greeks; few names are known, and there were no great figures, partly because artists had become humble craftsmen in the service of the state. Relief sculpture was the outstanding medium of this high-class propaganda. A fine example is the Arch of Titus, one of the sculptured panels of which (opposite) shows Titus marching in triumph through Jerusalem, with attendants carrying spoils from the Temple. This commemorated the conquest of Judaea in AD 71. The way in which the planes of relief are used to create the illusion of mass and movement is something that Greek relief sculpture

never achieved. Perhaps the best-known piece of Roman imperial relief sculpture is Trajan's Column (right) erected in about AD 113 to celebrate the victories of the Emperor over the Dacians. The column is 38 metres high, including the pedestal; the frieze ascends it in a continuous spiral with a total length of over 50 metres. It is packed full of detail and the style is clear and unpretentious: later, celebratory works of this kind tended to become grandiose and

pompous, but there is little trace of that on Trajan's Column.

Another common type of imperial propaganda was the portrait of the emperor, which appeared on coins as well as in busts and statues. The Greek artists who portrayed the early emperors found a brilliant compro-

Below:
Trajan's Column in Rome, about AD 113, once irreverently called the world's greatest strip cartoon.

mise between the idealized head of
5th-century Greece and the realistic
portraits of later times, as in the statue
of the Emperor Augustus (left),
which is clearly a portrait of an
individual yet by its clean classical
style suggests an almost superhuman
quality. Of course much depended on
the personality of the individual
emperor. The Emperor Claudius, in a
more than usually weak moment,
allowed himself to be portrayed as the
god Jupiter (the Greek Zeus), and
pretty silly he looks. The Emperor
Vespasian, a down-to-earth soldier of
peasant stock, foreswore all unnecessary pomp, and he appears as the
rough, tough, honest Italian he was.
The Emperor Hadrian, a devoted
admirer of Greek culture, not surprisingly appears looking rather like a
Greek hero.

Some remarkably realistic Roman
portraits come from Egypt in the 1st
and 2nd centuries AD (opposite). They
were painted during the life of their
subjects and after death were held in
place over the head of the mummified
corpse with wraps which left the
painting visible. The medium was
encaustic, in which pigments are suspended in melted wax, which can be
applied to wood. The faces are
realistic despite the exaggerated size
of the eyes, but the costumes are
indicated less carefully.

Apart from these portraits on
wood, the largest surviving group of
Roman paintings comes from Pompeii, as mentioned above. Examples
of the artistic taste of private citizens
exist in considerable numbers in the
sarcophagi, or stone coffins, which
became the customary resting places
for the corpses of the rich from about
the time of the Emperor Hadrian.
They were usually richly decorated
with relief sculpture, very often with
scenes from classical mythology, and
taken from Greek models. Sometimes
they are in coloured marble, which
the Romans had an un-Greek taste
for. These sarcophagi were the bread
and butter of many sculptors, and as
time went by they tended to become

larger, with more and more sculpture, which was frequently of a very high quality and a good deal livelier than most public sculpture. The Achilles Sarcophagus (right), now in the Capitoline Museum in Rome, dates from the 3rd century AD and was made in Athens. It is 1.3 metres high and depicts the scene among the womenfolk of the king of Scyros when the young Achilles, hidden there by his mother, Thetis the Nereid, is discovered by Odysseus and Diomedes (who detected him by the

Right:
The elegant Achilles sarcophagus, marble, probably made in Greece in the 3rd century AD. Museo Capitolino, Rome.

Below:
Roman mosaic of nymphs and sea monsters which once decorated a rich man's house in Roman North Africa. This example, from the late 3rd century AD, was found in Algeria.

interest he showed in their weapons). Figures of the dead man and his wife recline on top.

By this time (the 3rd century AD), the Roman empire was in decline, and classical art was declining too. However, the latter was not solely the result of the former. There was a powerful reaction to the classical tradition, stemming largely from the rise of new ideas, especially the Christian religion, which rejected pagan ideas and pagan art. Besides that, there was an obvious but not easily exlicable decline in quality, and signs of a preoccupation with the ugly and grotesque – a sign, some would say, of social decadence. The other side of this coin, however, noticeable in 3rd-century portraits, is an endeavour to get closer to the heart of things: portraitists were becoming more interested in the soul than the façade. But it was the victory of Christianity that proved most damaging to the classical tradition. The early Christians rejected practically everything in classical culture, and by introducing completely new sources of inspiration, changed the whole purpose and character of art. Nevertheless, the classical spirit lived on, into and through the early Christian and Byzantine periods, until the day when it was born again in the splendid dawn of the Italian Renaissance.

Early Christian and Byzantine Art

In the late 3rd century AD the Emperor Diocletian divided the empire into two halves, East and West. The eventual result was that the two developed into quite separate political units. The Roman empire in the West soon disappeared, while the Eastern or Byzantine empire (its capital at Byzantium, the modern Constantinople or Istanbul) lasted into the modern era, and was only finally destroyed by the Turkish conquest of 1453. With the collapse of imperial authority in Rome, the Christian Church was left to assume the dominance earlier exercised by the state. 'Render unto Caesar the things which are Caesar's, and unto God the things that are God's', Jesus said, and in the context of his time this was a revolutionary notion. In Rome, religion and the state were one. The emperor was divine, or semi-divine; temples were built to 'Augustus and Rome'. In every provincial town temples and statues glorified the gods and deified emperors; imperial officials were also priests of a sort. In this unpromising environment, Christianity grew up. At first it was merely one of many eastern cults, like the strange cult of Mithras, a powerful rival in Britain and others parts of the empire,

which helped to pave the way for the victory of Christianity in the Roman world by introducing monotheism (one god) and the vital moral principles of Good and Evil. But Christianity had certain advantages over pagan religions. It offered a deep spiritual life of hope, something that neither the secular religion of Rome nor the mystery cults of the east could do. It was naturally hostile to pagan religion, and in particular the concept of the divinity of the emperor aroused fierce opposition among the early Christians.

However, the Christians of the 4th and 5th centuries were not hostile to Roman civilization: such a thing was hardly conceivable, as no other form of civilization was known. They were Christians but they were also Romans – inhabitants of the Roman empire – and early Christian art differs from that of imperial Rome largely as a result of different economic circumstances. Since the early Christians were humble people of small means – slaves, craftsmen, women – there was scarcely enough money to create a Christian art. Moreover, they probably felt no need for it: the Jewish tradition from which Christianity sprang was against religious art.

There are exceptions, of course, but Yahweh's denunciation of graven images was not forgotten. The pagan statues and temples to be found in every town were, for their worshippers, the dwelling places of the gods, but for Christians they were the devil's works. Christians, therefore, had grave reservations against developing a parallel art form. Neither were there, to begin with, any churches, partly because the Christians did not have the money to build them, partly because to do so invited the hostile attention of the authorities, and partly because in architecture too the problem had to be faced of what form such buildings should take: they should certainly not resemble the temples of the heathen. The early Christian converts met in private houses, or the room of a house, in which, no doubt, they were often surrounded by inimical Roman decorations. The earliest churches, small, unpretentious and invariably built over in later times, have proved very hard to discover.

However, one excellent example was excavated in recent times at Dura-Europos, on the Euphrates, preserved by a fortunate chance. In 265 the Roman garrison happened to

Above:
The fresco paintings on the west wall of the synagogue at Dura-Europos, in Syria, early 3rd century, illustrating scenes from the Old Testament.

Left:
Painting on plaster on the wall of the baptistry, Dura-Europos.

Left:
A painting from the Catacombs, Rome, depicting the miracle of the loaves and fishes. First half of the 2nd century AD.

Opposite:
Roman Christian sarcophagus with scenes from the Bible between decorative columns. 4th century AD.

build a high earth rampart which covered a number of buildings, including a very early Christian church. Like many other towns, Dura-Europos also contained temples of the gods of Greece and Rome and of numerous eastern cults, besides a Jewish synagogue (opposite) which confirms the existence of Jewish religious art despite the ban on graven images. The Christian church was a simple building no different from others except for the addition of a baptistry, which had frescoes on the walls. Here were Adam and Eve in the Garden of Eden, Christ walking on the waters and other scenes from the Old and New Testaments; in another room, a frieze depicting pagan motifs, surviving from the days when the building was a private house, remained untouched. As one would expect, the style of the paintings is similar to that of paintings in the temples, but some of the characteristics of Byzantine painting are already apparent: the frontal pose of the figures, the absence of relief, and the spirituality of the faces.

According to Christian doctrine, at the Second Coming of Christ the dead would rise up and the body would come to life again. The latter therefore had to be preserved, and so burial was preferred to cremation. It may even have been Christian influence that caused the preference for burial among the Romans from the 2nd century onwards, since the earlier

Roman custom was for cremation. The first Christian cemeteries were located outside city walls, with the graves in rows marked by grave-stones, or stelae. In Rome itself, the Christians buried their dead in the underground network of tunnels outside the city known as the catacombs, where the tombs can still be seen. The galleries were often decorated with paintings (opposite), in a style similar to that found in private houses and often including traditional motifs as well as specifically Christian ones. The Christian images were usually symbolic, like the fish and basket of bread which illustrates the parable of the loaves and the fishes. Some motifs later to become very familiar made their first appearance here: the figure of the Good Shepherd carrying a sheep on his shoulders, for instance. By no stretch of imagination could these sketches be regarded as great masterpieces of world art; but their historical importance is nonetheless considerable. Some of them take some working out and would make no sense to anyone not fully conversant with Christian teaching; the fish and the basket might not be immediately comprehensible even to someone well read in the Bible, and others are more obscure. It may well be that the enigmatic quality of these devices was necessary in order to preserve secrecy and avoid persecution, and that their purpose was instruction for humble Christian converts who would not, as

a rule, be able to read.

The carved stone sarcophagus of the Romans was continued by the Christians without dramatic change; the same techniques, the same materials and tools were used, and even some of the motifs were the same: lions, winged *putti* or cherubs, and so on. Specifically Christian motifs are, as might be expected, similar to those in the paintings in the catacombs, usually with a typically classical background of vines or architectural columns (below). It is sometimes difficult to tell whether a particular sarcophagus is Christian or not because the nature of the subjects is not clear, and sometimes a traditional classical motif is adapted to a Christian purpose. The Biblical subjects range from the Temptation of Eve to the miracles of the New Testament, and they tend to be jumbled together in what looks like a rather arbitrary way, with no break between and the subjects sometimes overlapping each other. The apparently arbitrary sequence is probably to be explained by the prayers for the dead, which the carved scenes illustrate, and this would also account for the prevalence of particular subjects. The most splendid examples of early Christian sarcophagi were, naturally, made after Christianity had become an accepted religion.

The triumph of Christianity early in the 4th century was sudden. Only a few years before, the churches had

Above:
Mosaic from the vault of Sta Costanza
in Rome, with disciples of Bacchus
gathering the grape harvest. 4th
century.

been destroyed and the bishops executed by imperial decree. Suddenly, the Christian religion (and Christian art) became not only free, but the religion of the state. At the Council of Nicaea the Emperor Constantine presided over a council which included those bishops who had survived the persecution of just twenty years before. The triumph of Christianity was obvious: the churches built throughout the empire under Constantine proclaimed it. These included great basilica like St Peter's in Rome, the great churches of Constantinople, and sanctuaries built in sacred places. Most of these early churches have disappeared, unfortunately, and therefore there are comparatively few examples of the images that adorned them. Roman traditions were followed to a large extent, and motifs were appropriated without regard, probably without awareness, of their significance for the non-Christians who evolved them. The mosaics on the vault of Sta Costanza (above) in Rome combine Christian and pagan subjects and are surrounded by a classical geometric border. There are scenes of everyday life, such as the treading of grapes and the wine harvest, which were common in classical art. Only the symbolism is changed; this scene is no longer connected with the revels of Dionysus or Bacchus, but calls to mind the Christian Eucharist. There are also scenes hard to interpret in either pagan or Christian symbolism, for example, a cock fighting a tortoise, repeated more than once, which perhaps represents the conflict with the heresy of Arianism. Now and then, what appears to be a traditional Hellenic mosaic, such as a scene of fishermen, incorporates the story of Jonah being swallowed by the whale, or some other purely Christian motif. But besides all this, there is another scene at Sta Costanza which is truly Christian – Christ standing on the rock from which flow the rivers of paradise, teaching the word to the Apostles. The mosaic (opposite) in the apse of Sta Pudenziana (late 4th century) shows Christ enthroned, teaching his disciples, with two rather mysterious women in attendance. Behind him is the hill of Calvary and the cross, rising above Jerusalem with its Christian sanctuaries. The good condition of this mosaic, incidentally,

is the result of several extensive restorations; little of the original remains. Already, many of the features of Christian iconography are fully developed here – the dominating figure of Christ, and the Cross behind him as the emblem of pain and suffering turned into triumph. This mosaic was to inspire Raphael centuries later. It forms a well-judged climax to the church, the Cross marking the axis of a semicircle formed by the four beasts, emblems of the four evangelists (not fully visible in the illustration because of an obscuring arch). The treatment of the figures is still classical, but they are not conventional: each head is strongly individualized. In fact the work represents a considerable triumph over limited means. For mosaics are composed of little cubes of coloured marble and, though coloured glass was beginning to be used, the available colours were severely restricted. Here, however, skilful modelling is achieved by gradations of tone, to convey form and mass; even the buildings show painstaking efforts towards realism. This classical spirit was soon to disappear, along with the Western Roman empire; the Byzantine style, as we shall see, is more hieratic, conventions being fixed by religious tradition.

While the style of imperial Rome was disintegrating in the new social, economic and religious conditions, different developments were taking place in Byzantium. As the Roman Empire dwindled away and Rome became a mere provincial town, Byzantium flourished. For about a thousand years after the end of imperial Rome, the Eastern Roman Empire lived on. Its civilization was different. It retained the Christian religion in common with the West, although interpreting it in a markedly different way. The power and wealth of the Byzantine emperor resulted in an imperial architecture far greater in scale and in richness than anything that Early Christian Rome could produce; but this empire was also

influenced by the Orient and Byzantine art also reflected Eastern characteristics, with its hieratic approach, indulgence in bright colour and preference for complex surface patterns, which are most familiar to us in mosaics. The Byzantine style reached a peak in the reign of Justinian in the 6th century, and was spread far by his conquests and his even wider prestige as the inheritor of the Roman tradition. His general, Belisarius, conquered much of Italy and imposed on the classical culture of Sicily a layer of Byzantine culture that was felt for many centuries. But Byzantine influence is most clearly apparent in the mosaics of Ravenna.

The Emperor Augustus had located the headquarters of Rome's Adriatic fleet at the port of Classis, an

act which raised the status and increased the prosperity of nearby Ravenna. In the 5th century Ravenna was the primary residence of two emperors and acquired the status of a kind of capital, confirmed after the Justinian conquest of 540 when Belisarius made it the headquarters of the exarchate that represented Byzantium in the West. The art and architecture of Ravenna shows a mixture of Italian and Byzantine influence and, whatever the relative importance of the two traditions, the outcome is a collection of splendid buildings which seem

Below:
Part of the story of Jonah and the Whale, from a 4th-century mosaic at Aquilea, east of Venice.

quite magnificently decorated.

Mosaic pictures were to be the chief decoration of eastern churches for close on a thousand years. At Ravenna in the 5th and 6th centuries the tradition was formed and many of the technical and iconographical problems first solved. Floor mosaics had originated in Greece and became extremely popular in Hellenistic and

Below:
The remarkably accomplished composition of the vault mosaic in the Baptistry of the Orthodox, Ravenna. The central scene is of the baptism of Christ and it is surrounded by figures of the twelve apostles.

Roman times. It seems, however, that mosaic was seldom used for the decoration of walls, and though the lack of evidence – floors survive better than walls – makes it difficult to form a certain judgment, what evidence there is suggests that frescoes remained the favourite form of wall decoration. In the 4th century mosaic was used in monuments and memorials, and also, as we have seen, in the vault of Sta Costanza in Rome. The vault mosaics there closely resemble contemporary mosaic pavements, though soon afterwards, pos-

sibly earlier in some places, glass cubes began to be used instead of marble. These were not suitable for floors, being much more fragile than marble, but they were perfectly satisfactory for mural mosaics. White stone backgrounds gave way to blue and gold, as in the mosaic of the Empress Theodora and her attendants (page 91). The churches at Ravenna, and later Byzantine churches, gained a brilliance never seen before. Walls, apses, domes and vaults presented complicated and challenging opportunities which the decorators met with great imagination and skill. The motifs were not

Above:
The apse of St. Apollinare in Classe, Ravenna, 6th century AD.

always new. The procession of figures had been known since the Assyrians and the Egyptians: at first it was a military procession, later a triumphal one leading towards a god or king seated on a throne as in the Parthenon frieze (page 65). It was used with brilliant effect in the church of St Apollinare in Classe, Ravenna (above), in which the lines of saints and martyrs move along the walls above the arches of the columns for the whole length of the building from porch to apse, where their crowns are

offered to figures of Christ and the Virgin. Above, in the spaces between the windows of the clerestory, are figures of saints, situated like statues in niches, while above the windows are scenes from the Passion of Christ. The whole arrangement suggests an attempt to reproduce relief decoration in two dimensions: the Byzantines regarded sculpture, in general, as a minor art, though the 'graven image' was only forbidden in religious art, and even then for a comparatively short time.

The rise of the vault made possible an overall decorative scheme in which mosaic was employed to give the interior of the building an impres-

sive unity, with the bands around arches and windows, columns and mouldings integrated into a sparkling whole. Sometimes the figures among gilded foliage lose their identity, while others make a superficial impression of a patch of colour, only surrendering their detail at a closer look. Important developments were taking place with regard to the portrayal of the human figure, signs of which are evident in comparing the procession of saints and martys in St Apollinaire Nuovo. Since the 5th century, the stylization of draperies had been marked, but the faces still looked like painted portraits, with subtle shading and highlights. In the 6th century a new style developed, in response to new ideas. In representing drapery, modelling and colour shading disappear, to be replaced by a simple play of lines; folds do not completely vanish, but they are rendered in an increasingly sketchy manner. At St Apollinare in Classe the magnificent robes of the saints' dress on the north wall are presented as red surfaces, while the martyrs retain a certain relief, although the folds of their robes are simply drawn. It is to this emphasis on flat areas of colour that the famous mosaics in the choir of San Vitale at Ravenna of Justinian and Theodora (opposite) bringing gifts to the church owe their magnificent impact. The overall impression is of a brilliantly coloured surface, thanks to the rendering of the court dresses as sparkling swathes of colour. The faces of the empress and her attendants certainly bear some traces of conscious portraiture, but essentially the figures are elements in a brilliant pattern. The stiffness of the poses and the characteristic frontality of the figures does not disguise the fact that this too is a procession: the figures are moving towards Christ, at the end of the apse, yet it is the faces themselves that, in the end, make the strongest impact. They may be stylized: the nose on each face is simply a dividing line, and the eyes are large and staring, emphasized by the heavy eyebrows; it is easy to see here how icons developed. But the faces still have character: the more important figures, in this case the empress, clearly having more individuality

than her attendants whose faces are more automatically rendered.

The frontal pose of human figures, dictated by symmetry, was not universal. The martyrs of St Apollinare Nuovo, though almost frontal, are clearly indicated by the slant of the hem of their cloaks to be walking.

At Ravenna the Eastern contribution was superimposed on Western traditions, which is what gives it its particular distinction, but it is clear that we have come a long way from the art of the Roman world. A new aesthetic has been created in which realism recedes, colour takes prece-

dence over form, and two-dimensionality replaces the old care for modelling. The figures of prophets, saints and martyrs, confronting the congregation with their unwavering eyes, convey a sense of the supernatural, yet there is nothing sinister about the art of Ravenna, none of the frightening or the grotesque which was to figure so prominently in Gothic art. There are no scenes of devils with barbed tails, no visions of the damned being plunged into eternal hell fire; there are no shadows, merely a serene brilliance. This art records the victory of Christ and looks towards man's entry into Paradise. What hope and confidence must have been instilled in the worshippers confronting the scene portrayed in the apse of the church St Apollinare in Classe in the 6th century,

Below:
Detail from a 6th-century Byzantine manuscript of unknown origin showing Rebecca at the well and manifesting Hellenistic influence. Österreichische Nationalbibliothek, Vienna.

where Christ, open-armed, extends his blessing, amid a charming scene of Paradisal animals and fruit trees, and the souls of the saved, represented by sheep, enter upon their inheritance. There is really nothing like this in Western art.

By comparison with the mosaics, Byzantine painting has often been regarded as monotonous and so dominated by lurid colour as to be almost vulgar. Closer studies have revealed more subtlety, and different schools as well as changes in development over the course of time have been distinguished.

The eastern provinces of the Roman empire were influenced not only by Rome itself but also by other traditions from farther east, in particular from Mesopotamia and from the Persia of the Sassanids. The Eastern influence is observable in mosaics of the 4th century found at Antioch in Syria, and it became greater as time passed. Byantine art in turn was to have a powerful influence

on Christian art generally, to which these Eastern influences were transmitted, mingled with the older traditions of the Hellenistic world: the Ravenna mosaics displayed the confrontation and interpretation of these very different styles. Among traditional Christian themes there were to be some that were treated in a Hellenistic style and some in an Eastern style, and sometimes themes deriving from the one style were transcribed to the other. The Hellenistic style is elegant and flowing, with three-dimensional figures and careful use of light and shade, shaded colours and scenes in depth. Clothes are blown by the wind, faces express emotions. In the Eastern style, on the other hand, everything is depicted in two dimensions. Backgrounds usually consist of one strong colour tone, most often blue or gold, and any suggestion of landscape or architecture is indicated in a sketchy and strictly non-illusionistic way. Figures become flat outlines, and clothes are similar

patches of pattern, the lines representing folds rendered in an almost abstract way. Faces are strongly drawn, but flat and emotionless, the large eyes indicating that they are not dwelling upon the mundane incidents of this world but contemplating another world altogether, serene and supernatural.

The two approaches intermingle to a varying extent, partly depending on the medium, which may be encaustic – for painting wooden icons, miniatures illustrating manuscripts (often rather resembling icons), frescoes, or mosaics. These four methods naturally demand very different techniques. The artist in mosaic is much more restricted in general scope than the painter of a fresco and does not have the same opportunity for depicting detail as the miniaturist. Although the subject may be the same, there is obviously considerable difference in execution due to the medium. In mosaics especially, much of the effect of the work may derive from the material itself: the splendid gold backgrounds, for example. The majestic effect of the *Pantocrator* at Daphni in Greece (right) also owes much to the material. This figure of Christ as a powerful Eastern potentate, law-giver and judge is a common theme for the centre of the dome or apse in Byzantine churches. Many icons also owe their glittering splendour to their rich backgrounds of gold.

Sometimes artists made the mistake of attempting to reproduce the effects of one medium in another. It is no good a mosaicist striving for the vivid detail and atmospheric effects of, for instance, a fresco painter, but there is evidence that they did just that, that they tried to make small cubes of stone or glass look like paint, while some fresco-painters deliberately sought to make their frescoes look like mosaics, as if they were afraid that people would suspect the use of fresco was merely an economy measure by those who could not afford mosaics.

One might suppose that the 'eastern' style would be more frequently encountered in icons and mosaics than in frescoes or miniatures, since the latter are more 'western' techniques. But this is not the

Above:
The powerful mosaic of *Christ Pantocrator* at Daphni, 1100.

case; other circumstances, including the personal inclination or desires of the artist, were more important. The mixture of the two styles is universal, and the modern development of high-quality colour photography, which makes it possible to compare many works of art scattered over a wide area, has reinforced our awareness of the constant interchange. Static rows of saints, like the Fathers of the Church in a 12th-century mosaic in Palermo (page 94), alternate with scenes of great movement; but while the former shows some degree of life in the gesture of the hands, scenes like the Nativity or the Transfiguration show evidence of the static, monumental style taking over.

A tremendous crisis overtook Byzantine art in the 8th century. In 726 the Emperor Leo III removed the image of Christ from a gate of the imperial palace and replaced it with a cross. As he explained in an inscription below, he could not bear to see the living Christ represented by a figure that could neither breathe nor speak, and regarded a symbol as preferable.

Thus began the Iconoclastic crisis, when all figurative art was forbidden. Possibly the influence of Islam, which also has strong reservations concerning the representation of the human figure, had something to do with this development, but there were also many Christians who were worried by the accusation of idolatry. At any rate, for over a hundred years, the Iconoclasts were dominant. Not only was it forbidden to produce new works, but existing works of art were destroyed or removed, in churches and in other buildings, which helps to explain why our knowledge of Byzantine art before this time is so sparse. However, the ban was not fully effective, and the battle for and against images swayed back and forth before it ended, in 843, in the final defeat of the Iconoclasts, who had failed to win the support of the Pope, and the decoration of the churches had to be renewed all over again. Despite the length of the crisis and the disappearance of so much, there was no decisive break in the tradition of Byzantine art. Little change in style

Above:
A 12th-century Sicilian mosaic portraying three Fathers of the Church: St Gregory, St Basil and St John Chrysostom.

Left:
Mosaic of the Crucifixion in the monastery church at Daphni, Greece.

was manifest, and religious art in particular returned to its old traditions.

In the 7th century, the Byzantine Empire had been seriously attacked by the Saracens (Arabs) who, inspired by the Prophet Muhammad, swept into Syria and eventually overran all North Africa and Asia Minor right up to the Bosphorus. In 717-18 Constantinople itself was besieged, but the attackers were driven off with great losses by Leo III. Thereafter, the Saracen power receded, but the Byzantine Empire was further shaken by internal dispute in the Iconoclastic crisis, which was one of the causes of the final schism between East and West, confirmed by Charlemagne's coronation as emperor of the West in 800. However, the end of the Iconoclastic crisis a couple of generations later roughly coincided with a revival of Byzantine power. In 880 Byzantium regained its position in Italy; the ferocious Bulgars and the Russians were repelled by Basil II; the Arabs were driven out of Cilicia, northern Syria, Cyprus and Crete. Basil I founded the Macedonian dynasty which lasted into the mid 11th century. The Byzantine empire became great again, and Byzantine art spread throughout a wide area. The largely separate traditions of imperial and religious art came together in this period of revival: emperors once again appeared among the saints in religious pictures. At Hagia Sophia, the greatest church of Constantinople, new mosaics were

created to commemorate the accession of emperors, rather like the imperial statues of Roman times. The Emperor Romanos III appeared with the Empress Zoë, with the figure of Christ between them, in the south gallery (above). When Romanos died, Zoë married the Emperor Constantine II, and accordingly the head of Romanos was removed from the mosaic and replaced by a head of Constantine; no more convincing evidence of a trend towards realistic portraiture could be imagined. (This was not a new idea, however; imperial statues in Rome had been made with interchangeable heads.)

Some fine examples of the work of the Macedonian revival were discovered in the monastery church of Daphni in Greece, location of the *Christ Pantocrator* (page 93) mentioned above. The visitor to this monastery sees first a dome rising above gold and white walls in a setting of tall pines and cypress trees. Inside, the mosaics blaze with a light of their own, but their spirit is grave and respectful.

Above:
Mosaic from Hagia Sophia, Constantinople, 1030, showing the Emperor Constantine II and the Empress Zoë.

The Crucifixion (opposite), opposite the entrance, is sober, almost serene. The Christ on the Cross has eyes closed in calm acquiescence; the body is not wrenched into a tortured pose but suggests resigned acceptance of the sins of the world. The figure of St John is treated like a statue, though

95

Opposite:
This glittering Byzantine miniature of about 1078 shows the Emperor Nicephorus III flanked by St John and the Archangel Michael. Bibliothèque Nationale, Paris.

Above:
Central panel of an ivory triptych, showing Christ enthroned between the Virgin and St John the Baptist with apostles and saints below – a beautifully detailed piece of Byzantine workmanship of the 10th century. Musée du Louvre, Paris.

Above:
One of the churches in the extraordinary rock formations in Cappadocia, Turkey, hollowed out of rock to form the normal architectural features of churches.

the expression of the Virgin, on the other side, is full of silent suffering. A similar dignity marks the pictures of scenes from the Gospels in the niches beneath the dome. In general, the figures have a controlled, almost frozen appearance, which is yet not stiff or rigid.

In the 11th century the Byzantine Empire was threatened by the Normans, who had occupied southern Italy and were poised to expand into Greece and the Balkans, and more seriously by the Seljuk Turks, who had occupied Asia Minor and ad-

vanced to the Bosphorus. To combat this new Muslim threat, the Emperor called for aid from the Christians of Western Europe. He received more than he bargained for: his call gave the first impetus to the Crusades. Succeeding crusades were disastrous for the Byzantine Empire. Frankish crusaders were little better than barbarians, despite the presence among them of sincere and devoted men. They were racially prejudiced against Greeks and Levantines, and as Roman Catholics they were only slightly less hostile towards the Eastern Orthodox Church than they were to Islam. They resented the claim of the Byzantine emperors to the Holy Land, where they carved out short-lived kingdoms for themselves. The climax came in 1204: the Fourth

Crusade degenerated into a campaign of conquest against the Byzantine Empire and culminated in the capture of Constantinople, with looting on a massive scale.

The capture of Constantinople interrupted the development of Byzantine art in the capital for half a century, but the Byzantine Empire, and Byzantine art, did not die. The artists of Constantinople accompanied members of the imperial family to far-flung outposts of the empire where they set up their courts. There the traditions of Constantinople continued, and Byzantine art was spread even more widely. It acquired new inspiration and greater expressiveness in this period of dispersal.

One province where a new Byzantine art developed was Cappa-

docia, in Turkey. In parts of this region there are strange outcrops of rock, eroded into great misshapen cones, and in these rocks the people carved out houses and churches, including cruciform churches and even domes, which were lavishly decorated with frescoes. In some buildings there are only abstract geometric designs, no doubt dating from the period of the Iconoclastic crisis; most of the figurative painting (perhaps all of it) dates from the period of the Macedonian revival. Some can be dated as late as the 13th or 14th centuries, though there is a decline after the Seljuk invasion of the 12th century. The themes are similar to those of Constantinople, but they have a certain boldness of execution which is occasionally almost slapdash and a vigorous use of colour that belong to a local tradition. Figures tend to be very tall, taking up all available space, and no usable surface is left undecorated. There is very little refinement or originality of expression in these bold, simple pictures, and details in different buildings are realized in a similar way, suggesting long-accepted conventions or simple copying. It is the total impression that

is most memorable in these remarkable buildings.

During this period a delicate political role was played by the city of Venice, which was sometimes under Byzantine protection and sometimes hostile to it but at all times strongly influenced by Constantinople. This influence can be seen in the mosaics (and the architecture) of the famous cathedral of San Marco, which was begun about 1100. The mosaics date from different periods and have been much repaired and altered in the course of time, but the overall effect remains. The 11th-century figure of The Madonna (right) illustrates very well a Byzantine concern with decoration rather than illustration. The figure is a design, not a representation: the artist was not trying to portray a human being; he was presenting a symbol, expressing the superhuman nature of his subject, and at the same time fitting it into a scheme of architectural decoration. It is perhaps less easy for Westerners, accustomed to forms of art predominantly representational, to appreciate Byzantine aesthetics to the full.

In southern Italy, more particularly in Sicily, political developments

Above:
Christ's Entry into Jerusalem, 12th-century mosaic from San Marco in Venice.

Below:
Mosaic of the Virgin, San Marco, Venice.

caused a more complex mingling of styles. Early in the 9th century the Muslims from North Africa attacked Sicily and, in spite of checks, the Byzantine power was steadily pushed back. The Normans were brought in to help, but they soon established themselves as the dominant power. In the 12th century Sicily was ruled by a Norman dynasty which had to be treated as an equal by both the Eastern and Western empires. The impact of these very different civilizations created a complicated amalgam of influences in art in Sicily. For example, the basilica at Cefalu is in the western tradition, while the Church of the Martorana at Palermo is a typical domed Byzantine building on the inside but is largely Islamic in style on the outside. Surviving mosaics, of which there are a good number, are often the work of local artists following Byzantine traditions. They vary somewhat in quality, as might be expected, but there are particularly fine examples, probably by Greek mosaicists, in the church of the Martorana, where the Byzantine structure offers plenty of scope. The scene of Christ crowning the Norman king of Sicily, Roger II, is Byzantine in both theme and treatment. The similarity with, for example, Christ

between the Emperor Constantine II and the Empress Zoë (page 95) is obvious: the Norman king is shown wearing the robes of a Byzantine emperor. Roger himself took a commendably broad-minded view of artistic differences. The chapel in his palace has a Byzantine dome and Byzantine hieratic figures of saints, but a Moorish ceiling. The total effect of the mingling of styles in Norman Sicily, if occasionally bewildering, is rich and exotic.

Byzantine artistic traditions were perhaps most important in the Slavonic countries, where they continued until quite recently and, in some respects, continue still. The paintings and icons of Russia in the period of the Renaissance in Western Europe show an unbroken tradition going back to 6th-century Byzantium. When the Slavs accepted Orthodox (Eastern) Christianity they also adopted Byzantine art, and it is possible, in Yugoslavia for instance, to trace quite precisely the border between Roman Catholic and Eastern Orthodox influence by the architecture of the churches – the basilica in the former and the domed church in the latter. In Serbia, there are particularly fine paintings in churches at Milesevo and Sopocani which date from the time

when Constantinople was eclipsed by the Franks, prompting the thought that artists in flight from the Franks set up their studios here. Byzantine art of this period was more expressive: the earlier serenity had largely been replaced by consciousness of sorrow and suffering, in response, no doubt, to the troubled times. The marvellous painting of the Annunciation, which dates from the early 14th century and which comes from a church famous for its frescoes at Ochrid in Macedonia, preserves the traditional reserved expression which is comparatively unusual at this date, and may be due to the fact that this is probably the work of an artist from Constantinople. It is a double-sided icon (the other side shows the Virgin and Child), of the type carried on a pole in religious processions. Its elegant beauty has made it one of the best-known of all Byzantine paintings.

In the 10th century the Russian state which then had its capital at Kiev was converted to Christianity. There had been contacts, sometimes friendly sometimes not, with Byzantium for a long time before that, and it is not surprising that the religious art of Kiev should appear Byzantine. Yet the way in which Byzantine art became, without a break, the art of the Slav peoples was a momentous development. It was of course due chiefly to the Orthodox Church, but also to the prestige of the imperial city of Constantinople, which stood like a beacon of civilization in Europe's so-called 'Dark Ages', and attracted Arabs, Turks, Bulgars and Franks in much the same way as, in an earlier period, the civilization represented by the city of Rome attracted the Barbarians.

Byzantine art in its homeland went through one further period of glory in the 14th and 15th centuries, before Constantinople's final fall to the

Turks. This period is sometimes called the Palaeologue Renaissance, after the Palaeologue dynasty which drove out the Franks in 1261 and proved strong enough to resist all attacks until 1453. The mural paintings of this final period revealed a new blend of the classical and hieratic styles, with a more openly emotional treatment of subjects, a greater sense of rhythm and dramatic tension, and a greater emphasis on picturesque detail; but all was still firmly rooted in the old traditions. It spread from Constantinople through all the countries where Byzantine influence reigned, and its greatest surviving works are to be found in the Balkans and Russia. Thus the life of Byzantine art extended far beyond the fall of Constantinople and the extinction of the Byzantine empire. In the religious art of the Slavs it had established principles that lasted for centuries, and in the Orthodox monasteries like those of Mount Athos, not only were the old works reverently preserved, but new works were produced following the old pattern, preserving the Byzantine tradition of religious art and icon painting down to the present day.

The significance of the Byzantine style in the history of Western art is considerable, since Constantinople kept alive a civilization inherited from Rome, though transformed, during the so-called Dark Ages. But it also influenced Western art more directly, and its influence extended farther west than Ravenna or Sicily. Charlemagne, after all, visited Ravenna.

The people who were the inheritors of Roman civilization took their artistic, especially their architectural, models from Roman tradition; but they also had artistic traditions of their own, though these were chiefly confined to what are called the minor arts. The basilicas and carved sarcophagi of 4th-century Gaul are no different from those of Rome, but the weapons, drinking vessels, jewelry, and so on are quite different. These objects were decorated with linear, geometric patterns, owing nothing to the Mediterranean world.

The British Isles contributed new themes and new methods of decoration which, through the medium of illuminated manuscripts, had a wide

Above:
The Journey to Bethlehem, from the frescoes in Sta Maria in Castelseprio, north Italy, which, variously dated from the 7th to the 10th century, seem to look forward to Giotto.

103

influence. St Columba himself copied manuscripts, and the Irish monastic tradition for which he was largely responsible, considered old-fashioned by 'Roman' Christianity, produced such extraordinary works as the Book of Kells (page 106). The origins of this art are a matter of argument, but it clearly owed much to ancient Celtic tradition, manifest in the decoration of a sword scabbard (page 107) from County Antrim, made before the Roman conquest of Britain, which bears a marked similarity to the decorative borders found in the Book of Kells. In this Irish manuscript art, with its spirals, bands, dots and ribbons, including animal forms that are so distorted as scarcely to be recognized as such, we are even farther from the world of nature than Byzantine art.

A new wave of creative energy swept over Europe in the age of Charlemagne (late 8th and early 9th centuries), and people naturally looked towards the one Christian centre that had maintained a constantly high level of artistic creation. When Charlemagne wanted to build a chapel in his capital at Aachen, he sent his craftsmen to Ravenna to study the design of San Vitale, though the resulting building owed almost as much to Roman traditions and something to local innovations. The Byzantine style is prominent in Carolingian manuscripts, and as late as the 11th century, churches in Western Europe were decorated with symbolic figures that certainly owe something to Constantinople, rather more, perhaps, than they owe to classical Rome. The frescoes in the little chapel at Castelseprio (page 103) in Lombardy are truly Byzantine. They are probably the work of Greek artists from Constantinople in the 10th century (though there is some argument about the date, some authorities believing that they are much older). Like the similar frescoes at St Germain d'Auxerre, they have a good deal of liveliness and charm.

Charlemagne set up a workshop at his court for copying manuscripts, in which Irish and Mediterranean influences are evident. The book which celebrated the Emperor's return from Rome after the baptism of his son

Right:
Detail of a psalm from the Utrecht Psalter. The psalm is Psalm 28: 'Unto thee will I cry, O Lord'. Bibliotheek der Rijksuniversiteit, Utrecht.

Below:
Miniature of St Mark, from a Carolingian manuscript presented to a monastery by Louis the Pious in 827. Bibliothèque Nationale, Paris.

Pepin was written in gold and silver on purple (the imperial colour) parchment, like the manuscripts of Constantinople. There followed a succession of marvellous works, some of which show some awareness of the techniques of classical painting. The Utrecht Psalter (page 104) of about 820 contains a mass of realistic figures against a background of more or less visionary landscape or architecture. The most remarkable thing about it is the brilliant draughtsmanship. Though it harks back to ancient traditions (compare, for instance, the Crucifixion at Daphni (page 94)), it represents something new in Christian art, and carries us out of the Early Christian period into the world of the Middle Ages.

Above:
The Pepin Reliquary, given to the Abbey of Conques by Pepin of Aquitaine in the early 9th century. The body is wood, covered with beaten gold and inlaid with precious stones. Trésor de l'Eglise, Conques.

105

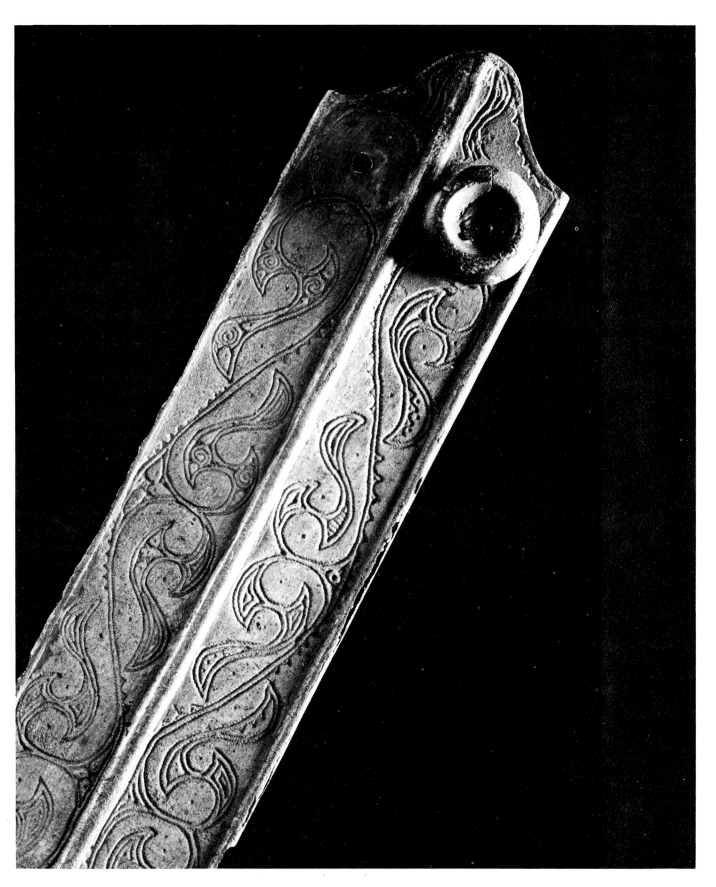

Medieval Art

In terms of European history, the Middle Ages lasted about a thousand years. It began around the time of the breakdown of the Roman Empire in the 4th and 5th centuries, and ended with the period of the Reformation, the invention of printing, the discovery of the New World and the formation of 'nation-states' which created the basis for the modern political map of Europe. The term 'Middle Ages' was first used in the 16th century to describe the long period between the world of classical antiquity and the current post-Renaissance world; the intervening centuries were comparatively little known and seemed markedly less important. But of course the Middle Ages were not just a worthless gap in the history of Western European civilization. The Renaissance was not, as some contemporaries regarded it, a reconnection with the classical world that disregarded all that lay between; on the contrary, the Renaissance was in a sense the culmination of a long process which, in fits and starts, had been going on throughout the Middle Ages.

Civilization was brought to the lands of Western Europe when they were part of the Roman Empire, and they had no separate identity until that empire was disintegrating. By the end of the 3rd century it was already proving impossible to govern: the Emperor Diocletian divided it into Eastern and Western parts and in 330 Constantine founded the city named after him as capital of the Eastern Empire. For a century and a half this division continued, but in 476 the last Western emperor was deposed. In theory that left the Eastern, or Byzantine, emperor supreme, but in fact he had lost control of the western provinces, where various more or less independent barbarian kingdoms were formed. The Visigoths established themselves in Spain and southern Gaul (France), the Vandals in North Africa, the Ostrogoths in Italy, and the Franks in northern Gaul.

As we have seen in the previous chapter, the Byzantine Empire lasted throughout the Middle Ages and remained in contact with Western Europe. During the 6th century the Emperor Justinian, builder of Hagia Sophia and formulator of a revised code of Roman law, destroyed the Ostrogothic kingdom in Italy and drove the Vandals out of West Africa; parts of southern Italy remained within the Byzantine compass until the 11th century. Until the 8th century the Pope in Rome looked to the Byzantine emperor as the chief secular power of Christendom and later, during the 11th and 12th centuries, thousands of Western Europeans visited Constantinople as crusaders or merchants; western European states were founded in the Middle East by crusading leaders.

Nevertheless, the forces that divided East and West were greater than those that united them. For north-west Europe, the link with Byzantium was often comparatively remote, while in general cultural differences were considerable and grew more marked as time went on. In the West, the language of the Church, of government, and of scholarship was Latin; in the East it was Greek. Though both were Christian, different forms of religious organization and even doctrine developed.

The Germanic kingdoms established in the West when the Roman Empire fell were mostly rather short-lived. The Vandal and Ostrogothic kingdoms were destroyed by Justinian; the Visigothic kingdom was destroyed in the early 8th century by

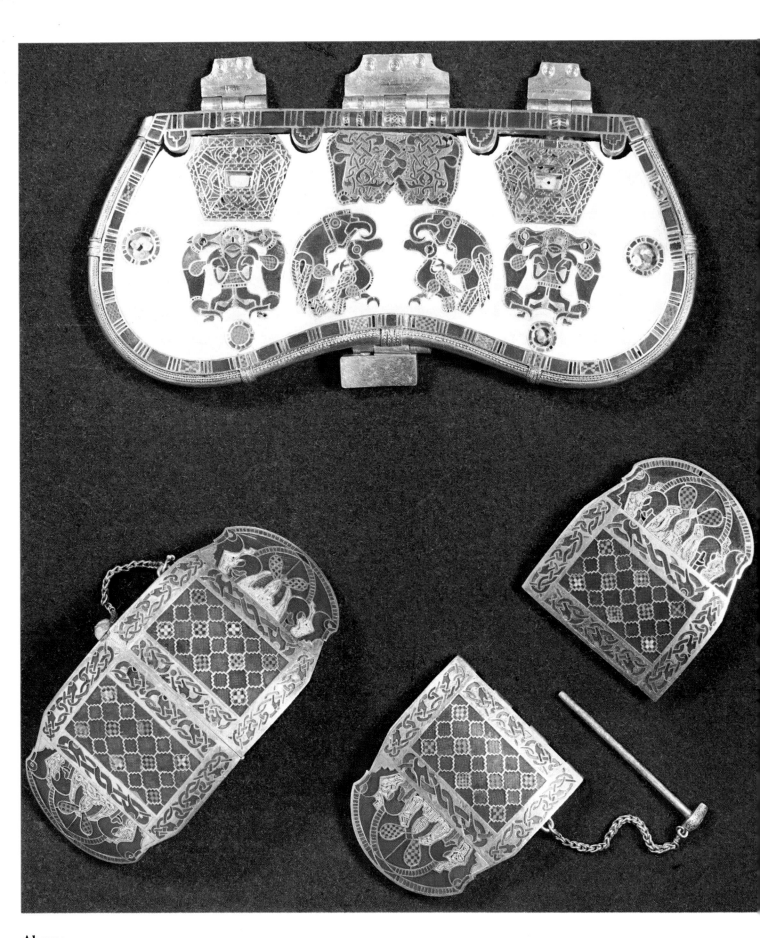

Above:
Part of the treasure of the Sutton Hoo burial ship, dating from the first half of the 7th century but only discovered in the 20th. These clasps and buckles of gold, glass and semi-precious stones show the richness of a British court at the beginning of the Christian period. British Museum, London.

Muslims, who also deprived the Byzantine Empire of much of its territory. In Western Europe, the advance of Islam was checked by the one Germanic kingdom that had taken firm root – the kingdom of the Franks. In 732 Charles Martel, king of the Franks, defeated the Muslims at the battle of Tours, preventing their expansion farther north. Under the Carolingian dynasty, the Frankish kingdom was stabilized and expanded, reaching the height of its power with the symbolic coronation of Charlemagne as Roman emperor in 800 by the Pope.

The spectacular Carolingian achievements were, however, transitory. Under his successors in the 9th century, Charlemagne's empire broke up in civil war, while Western Europe came under fresh attack from the Magyars in the east, the Muslims in the south and, most destructive of all, the Vikings from the north-west. At the same time, the development of the form of society which we call feudal led to the weakening of central government.

The most influential force in medieval Europe was the Church, and religion dominated life and art. This fact gave rise to ambiguous attitudes towards the classical, pre-Christian past. On the one hand there was a feeling that pagan culture was sinful and dangerous, and at best had no relevance to a society which had seen the True Light. On the other hand, it was possible to see classical culture as the precursor of Christianity, in which case classical learning could be regarded with the same respect as was accorded to the Old Testament, also a precursor of Christianity. There tended to be revivals of classical culture, though on a much smaller scale than the Renaissance, at different periods; indeed, these revivals had begun in the classical world itself – for instance, the Hellenicism of the Emperor Hadrian. On the whole, Christianity had little use for classical art. The medieval Church did not think of God as an ideal human figure, as the Greek sculptors of the 5th century had shown their gods. An art with a more transcendental flavour, conveying religious meaning by symbols, was appropriate, something

like the art of the Ravenna mosaics perhaps. However, as we have seen, Early Christian art was immensely varied, sometimes near classical in spirit and showing a great tolerance of pagan influences, sometimes, as in Byzantium, far removed from naturalism.

The first notable revival of classical learning (no other was recognized) in Western Europe took place in the time of Charlemagne. At that time contact with Byzantium was slight, due to the Iconoclastic crisis, and this helped to ensure that the styles of art established during the 'Carolingian renaissance' came from classical traditions. These were mixed with other influences however, including Anglo-Saxon (Charlemagne's chief assistant in his cultural planning came from

York), as well as Germanic and Early Christian styles.

After Charlemagne, the Carolingian empire split up, the two main divisions being roughly equivalent to Germany and France, but in the following century (the 10th) the idea of the empire was revived again with the coronation of the German king Otto I at Rome, and for a century or so it looked as though the future of Europe lay with the Germans. Otto revived the imperial art of the Carolingians, but with some differences.

Above:
This detail from a Renaissance painting
shows a magnificent cross and altarpiece
of the 7th century at St Denis. National
Gallery, London.

Above:
The head from a wooden crucifix in Cologne Cathedral, carved in the 10th century and probably painted. Large figures in wood predated stone sculpture.

Opposite:
Altarpiece from Basle Cathedral, early 11th century. The gold is inlaid with precious stones, and the figures are depicted in high relief. Musée de Cluny, Paris.

Below:
An initial letter from an Anglo-Saxon Psalter, late 10th century. British Library, London.

Above:
A page from a Gospel Book of the early 11th century which displays the strong influence of Eastern styles. Bayerische Staatsbibliothek, Munich.

The Byzantine influence was more evident (Otto II married a Byzantine princess), and the beginnings of the style known as Romanesque (i.e. 'in the Roman style') were obvious. There was a similar artistic revival in Anglo-Saxon England about the same time, in which also distinctly Romanesque elements can be recognized alongside Anglo-Saxon motifs, as in the initial letter from an Anglo-Saxon Psalter (page 112). In France

too, developments foreshadowed the emergence of Romanesque: the great abbey of Cluny was founded in 910, and soon afterwards an agreement was made with the Norsemen which allowed them to settle in Normandy; in a generation or two they became the people we know as the Normans. Cluny was the symbol of a great movement of ecclesiastical reform and renewal of Christian values which was to find its expression in

Romanesque art and architecture, while the Normans were to prove the most successful people in feudal Europe, and the greatest builders. In Britain, the Romanesque style is known simply as 'Norman'.

Although the styles of most of the cultures of earlier times had been affected to a greater or lesser extent by outside influences, they were all essentially homogeneous. Roman art was basically the same in Italy

and in Britain; Byzantine art spread equally far without losing its character. The same cannot be said for what we call Romanesque art. The term describes the art of Western Europe in the 11th and 12th centuries, and although the different Romanesque styles in various regions had much in common, they were far from identical. It is easy to distinguish German Romanesque from that of France or Italy, and it is also possible to detect different styles in the same country. This was largely the result of the decentralization caused by feudalism. For all practical purposes the Duke of Normandy was an independent ruler, however devoutly he might pay homage to the King of France. Moreover, travel between different regions was difficult, the transport of building materials even more so; on the whole, disparities in style are less remarkable than the speed with which cultural ideas spread in medieval Europe.

There was one great unifying factor, and that was the Church. The Romanesque period is the great age of the Roman Church, and although there was a 'Holy Roman Emperor', he was scarcely more than the overlord of Germany and Italy; he certainly had far less influence as a universal power than the Pope, who was able to confine him to an inferior position – symbolized by the homage of the Emperor Henry IV to Pope Gregory VII at Canossa in 1077. Romanesque art is largely, though not exclusively, the art of the Church, especially of the monasteries, which stood out like beacons of learning in a rather savage world.

It is exceedingly difficult to define Romanesque art. In some respects, and especially in architecture, it can be seen as the link between the classical and the Gothic styles: it has many elements of the classical but is not yet itself classical; it has many elements of the Gothic, but is not yet itself Gothic. But it would be possible to list many Romanesque buildings which do not foreshadow Gothic, and some which have little about them

Left:
Relief carving of Isaiah at Souillac,
early 12th century.

Above:
Carved capital on two columns from an abbey at Toulouse, late 12th century. Musée des Augustins, Toulouse.

Right:
Tympanum of the Prior's Door at Ely Cathedral, about 1140.

that is classical. Romanesque art also includes northern traditions having little or no connection with the classical; in Spain particularly it is influenced by Muslim style, in many places by Byzantine art, and so on.

Apart from architecture, which is not within the scope of this book, most people would agree that the most interesting aspect of Romanesque art is its sculpture. Part of the reason for this is the fact that sculpture on a large scale had to be rediscovered; it was not part of a continuing tradition. Therefore, early Romanesque sculpture varied considerably in style and technique, and many short-lived local schools appeared which disappeared as quickly as they were formed, or were overtaken by new developments. Some attempted to capture physical movements, as in the figure of Isaiah (opposite) from the abbey church at Souillac. Others tried to convey the helplessness of mankind in the grip of fate. Sculpture changed very rapidly within a short time, and before a much longer period had elapsed it had broken away completely from its Romanesque origins.

Medieval sculptors, like the sculptors of ancient Greece, were concerned with using the dimension of depth, which is sculpture's chief advantage over painting, to achieve greater realism; the revival of monumental sculpture in the 11th century meant therefore a step toward

representational art. From this point of view, the stylized patterns and decoration of Romanesque sculpture which, for us, are one of its most attractive features, were redundant. The Greeks had worked out their ideal naturalism in sculpture for themselves, but the medieval sculptors had at least some guidance in what survived of classical sculpture. In southern Europe many Roman buildings were still standing, with relief carvings and statues, and it is not surprising that in Spain, Italy and southern France Romanesque sculpture frequently employs easily recognizable motifs from antiquity. A capital from Toulouse (above left), though thoroughly Romanesque in its general arrangement, depends on classical art for its motifs, which include a centaur. In the north, however, there were far fewer classical remains, and what did exist was generally of poorer quality. In this region, sculptors found their motifs elsewhere, particularly in paintings, which means almost without exception the work of the illuminators of manuscripts in the monasteries. The capitals in the crypt of Canterbury cathedral were clearly carved by

someone who had looked at the ornamental initial letters painted in the sciptorium. The patterns carved on the arches of doorways, like the Prior's Door at Ely (above), were taken from the early Gospel books. Probably such patterns were first simply painted on a flat surface; carving came later.

However, the carving of awkward architectural details like the capitals of columns and the recessed tympana of doorways posed different problems from the decoration of manuscripts. The Ely door shows how the sculptor overcame the problem of filling the semicircular space of the tympanum gracefully, and also illustrates the skill with which Romanesque sculptors integrated sculpture with architecture, so that the carvings seem part of the masonry, an effect stemming partly from the fact that carving was done on stone already in place. The church as a building was intended to be a living image, a vital picture of the Christian religion from Genesis to the Day of Judgment.

Most Romanesque sculpture is relief carving, but its most striking achievements came with the approach to sculpture in the round, a

Opposite:
An early 12th-century painting of Christ in Majesty, from a chapel belonging to the abbey of Cluny at Berzé la Ville, whose monumental style had a strong influence on Romanesque painting.

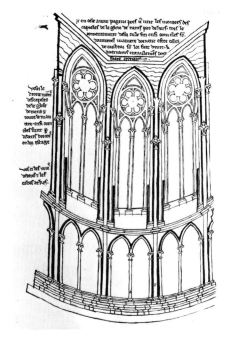

development which, derived from classical art, was first seen in southern Europe and spread steadily north. It was encouraged by the practice of making doors and windows with many decorative columns; most of the early figure sculptures are found on doorways. When carving a column, it was inevitable that figures should appear almost totally in the round because of the shape of the basic structure, and it is possible to trace the progress by which reliefs became higher and higher until they became virtually free-standing statues. The culmination of this development can be seen, for instance, in the figures

Left:
A page from the sketch-book of Villard d'Honnecourt, showing a sketch of a window at Reims.

Below:
Figures from the west front of Reims Cathedral, about 1220, showing the Visitation.

from the west front of Reims cathedral (below) which have finally broken away completely from the building. The pose and the drapery of these figures suggest that the sculptor must have had direct access to classical examples, but the chief innovation in this area came not from sculpture but from metalwork, especially the work of Nicholas Verdun in the late 12th century, whose elaborate altarpieces show a profound understanding of classical conventions. Early relief work in metal was done by beating strips of the metal over wooden cores, but by the middle of the 12th century casting had become normal, and this method encouraged greater movement and gesture than carving in stone. The smaller scale also encouraged metalworkers to show off their talents. Moreover, sculptors were originally masons: the same men built the buildings and made the carvings. They were a class apart from most medieval craftsmen, partly because they often worked in comparative isolation, but during the Romanesque period, sculpture gradually became distinguished as a separate craft from its parent masonry, much as the sculpture itself gradually became divorced from the building.

In drawing and painting too there was a movement away from two-dimensional representation, a movement based on the conventions of drapery (opposite) in classical sculpture and influenced more and more by contemporary metalwork and sculpture. The use of pattern books was common in the Middle Ages, and helped to spread stylistic ideas. The sketch book of Villard d'Honnecourt, a mason by trade, who was at work in the early 13th century, is a rare surviving example of a craftsman's plans (above left). His sketches might well be a model for a sculpture; it is interesting to compare the drapery style as it appears in d'Honnecourt's sketch book with the statues at Reims.

Romanesque manuscripts can usually be distinguished from earlier ones by the firm, easy lines of the drawing, very different from the feathery outlines of Anglo-Saxon drawing. Romanesque drawing uses line in the same way as a glass-painter or an

117

Above:
Detail from a baptismal font by Rainer of Huy, early 12th century, in cast bronze, possessing a remarkable clear, classical quality. Church of St Barthélemy, Liège.

Opposite:
The Gloucester Candlestick, 1104-1113, 58 cm high. Victoria and Albert Museum, London.

enameller, to mark the border of colours, as in the Bury Bible. The manner of representing the drapery here is a convention known as the 'damp-fold' style, which possibly bears some similarity to Byzantine conventions, though the sinuous double lines suggesting solid flesh beneath are novel. The same style is found in metalwork, and perhaps originated there. The Paderborn altar, the work of Roger of Helmarshausen, in silver with pearls and precious stones, was made in about 1100, and is one of the earliest indications of the 'damp-fold' style.

Romanesque illumination is also distinguished from its predecessors by a taste for strong colours (Anglo-Saxon illustrators generally preferred pale tints). Though it would not be difficult to find exceptions to the rule, the strong tones of the Bury

Bible are characteristic. This development can be followed more or less chronologically by tracing the succeeding copies made of a particular work, such as the Utrecht Psalter. The drawing and the colouring become stronger over the course of two hundred years, and the similarity between the earliest and the latest copy is remarkably slight: the relationship would hardly appear were it not for the copies intervening.

One of the difficulties in pursuing sources and trends of Romanesque style, or of many other artistic developments, arises from the fact that physical circumstances vary, and the need for economy (or the relative absence of such a need) may affect style. It is noticeable that colours generally appear most lavish when no one was troubled about costs. There was an effort to capture in painting the effects of stained glass or enamelling, a craft which was particularly attractive to medieval people and was brought to a high state of accomplishment in the Romanesque period. Enamelling is essentially the process of giving added brightness to metal by glazing. In Romanesque enamelling, the glaze was usually translucent. The love of brilliance, notably an intense admiration for jewellery, was what

prompted, or at any rate encouraged, a preoccupation with Byzantine art in the 12th century.

In general, metalwork was of great importance in the decorative arts of the 12th century. This importance sprang partly at least from the fact that the objects of the smiths' craft were primarily the most sacred objects of the Church – altars, altar cups and candlesticks, crosses and reliquaries (containers of various sizes for the relics, alleged or real, of saints, which were the most valuable possessions of many churches and monasteries). Next to the churches themselves, these demanded man's highest skills, and were usually made of the most precious materials. The Gloucester Candlestick (opposite), now in the Victoria and Albert Museum in London, has an inscription which tells us that it was made at the command of Abbot Peter of Gloucester, which enables it to be dated quite precisely to 1104-13, the years of the Abbot's rule. The cast-bronze font by Rainer of Huy (above) is about the same date; it was made not before 1107 and not after 1118 for the Church of St Barthélemy in Liège. It makes an interesting contrast with the Gloucester Candlestick, having a calm classical purity that is almost totally

119

absent from that work. The reliquary (above) from Trier cathedral is a century, or slightly more, older, and shows the continuance of Carolingian and Ottonian artistic traditions. It was made for the foot of St Andrew, which was contained in the hollow gold foot on the top of the shrine (elsewhere arms, or parts of arms, were similarly housed in imitation arms). The Trier reliquary is smaller than a photograph makes it appear – about 31 cm in height. It is made of gold with ivory panels and ornamented with precious stones and enamel. It is something of a miracle that this precious object – plus a very few like it – has survived to the 20th century. In time, churches, with their increasingly elaborate architecture, began to look more like shrines, while shrines increasingly took on an architectural form until, in the Gothic period, the two came to have the same form.

Romanesque used to be regarded as a crude and half-formed forerunner of Gothic art, relatively uncouth compared with the refinement of

Gothic, and there is a sense in which Romanesque is merely an incomplete form of Gothic. The pendulum of taste has swung the other way since the 19th century however, when this view was held, and some people prefer the comparative primitivism of much Romanesque decoration and the great strength of its buildings to the lighter and more elegant style which grew out of it.

The ordinary person asked to describe a medieval work of art will almost certainly describe something not Romanesque, certainly not Byzantine, but probably Gothic. The popular conception of medieval art is Gothic art. And the type of art most likely to spring to mind is not painting, nor sculpture, but architecture. It is in terms of architecture, in fact, that the distinction between Romanesque and Gothic is most easily made, and the decisive event that is traditionally held to mark the beginning of the Gothic is the building of the Abbey of St Denis, near Paris.

The term Gothic was originally a term of opprobrium, meaning much

Above:
Miniature from a Paris Psalter of about 1200. It shows the movement away from Romanesque tradition and the evolution of the Gothic style. Corpus Christi College, Cambridge.

Below:
Figures of apostles from the frieze in the apse of S. Clemente in Rome, 12th century. The style is close to that of the Early Christian period.

the same as 'Vandal'. The latter word has retained its meaning, but 'Gothic' has changed altogether; since the Gothic style had nothing particularly to do with the Goths, it is a very inappropriate name anyway, and the older name of 'Frankish' or 'French' work would be more suitable. The luminaries of Renaissance Italy, however, regarding the Middle Ages as barbaric, dubbed it 'Gothic' in disgust and Gothic it remains.

Like the Romanesque, the Gothic varied from region to region: Gothic cathedrals in England, France and Spain could never be confused, yet the contrasts in style are much less than in the Romanesque period. Although it covers such a long period and such a wide area, Gothic style is more homogeneous than Romanesque. This was partly due to the bands of craftsmen who travelled from place to place as opportunities for building arose, and partly to changing political and social conditions, especially in France. Royal government was growing in power and prestige, and the great provincial rulers were a little less independent than they had been. Under Philip Augustus, France attained a degree of unity unknown before, and despite the attacks of the English and the existence of a rival to the French kingdom in the dukedom of Burgundy, the emphasis was more on royal government and centralization. The rise of town life was also significant. Romanesque art had been largely the product of the monasteries; the centre of life in the new towns was the cathedral, which was a civic as well as a religious building, a meeting place, a storehouse, a fortress, and a social centre as well as a place for priests and services.

So far as sculpture is concerned, it is difficult to mark the dividing line between Romanesque and Gothic, if only because those names are themselves imprecise. The figures at Reims (page 117) have been discussed in terms of Romanesque tradition, but they are definitely Gothic. The Gothic style, at least in architecture, may have begun about 1150, but there are 'Gothic' works earlier than that date and plenty of 'Romanesque' ones later. Some works would be called 'Romanesque' by one authority and 'Gothic' by another. Sometimes these labels can seem more of a nuisance than a convenience.

Like Romanesque, Gothic sculpture is mainly ecclesiastical, and it is hard to appreciate it fully without some knowledge of its purpose in medieval society. Its purpose was educational – to teach and glorify the Christian religion. That does not mean that the subjects are exclusively Biblical; everything in the world that stands for the glory of God may be admitted, including plants and animals, symbolic figures representing the arts, or the seven deadly sins for that matter, though most history commemorated in sculpture is sacred history. As in Romanesque or Byzantine art, both the subjects and the way in which they are depicted were rather strictly governed by iconography. For example, in Gothic art, God, the angels and the apostles always have bare feet, while others are shod; this was conventional, and to depart from such a convention was not so much a question of ignorance or bad taste but rather one of heresy.

To a large extent the Gothic style is the visual expression of the movement for religious reform and spiritual renewal which, beginning in the 11th century, reached its peak in the 12th century. It flourished particularly in France – that is, the area of France ruled by the French king; the king of England ruled a large portion – and reached its height in the reign of St Louis (1226-70). By that time the grip of the Church on Christian Europe was greater than at almost any other time; there was an unprecedented period of church-building, and men flocked to give their money or even their lives in the Crusades. The Church dominated the existence of ordinary people to an extent that we find hard to comprehend: an old woman carrying firewood laboriously to her house would think of Christ carrying his Cross; a monk in France

cut his apple into three parts before eating it in memory of the Trinity. Sculpture was one of the instruments of the Church: it illustrated its beliefs and doctrines in every new cathedral and church, bringing the message to ordinary people who, of course, entirely lacked all the media of mass communication that we have become accustomed to. One result of this function of sculpture was that events had to be depicted in a way that was accessible to the ignorant and often illiterate. This explains the popularity of such subjects as sowing the seed or reaping the harvest, matters which everyone understood. Figures became

Above:
Stained-glass window from Chartres Cathedral. Chartres has perhaps the finest surviving collection of early Gothic glass, with its strong reds and deep, mysterious blues, which modern methods have never been able to recapture.

123

more human; the remote, mystical element in much Romanesque sculpture almost disappeared, and saints became recognizable as ordinary mortals, with the faces of men or women you might see in the street rather than the hieratic features of earlier statues of saints.

As in the Romanesque period, sculpture was in the main confined to doorways, porches, tympani, and so on, but the porches and façades of churches had become very much larger, offering far greater scope, as in the west front of Wells cathedral (page 127). These buildings, especially in France, were usually set in the midst of the town, not hidden away in some remote location like the monasteries. The sculptures were thus placed where everyone could see them as they went about their daily business. Since they depicted examples to be followed, lessons to be learned, or dangers to be avoided, it is not surprising that they became more realistic in style. The sculptors found that man's relation to God, and indeed God himself, could be depicted in human terms, and thus they returned to a kind of humanist art not seen since classical times. The degree to which they took classical examples as their models is open to argument; undoubtedly they copied classical forms, though the Gothic conception of the classical was very unlike that of the Renaissance. The figures at Reims (page 117) actually had Roman statues as their models, though of course they were not trying simply to portray the Virgin Mary as a Roman lady. At this stage, they were not quite certain what they were aiming at, and because we know that two or three centuries later classical art was to be dramatically revived in the Renaissance, we may impart to such works as the Reims figures more significance than we should. They were perhaps the finest works of their time (early 13th century), but it is an interesting

fact that in an age of much imitation and common models, the Reims statues were seldom copied elsewhere. In fact this incipient 12th-century classical revival proved a dead end: classical art was pagan art, and probably the Church disapproved. Gothic sculpture developed in another direction.

Although the Gothic sculptors, like the Greeks, aimed to portray realistic human figures, their aims were of course quite different. They were not aiming at an ideal kind of human beauty. On the contrary, the Church frowned on such an idea. The body was a temporary vehicle and a rather unsatisfactory one, at odds with the soul, which was of true importance, and liable to gross and sinful desires.

Gothic sculpture aimed to express emotion and personality, to mirror the soul, so to speak, an effect achieved by gesture and movement, as well as facial expression. In this respect, Gothic sculpture was not so far from Hellenistic, as distinct from Greek, ideas, yet the resemblance is misleading. Gothic sculpture developed in its own way, without much help from earlier styles.

In the middle of the 13th century, three important programmes of sculpture were carried out in the German cathedrals of Bamberg, Strasbourg (now in France) and Naumburg (none of them, incidentally, truly Gothic buildings). Until this time, there had been very little large-scale sculpture in Germany,

Above Left:
An example of Gothic realism: the statue of St Elizabeth from Bamberg Cathedral, about 1235.

Above:
A detail of the tympanum at Bamberg Cathedral in which the sculptor attempted to convey emotion through facial expressions: as the scene is the Last Judgement, and the grimaces are meant to show grief and torment, he did not quite succeed. About 1235.

and what there was appears to have derived more from Italy, where the Gothic style was less prevalent, than from France, the birthplace of Gothic. The sculpture of these three buildings, however, is in the High Gothic style, and derives from France, especially at Bamberg.

Before the Gothic sculptors arrived, Bamberg had a carved choir screen in a strong and lively Romanesque style, which was probably derived from manuscript illuminations. This local school made its mark on the new style, which appears to have come from Reims. The figure of St Elizabeth (above) at Bamberg has an obvious affinity with the figures at Reims (page 117), but the free and lively movement of the draperies at Bamberg may be due to local influences. Another development is the marked individuality of the face, which is that of an old woman, tough and trouble-hardened, which by contrast makes the works of the Reims sculptor appear almost bland. The attempt to convey emotion and feeling in the subject did not always work very well even at Bamberg. In the scene of the Last Judgment (above right) which decorates the tympanum of the north porch, the Saved and the Damned

express their feelings at the news of their fate. The smug grins of the Saved, shown in the photograph, are convincing, but something has gone badly wrong with the attempt to convey the horror of the Damned who appear grotesquely amused at their prospects.

Surer hands were at work in Strasbourg, where a different kind of subject is tackled on the tympani of the south transept with striking success. Above the twin doorways are scenes of the Coronation and Death of the Virgin. In the latter, expressions of grief have been well managed, the sculptor having wisely determined to turn the corners of the mouth down rather than up. Below, the doorways are flanked by three statues, representing the Church, King Solomon (between the two doors) and the Synagogue (right). The two female figures (the Church and the Synagogue) have to register triumph and defeat respectively, and the sculptor has managed the latter in an interest-

Right:
The Synagogue figure from Strasbourg, about 1230, a technical *tour de force* portraying the triumph of the Church over Judaism. Musée de l'Oeuvre Notre-Dame, Strasbourg.

Above:
The Crucifixion, after 1249, from the
Rood screen at Naumburg Cathedral.

Christ is indeed the 'gateway'. The
figure is meant to arouse sympathy in
the spectator: the body is wrenched in
pain and the face is full of suffering,
while at either side, as Christian
iconographic tradition dictated, stand
the Virgin and St John, displaying
acute but restrained grief, as they
indicate, by gesture, the Saviour on
the Cross, adding to the impression
of pathos. Here is a quite different
conception from Romanesque
renderings of this motif, in which the
Crucifixion is treated not as the
suffering of a man but the triumph of
a god. Scenes from the Passion are
illustrated above in a strikingly realistic way, with little details such as
Pontius Pilate washing his hands, or a
disciple at the Last Supper helping
himself to bread, vividly caught.
Faces express character: Pilate's is the
face of an irresolute man, the High
Priest looks extremely sinister.

Passing through into the choir at
Naumburg, the visitor finds himself
among very different scenes. Here are
statues of historical figures rather
than strictly religious subjects. As
most of the people represented would
have been dead long before, they
cannot be actual portraits, yet so
realistic are the faces that it seems
certain that the sculptor used living
models.

There is no question that the
sculpture at Naumburg was the work
of one man, though he is known only
as 'the Master of Naumburg' (he
would not have done all the actual
carving with his own hands). He
attained a degree of realism that no
one had even attempted before, and
which could hardly be excelled. Later
German sculptors, striving for even
greater expressiveness than the
Master of Naumburg, tended to degenerate into caricature, producing,
for example, Crucifixions so horrible
in their gross emphasis on physical
agony that they resemble the more
ferocious examples of Polynesian
masks or works that are so self-con-
sciously expressive that the actual
feeling is trivial. There was in fact no
one who quite measured up to the
standard set at Naumburg until the
late 14th century, when Claus Sluter
broke away from the fine and frothy
style which had then become fashion-

Above:
Virgin and Child from the doorway of
the Chartreuse de Champol, School of
Klaus Sluter, c. 1400.

able in favour of more monumental,
emotionally highly-charged work
which, whether the artist himself
knew it or not, fell closely into line
with the Naumburg tradition.

The suggestion of a body beneath
the clothes which is easily detected in
the Synagogue figure at Strasbourg is
another unusual feature of that remarkable work. There are almost no
nudes in Gothic sculpture and the few
examples we know are not very
successful. Sculptors were more interested in the drapery than in the body
underneath; when they sketched out
their plan on the block of stone they
were to carve, they drew a frontal
outline only, and although we have
seen how fully independent statues
gradually emerged from carved reliefs, in a way Gothic statues never
did become completely divorced from
the wall, always retaining a suggestion of relief, certainly by comparison with the fully rounded free-
standing statues of classical Greece.
But part of the reason for this was that

ing and successful way, by giving the
body a twist that, although anatomi-
cally doubtful, is highly expressive of
dejection; defeat is also signalled by
the broken spear carried by this figure
and by the closed eyes, subtly visible
through the blindfold. An interesting
feature of this figure is that it has a
markedly different appearance if
viewed from the side instead of the
front. The head which seemed to be
drooping dejectedly then looks as if it
is lolling rather horribly from a
broken neck, while the body has an
unnatural twist. It would be pre-
sumption to suppose that this is just a
dramatic accident.

At about the middle of the 13th
century, shortly after the sculptures at
Bamberg and Strasbourg, the west
choir of Naumburg was built with an
unusual screen. A carved Crucifixion
forms the central pillar of the doorway, so that anyone entering the choir
has to pass under the arms of Christ (it
was normal practice to have a Crucifixion on the screen, but it was usually
raised high above the ground). Here,

Above:
The Last Supper, by the Master of Naumburg, after 1249. The figures are remarkably unposed, caught at a moment in time almost like a photograph, and the screen of which this is a detail is one of the great dramatic masterpieces of Gothic sculpture. Naumburg Cathedral.

Below:
The west front of Wells Cathedral. In the niches are carved figures, 13th and early 14th centuries.

Gothic statues, and sculpture generally, were normally placed against a wall, very often in niches, like those on the west front of Wells Cathedral in England (right).

The rise of royal and noble dynasties in medieval Europe was responsible for a vogue for splendid tombs, similar in form to the reliquaries in which were housed more sacred remains, but tending more and more to include a sculptured figure of the dead person. The most imposing examples are, naturally, royal tombs, but by the 14th century even a humble knight of the shires might be so entombed, as many a parish church attests. This custom was an important source of employment for sculptors, and so great was the demand that a

Above:
Tomb effigy of Edward II in Gloucester Cathedral.

Left:
The choir stalls at Chester Cathedral, about 1380, characteristic of the fondness for elaborate carved decoration of architectural forms in the later Middle Ages.

number of workshops sprang up to cater to it. The early examples of Gothic bronze and marble effigies, like that of King Henry III in Westminster Abbey, simply represented the king as an idealized monarch, in a style familiar from contemporary manuscripts. It was not until the 14th century that realistic portraits were attempted. The effigy of Richard II, for example, is clearly taken from life: we should recognize it as such even if we did not have other portraits of the king for comparison. However, realistic portraiture remained comparatively rare before the Renaissance. The numerous tombs of Crusader

Above:
One of the famous tapestries at Angers in France, begun in 1377. Tapestries were one of the finest productions of medieval art, but in many cases time has not been kind to their colours, and an effort of imagination is needed to recapture the glories of the musty hangings in dark museums. Angers is a fortunate exception. Musée des Tapisseries, Angers.

Left:
Virgin and Child, probably the most popular subject for Gothic artists. This early 14th-century statue is in the Cathedral of Notre Dame, Paris.

knights were made with a simple stock figure, and most look pretty much alike. To be fair, these were not works of great artistic merit, but they have considerable importance, firstly because they kept sculptural traditions alive in districts where other opportunities were declining – when the great age of cathedral building was over – and secondly, because from them the great vogue for memorial statues, divorced from the actual tomb, was to develop. These represented the main source of sculpture right up to modern times.

Although Gothic sculpture was predominantly religious, it was not exclusively ecclesiastical. In 13th-century France a court art developed in which the austerity of early Gothic sculpture was entirely abandoned in favour of a fashionable elegance, with affected gestures of the hands and sometimes rather unpleasantly complacent facial expressions. So far as sculpture is concerned, the most notable examples are small works in ivory or some other material, sometimes narrative pieces based on romantic legend, which were often placed in an architectural setting. Private chapels were furnished with similar works, Madonnas in ivory, silver, and painted wood or stone being the most popular. Tapestries, like the famous ones still to be seen at Angers (above), might be placed in this category of 'luxury art'.

129

Although the Italians were fundamentally unsympathetic to the Gothic style, there is some Gothic art in Italy, especially in regions influenced by French taste, which included parts of northern Italy and the Angevin kingdom of Naples. Nevertheless, Italian Gothic had a distinctive character of its own and, as in Italian art generally, it was not so much a particular style or movement as the work of individual artists that was important. In northern Europe, Gothic art was most frequently anonymous, or the work of a certain school, while in Italy the finest works are those of particular artists, especially the Pisano family.

The founder of the family, Nicola Pisano, was at work on a pulpit for the cathedral of Siena in the middle of the 13th century. The work was probably based on classical sarcophagi and is in the classical tradition, but later pulpits show much more of the French Gothic influence. This no doubt reflects the growing French political influence in northern Italy, though Giovanni Pisano, Nicola's son, may have visited France himself at some time. It is in Giovanni Pisano's work that the Gothic influence becomes most marked, with movement and expression strongly emphasized, in contrast with the rather stiff, formal figures of his father. In his later work, Giovanni's depiction of emotion approaches hysteria, but other members of the family produced works in a more approachable style, clearly deriving from France.

In the Middle Ages, sculpture and flat areas of wall inside churches were frequently painted. This sometimes comes as a surprise to people nowadays, although in the past few years there has been a trend in favour of restoring such colours where feasible; but the idea that Gothic art was rather grey and dull is completely untrue. The love of bright colour which was a feature of Romanesque art continued into the Gothic period. In spite of that, painting remained a minor art. People preferred to decorate their walls, if they had means to do so, with tapestries rather than pictures (they were warmer for one thing). Painting was seen largely as a matter of applying areas of colour, as gorgeous as possible, and painted pictures therefore were two-dimensional, with little or no attempt at modelling. It appears to have been considered an adjunct to sculpture, a poor substitute – a painting was cheaper than a statue.

There were of course places where painting was the only possible method of ornamentation, for example in books and manuscripts. In manuscript illustration, as in architecture, France took the lead in 13th-century Europe. It was becoming more of a professional craft, and we know some of the artists by name. At the same time script became finer and the whole format smaller. This may have been at least encouraged, if not exclusively caused, by the need of members of the new itinerant religious orders, the friars, for works that could be more easily carried about. The miniatures are often framed in an architectural setting, and the figures are more realistic. Hatched backgrounds in gold and strong colours were becoming popular towards the end of the century. The Maciejowski Old Testament (opposite) is a lively example of the 13th-century French illuminator's art. The scenes illustrated are The Drunkenness of Noah (with foliage reminiscent of carved details on capitals, bosses, etc.), The Tower of Babel (providing a handy illustration of medieval building methods), The Sacrifice of Isaac (note the angel grabbing Abraham's sword in the nick of time), and The Children of Israel Led into Captivity. (This manuscript was presented to Shah Abbas the Great by a papal mission early in the 17th century, and Shah Abbas had the Latin text translated into Persian.) The Gothic love of fancy and the grotesque often found expression in miniatures, where one may find all kinds of exotic animals making their appearances and delightful conceits like sportive mermaids or a rabbit playing a harp. ·

Left:
GIOVANNI PISANO's depiction of the Nativity, from the pulpit of Pisa Cathedral, 13th century.

Opposite:
An illuminated manuscript of the Old Testament, made in Paris, given to Shah Abbas the Great by the Pope in 1608. At Shah Abbas's request, a Persian translation was squeezed into the margins. Pierpont Morgan Library, New York, MS 638, folio 3.

...valiter Noe vineam plantauit. et i- | ...turre babilonis ... erigit. er... er al...
ebrius. a(c) nudatus. ab uno filio(rum)... | ...spiritu(m) sapia(m) humana(m) ofundit in
...onobus ... contegitur | lingua(s). ne se muicem hedificantes intellig-
 | ...Atqui ita ceptum opus non possit impleri.

Craliter Abraam iubente deo summi. obe- | uomodo excitus Regis Elamitarum cali-
diens sacrificare filium suum unicum uo... | ...orum trium regum. uicto rege gomorre cu(m)
...et iam eleuato gladio ut feriret. ab angelo | aliis quatuor regibus. captiuos ducunt. z i(nter)
...etrahitur. et aries pter spem oblatus sacrifi- | alios Loth nepotem abrahe.
...o cistitur...

פהם ייריא יצחק חקם

נלי ודי פארסאה בר עבר רוח וחדי...
...מויד ודאתא ודדין אלתכסבסה אלחנית...
...וס אחמיר דאזהס

It was in Italy that medieval painting made its most noticeable advances. We have seen how in the 13th century Italy came increasingly under the influence of northern Europe, especially France, and was drawn away from her traditional sources of artistic inspiration – the world of antiquity and Byzantium. The Gothic style appeared in Italian architecture as early as 1220 and somewhat later in sculpture, notably in the work of Giovanni Pisano. The case of painting was rather different, for it was native Italian innovation rather than northern influence that was decisive. A tradition of painting already existed, though it was not strong, which imitated Byzantine mosaics, and this tradition is still evident in the work of Duccio di Buoninsegna (c. 1260-c. 1319) and the Siena school. But the art of Duccio, and more particularly his disciples such as Simone Martini, is much more human and naturalistic than anything in Byzantine art. Duccio apparently preferred to work in tempera rather than fresco (the technique of wallpainting on unset plaster), the other main medium of Italian painting, and a number of his wooden altar-pieces still survive. In preparing a tempera, the artist first covered the panel, usually of poplar wood, with plaster, giving a smooth, hard finish on which he drew his design. Next, gold leaf was laid on those areas where it was required, and the figures sketched in *terra verde*, a greenish pigment that gave body to the final colours, which were prepared by an apprentice in little pots, mixed with white of egg to bind them. More vivid colours were possible than with fresco, and tempera also had the advantage of making corrections less of a headache than in fresco, where the plaster had to be scraped off and a fresh start made. Duccio's *Entry into Jerusalem* (right) was painted in 1308-11. Although he was fairly conservative by comparison with some of his immediate successors, many of the new qualities can be seen in this work.

Opposite:
Jean II, about 1360, the earliest surviving example of a French painting on panel, showing the arrival of realistic portraiture. Musée du Louvre, Paris.

Above:
Duccio's *The Entry into Jerusalem*, about 1310. Museo del'Opera del Duomo, Siena.

The figures are flattish (Christ, as convention dictated, is larger than the others), but there is a clear recession in the crowd emerging from the city gate and the buildings beyond. The novel achievements of Italian Gothic paintings are already apparent in the way the figures are integrated with the architectural background and the evident three dimensions of buildings. There is, however, less emotion in the human figures than in those of contemporary Florentine painting; more than a trace of the austere Byzantine tradition remains.

It was in Florence that the most startling breakthrough was made, and the foundations laid for European painting for the next five hundred years. Giotto di Bordone (*c.* 1266-1337), the leader of the Florentine school, was slightly younger than Duccio. In his frescoes devoted to the life of St Francis (below), the subject-matter, with its emphasis on the saint's love of nature and the humanness of Christ, was influential in destroying Byzantine convention and encouraging a more emotional style. Giotto uses landscapes and architecture to perform a new function. The

building in the background as St Francis renounces his worldly wealth acts like a backdrop of a theatre stage, filling the empty space which, in Byzantine art, would have been a blank sky of gold. However, the building is not just a space-filler. The Romanesque pavilion, its foremost corner precisely in line with the figure of the saint and its roof-line receding, emphasizes the great divide between his former, worldly associates and his new, spiritual companions. At the same time, the shape of the building perfectly fits the available space. There had been nothing like this in post-classical art.

Most of Giotto's work ('school of Giotto' is usually a safer description because many of the works were done or finished by his pupils) was frescoes. Italian churches had smaller windows than the churches of northern Europe, where the light is generally gloomier, and the stained glass of the northern Gothic churches provided all the pictorial colour needed. In Italy there was greater scope for murals. In the Arena chapel at Padua, Giotto lined the walls with his designs, the paintings arranged in

three rows, separated horizontally by ornamental bands and vertically by figures representing the Virtues and Vices. The figures are clearly three-dimensional, unlike contemporary Sienese figures, with mass and volume conveyed by delicate shading. Giotto is not a total realist (but then perhaps no painter is), as he simplifies details for the sake of overall design, and his settings remain simple and stage-like. Movement usually takes place from side to side, not in depth, and the setting is always firmly subordinated to the figures. Emotion is intense, and Giotto's warm human sympathy always evident, but there is none of the near-hysterical emotion indulged in by some of his successors. In fact, though Giotto may be a primitive in terms of the High Renaissance, he was far ahead of his time, and the temporary decline in Florentine painting after his death is evidence of his extraordinary qualities.

Below:
GIOTTO, *St Francis Renouncing his Inheritance*, after 1228. Bardi Chapel, Santa Croce, Florence.

The World of Islam

Islam is not only a religion, it is a civilization. Its founder, the Prophet Muhammad, was also a law-maker, a general and a political leader, and the caliphs ('successors') who came after him inherited his powers of universal leadership. The Muslim empire was not acquired by religious conversion, but by military force and good government. The pre-Muslim Arabs were a simple people, who lived a hard life with little education or cultural tradition. Though they included some converts to Judaism and Christianity, their religion was a primitive kind of polytheism. But they did possess a highly poetic language and a poetry of complex rhythm, celebrating the nomadic life of war, hunting, women and wine and denigrating their enemies, and this was to prove a powerful inheritance in Islam.

Muhammad aimed to restore the religion of Abraham, a belief in one God and in a future life. As his influence increased, the authorities in Mecca began to fear him and resent his denial of their gods. The Muslims were persecuted, and in 622 (the first year of the Muslim calendar) Muhammad undertook his famous *hejira* ('flight') to Medina, where he found a welcome. From Medina he attacked his enemies in Mecca, eventually capturing it and taking over control, the first act in a remarkable imperialist expansion. Muhammad destroyed all idols in Mecca and sent word to the rulers round about that they should adopt Islam or be destroyed. He died in 632, but the tremendous impetus that he had begun continued. Inspired by his word, the Arabs swept into Palestine, Iraq, Syria and Egypt. Persia was conquered and converted; Islam spread east into the northern Indian peninsula and west across the length of North Africa and into Spain. Within a hundred and fifty years of the Prophet's death, Islam had conquered half the known world.

The conquests made Arabic an imperial language. To meet the new requirements of a vast empire, it changed and expanded, evolving new words and sometimes adopting foreign ones. Having already a rich and dynamic tradition, it became the universal language of Islam, and remained the chief unifying force in the Muslim world long after the exclusively Arab kingdom had disappeared. It was the language of the Quran (Koran), the Islamic 'bible', and its form of writing became the single most important feature of Islamic decoration, giving rise to an enormous range of abstract, linear ornament, which is characteristic of virtually all Islamic art.

It is important to grasp that Islamic art is just that – the art of Islam. It is not the art of a particular people nor of a particular country. The Arab empire incorporated a vast number of different peoples with different traditions, and it was, through succeeding years, subject to invasion or influence from other alien cultures. Islamic art remained, like Islam itself, to a large extent unaffected by political or geographical frontiers, but it was influenced by various different cultural traditions within it, most notably Arab, but also others, especially Turkish and Persian.

From the 10th to the 19th century a large part of the Muslim world was ruled by Turkish peoples, and it is therefore not surprising that Turkish ideas and traditions have made a large contribution to Islamic art. There is a distinctly Turkish iconography based on long traditions of design, figurative and non-figurative, which originated in the east. The Persian contribution is no less distinguished. Persian literature, more subjective, more lyrical and more mystical than Arabic, formed the basis for the major schools of Muslim painting that developed in Iran, in which the imagery is poetical and abstract, or semi-abstract. It is sometimes feasible to distinguish these Arab, Turkish and Persian elements in Islamic art, but they are often inextricably mingled, so that attempts at precise classification are impossible, while at almost all times and in all places in the Muslim world many basic features of art and architecture are shared in common, creating a supra-national culture which has no equivalent in history except in Roman civilization.

The many different peoples who were incorporated in the world of Islam thought of themselves first and foremost as Muslims rather than Turks, Persians, or Arabs. Educated men knew and spoke Arabic. They all met together in the mosque, the

Muslim place of worship that with only minor differences followed the same plan throughout the Muslim world. When they prayed they all turned towards Mecca, which was represented by the central niche, or mihrab, in the wall of every place of prayer. They all shared Muhammad's simple teaching and recognized one infinite and all-powerful God (Allah). They all expected to stand equal before Allah on the day of judgment. Religion was the great agent of cohesion, and religion, inasmuch as it can be separated from other elements, was the most important factor in Islamic art.

The awareness of the infinite, the antithesis of the short earthly existence of man, finds expression in most forms of Muslim art, especially in the form of the infinite pattern which may be applied to any surface, from a small box to a vast dome, regardless of the physical form. Such patterns seem

to deny the form of the object, and a world is created in which (for example) the solid structures of architecture – walls, arches, domes – are disguised under a blazing pattern of ornament, a world of fragile fantasy. This convention is quite different from – in fact opposed to – most artistic traditions of Europe.

Islamic decoration was made up of naturalistic or abstract geometrical forms and of Arabic calligraphy, which found its way into every kind of decoration. There are many forms of script in Islamic calligraphy, but the two main divisions are called *Kufic* and *Nashki*. The earliest form of *Kufic* (named after the town, south of Baghdad, where it is said to have been invented) was angular and strongly vertical. More elaborate versions, in which stylized leaf and floral forms are added to the vertical strokes, are called foliated and floriated: they were developed in Egypt in the 9th

Right:
Ceramic bowl with calligraphic decoration. Victoria and Albert Museum, London.

136

century. *Naskhi* is a cursive script, which replaced *Kufic* from the 11th century on, beginning in Baghdad. Other forms of cursive script are *Thuluth*, a more mannered version of *Naskhi*, and *Nastaliq*, the Persian script of the 15th century, perhaps the most elegant of all, in which the dominant movement is horizontal rather than vertical.

Anyone at all familiar with Muslim architecture is aware that, predominantly, the decoration is of abstract design. Muhammed had condemned idols, and for that reason no figurative art is to be seen in mosques. This convention extended to the other arts. Among the sayings of Muhammad is a warning that makers of images will be punished on the Day of Judgment because they have dared to create creatures, which is the prerogative of God alone. But the real object of the Prophet's warning was the maker of false images – religious idols. Except in the purely religious sphere, figurative representation was not forbidden in Islam, although, at certain times and in certain areas, there was a prejudice against it.

The caliphs who succeeded Muhammad were elected at Medina, but after some years a struggle broke out, degenerating into murder and civil war, between the Shiites, who regarded the descendants of Ali (Muhammad's son-in-law) as rightful caliphs, and the Sunnites, who believed the caliph should be elected on a somewhat wider basis. A Sunnite dynasty of desert people known as the Umayyads eventually emerged victoriously from this conflict, and their dominance was confirmed when Ali's son, Hassan, surrendered his claim to them. They moved their capital to Damascus and engaged in constant war with Byzantium, no doubt in the knowledge that a 'Holy War' has a powerful fortifying effect on popular support.

The importance of this move from the art-historical point of view was that it brought the Muslims into direct contact with the heritage of Greece and Rome, as well as with Persian and other Asian artistic traditions. In Islam, such intermingling of cultures almost invariably resulted in artistic ideas that, whatever they

owed to more or less alien sources, were highly original. The process can be observed in the first great Muslim building, the famous Dome of the Rock in Jerusalem (below), built in 691 and intended to demonstrate the superiority of Islam over Christians, Jews and others. Both the form of the building itself and the decoration – mosaics, carvings, and so on – owe much to Western tradition: first impressions of the interior suggest a palace of the late classical period. A closer inspection reveals not only realistic designs of classical inspiration but also abstract motifs of a kind that were to be repeated in Umayyad mosques and palaces over a wide area of the Middle East. The floor mosaics contain beautiful and realistic fruit trees and classical acanthus

Below:
The Dome of the Rock, Jerusalem. It was built at the end of the 7th century, though the tile decoration on the outside belongs largely to a 16th-century restoration. Originally, it was intended to replace the Kaaba, the sacred shrine at Mecca, as the chief centre of Muslim pilgrimage.

scrolls as well as candelabra-like trees and palmettes deriving from motifs of Sassanid (the defeated Persian dynasty) origin. (There is not so great a 'culture-clash' as might be supposed, since Sassanid art itself incorporated orientalized Hellenistic motifs.) In other buildings of the Umayyad period, the late classical influence is even stronger. Sculptured architectural details such as the capitals of columns are esentially Roman in form and execution, and some floor mosaics in Umayyad palaces have geometrical patterns that are of Byzantine origin. The subject of these early mosaics, and of the few wall paintings that survive, are generally peaceful scenery with fine trees and meadows, sparkling lakes and attractive buildings – sometimes almost identical with the buildings in the Ravenna mosaics (pages 89-91) – which, for all their dependence on western art, are intended to demonstrate the great benefits conferred by Islam – peace and prosperity.

One form of architectural ornament that owed less to classical tradition was the plaster panel, found in an apparently endless variety of patterns. Classical motifs may still be clearly evident, for example the ubiquitous acanthus motif in the reconstructed ceiling belonging to a gate of the palace of Khirbat al-Mafjar (early 8th century), but the human heads come from oriental-hellenistic art, and resemble the stucco sculpture of Central Asia of a slightly earlier period. In general, the Sassanid element in the elegant plasterwork of this type is much more obvious, and there is a perceptible movement away from naturalistic forms towards more stylized, and eventually abstract versions. Besides relief work, there was some sculpture in the round made in plaster, usually of figures to stand in niches.

The minor arts such as glass and metalwork show a similar mingling of styles. Altogether, the Umayyad period displays a new and potent cultural force at work in an environment still largely governed by post-classical tradition. The Dome of the Rock is basically a western type of building, but Umayyad mosques are something new. In decorative art, too, the Umayyads take ideas from pre-Islamic cultures and fashion a new tradition of their own.

The restful peace depicted in mosaics as the blissful result of Muslim rule was somewhat misleading as far as the Umayyads were concerned. Their major weakness was the recurrent conflict between the Arab tribes of the north and south, in which the Umayyads themselves were eventually forced to take sides. The Caliph became a partisan figure, relying on one side or the other, which greatly reduced his prestige. More centralized control was restored by Abd al-Malik towards the end of the 7th century, but the main problems remained unsolved. The failure of an expedition against Constantinople brought a moment of peril, and though the immediate crisis was overcome, a legacy of grave financial difficulties remained. After the death of the tough but mean and tax-grabbing Hisham (743), the Arab kingdom went into rapid decline. The final revolt began in 746 when the black flags of the Abbasids were raised in Persia. The last Umayyad force was defeated in 750 and the Arab kingdom disappeared. The revolutionary Abbasids gained the caliphate, and moved the capital from Damascus to their own chief city, Baghdad, founded by al-Mansur in 762. The Abbasid dynasty retained the Baghdad caliphate until the 13th century, but during that time various other groups established more or less independent kingdoms in other parts of Islam.

To describe the Abbasid victory as the triumph of the Persian element in Islam is somewhat misleading, since the Abbasids were not all Persians and in the early Abbasid period there was an influx of Turkish peoples who had a strong influence on art, especially after the removal of the capital from Baghdad to Samarra in the early 9th century. The Abbasid caliphs were enthusiastic patrons of the arts, and were responsible for a rich material civilization. Almost nothing survives of Abbasid Baghdad and little of Samarra, but what does remain, including the great mosque of al-Mutawakkil, the largest ever built, is impressive enough.

Mosques, monuments and palaces were decorated with richly inventive wall paintings, tiles and plasterwork. The plasterwork of Samarra shows successive styles moving steadily away from the classical tradition until all traces of classical influence finally disappear; naturalistic ornament is banished and abstract linear design takes over. This total break with the classical tradition is marked also by a change in technique. Early plaster decoration was carved in high relief, gaining dramatic effect from contrasts between light and dark. In the later phase, the designs are not carved but moulded, and the light-and-dark effect is abandoned in favour of flat, repetitive pattern. This type of plaster decoration was later to be found throughout Islam, east and west.

Wall paintings, like that of the serving girls from the ruins of the Jausak Palace, Samarra (which was restored in modern times) often display classical motifs – hunting scenes, fights between men and animals – but in a style deriving from Central Asia. The large faces with almond-shaped eyes and scalloped fringe are characteristic, as are the strongly drawn outlines and the stylized rudimentary indications of drapery.

Perhaps the most important development was in pottery. The type of decoration known as lustre (below) was apparently first developed by the potters of Baghdad. This technique involves the application of a

metallic pigment over the glaze, giving a sheen that looks like metal, and was probably intended to do so: clay vessels are obviously cheaper than silver or gold or even bronze. Lustreware was made in various colours, though the most common was a brownish green, and figurative subjects were often adopted from the 10th century in Baghdad; elsewhere, patterns were abstract. Lustreware was to become an Islamic speciality, and remained popular until recent times.

Another interesting type of pottery came from Nishapur and Samarkand, under a local dynasty known as the Samanids. This was slip-painted, which meant that the design was painted on the body of the ware in liquified coloured clay before glazing (left). Human figures, as well as birds and animals, appeared as decoration on the pottery, usually drawn rather clumsily.

There were a number of other minor dynasties that encouraged artistic production in the 10th century, such as the Buyids in Iraq and Iran, particularly famous for their metalware (left) and their intricately patterned silks. But it was the Umayyads who established the most significant dynasty independent of the Baghdad caliphate, in Spain.

The Arabs conquered Spain early in the 8th century, but for a generation or two it remained a cultural backwater in the world of Islam. When the Umayyads in Syria were overthrown by the Abbasids in 750 one of them, Abd al-Rahman I as he became, escaped the massacre and made his way to North Africa. From there he crossed to Cordoba in Spain where his remarkable qualities of leadership enabled him to suppress the warring Muslim factions already there and create an independent caliphate which lasted for three centuries. Internal reforms established

good government in the hitherto anarchic conditions of Muslim Spain and a standing army enabled him to repel the attacks of the Abbasid caliph and other enemies. The Umayyad caliphate in Cordoba lasted for three centuries, and the city became the most important cultural centre of Islam, rivalled only by Baghdad.

Abd al-Rahman I is remembered chiefly for his construction of the Great Mosque of Cordoba (much enlarged by his successors), an elaborate, glittering building of arched colonnades decorated with stucco and mosaics, lace-like plasterwork and stone, which combines a fantastic richness of detail with an overall effect of peace and calm. The semi-abstract floral designs carved in a flattish surface against a background that recedes into shadowy depths also appear on quite small objects, such as an ivory box (above right) measuring only 10 cm by 20 cm, or on silks. There is comparatively little figurative art in Umayyad Spain, especially in the early period, in spite of the fact that it was in closer touch with the classical heritage and relatively unaffected by Central Asian tradition. Naturalistic motifs do appear, but they are refined and abstracted and so sometimes hard to recognize.

Egypt had enjoyed a prosperous period in the late 9th century under the Tulunid dynasty, but when they were overthrown in 905 political chaos ensued with resulting cultural decline. But Egypt was soon to rise again, under the Fatimids, a Berber dynasty belonging to the Shiite faction, which had previously been established in Tunisia. Under the Fatimids western Islamic art reached its highest peak, excelling even Spain in its variety. A tradition of figurative art, derived from Iraq, reached perfection, and there was much use of calligraphic elements to ornament such details as windows and niches. Paintings also decorated buildings, though the finest surviving example of Fatimid painting on a large scale is outside Egypt, in Sicily, where Fatimid artists were employed by the Norman king Roger II to paint the ceiling of the chapel (right) in his palace. The wooden ceiling, in the honeycomb or stalactite style, con-

Above:
An Umayyad carved ivory box made for Abd al-Malik in 1005, from the Cathedral Treasury, Pamplona.

Below:
The interior of the *Cappella Palatina* in the *Palazzo Reale* at Palermo, with part of the wooden, painted, stalactite ceiling of Fatimid workmanship.

tains scenes of court life as well as non-figurative designs. Motifs can be found suggesting influence from Norman Sicily, Fatimid Egypt, or Abbasid Iraq, proof of the comparative unity of Mediterranean culture in the 12th century; but the style is virtually identical with that of Samarra.

Apart from this magnificent work, Fatimid painting is known mainly from pottery. There was already a strong tradition of pottery in Egypt, the Tulunids having apparently brought potters from Iraq, and under the Fatimids Islamic pottery made great progress. Lustreware, typically in a deep brown, was much favoured, and can be distinguished from similar ware in Iraq only by the clay, which is coarser and darker than that of Samarra. Fantastic birds, animals and human figures were common subjects on Fatimid lustreware, which in the late 11th and 12th centuries were painted in a very accomplished style. Christian motifs and Coptic

Opposite:
Wooden *mihrab* from a Fatimid mausoleum, 12th century. Museum of Islamic Art, Cairo.

Below:
Lustre-painted Fatimid bowl, an interesting mixture of formal pattern and lively realistic detail, Egypt, 12th century. Museum of Islamic Art, Cairo.

priests sometimes appear, as well as scenes from contemporary life, such as a cockfight on a gold lustre bowl. Some of the artists' names are known: there was a man who signed his name, Sa'ad, on a large number of vessels painted in brown or yellowish lustre around 1100.

It is clear that painting on pottery was derived from wall paintings and miniatures which have not survived. We know there was keen rivalry among painters from Baghdad and Cairo because of a story telling of a competition between two painters of the rival schools in the mid 11th century. They were asked to paint a dancing girl in a niche in the wall and to show her passing through a door – a nice technical challenge. Both painters solved the problem in the same way by contrasting the girl's dress with the background to suggest movement, but it was the Egyptian painter who was judged the winner.

Ivory and wood carving, like painting, followed the Abbasid style, but a new type of abstract decoration of large surfaces apparently developed independently in Egypt. It was based on the principle of infinite systems of linear patterns, superimposed on one another to form geometrical figures, such as polygons or triangles (left). This was the infinite pattern that was to play so important a part in Islamic art from that time onward. It is curious that this totally abstract pattern was developed in Fatimid Egypt which, in other respects, was notable for its extensive and varied figurative art.

Meanwhile, in south-western Asia, a new power had arrived upon the scene, the Seljuk Turks. They were originally just one group from the Turkish peoples who migrated into Iran from Central Asia. As the power of the Baghdad caliphate declined they grew in power and importance, gaining control of Iran in the mid 11th century and eventually dominating most of the Muslim world, until the Mongol conquest of the 13th century.

The Seljuks were great builders, erecting large and gorgeous mosques in Isfahan and elsewhere, and developing new architectural structures. Their buildings were decorated

143

Above:
A bowl in *minai* ware from Iran. The battle scene was probably copied from a Seljuk painting, about 1200.
Smithsonian Institution, Freer Gallery of Art, Washington, DC.

with plasterwork and patterns in brick on a large scale, with whole mihrabs cast out of plaster. But the most extraordinary effects of architectural decoration in Seljuk Iran were achieved by the use of lustre tiles. By covering entire surfaces with a glassy sheen, solid masses of brick or stone were dissolved into a shimmering, insubstantial form.

Under the peaceful and prosperous Seljuk rule, Iran enjoyed something

Left:
This fine brass basin (the photograph is taken from above) is a rare example of Seljuk enamelled metalware. Tiroler Landesmuseum Ferdinandeum, Innsbruck.

have been responsible for the painted pottery and the illuminated manuscripts (although only one solitary Seljuk manuscript exists for comparison). Courtly and hunting scenes are favourite motifs, though sometimes there are abstract designs of arabesques or geometric patterns.

A moulded vase (below) is an outstanding example of another type of pottery, associated mainly with Kashan. The figurative pattern is in high relief, and the vessel is unusually large (65.4 cm high). Originally, it was probably gilded all over. The Kashan potteries, again probably under the influence of Chinese porcelain, also produced openwork vessels and displayed a wide range of other techniques, including vessels disguised as modelled figures, human or animal.

Of other works of decorative art that have survived from the Seljuk period, the most striking include brass and bronze ware with silver inlay, and bronze and plaster sculptures in the round. In Asia Minor, the earliest-known knotted rugs were produced under the Seljuks, the beginning of an art form so closely associated with the world of Islam. They were first made, much earlier, probably as shaggy floor coverings for the tents of the nomadic Turkish peoples from Central Asia, but by the Seljuk period they had acquired a decorative function. They were mainly in red, blue and natural colours, with abstract designs derived remotely from floral motifs and borders based on the Kufic script. Wood carving was also an art developed to a high degree in Seljuk Asia Minor. Beautiful objects such as lecterns carved in a high-relief pattern of scrolls survive.

From the end of the 11th century, the Seljuk Empire had begun to break up. Central rule was weakened by civil war, and in the 12th century dangerous pressures built up from the Ismaili sect known as the Assassins

of a golden age. Pottery became a major art form. Experts distinguish seven main types of pottery, including white ware, derived from Sung porcelain, and closely resembling it although Muslim potters had yet to learn the secret of making true porcelain. Many potters emigrated from Cairo after the fall of the Fatimid dynasty in 1171, establishing a taste for lustreware, which now more often had a lustre ground than a lustre design, leaving the area of the pattern in reserve. The chief centre of Seljuk lustreware was Rayy, near Iran, though its products were later surpassed by Kashan, where production continued unabated throughout the Mongol period. A speciality there was the making of mihrabs from panels of moulded, lustre-painted tiles.

A type of Seljuk pottery especially admired in the West is the so-called *minai* ('enamel') ware (opposite). It was painted over the glaze in a variety of colours, usually blue, green, brown, black, a dullish red, white and gold, and the colours fixed by a second firing at low temperature. Designs were closely related to miniature painting, and the same artists may

Above:
Large ceramic vase from Seljuk Iran, about 65.4 cm high, 13th century; such pieces are comparatively rare in Islamic art. Smithsonian Institution, Freer Gallery of Art, Washington, DC.

145

146

Above:
Metal basin known as the *Baptistère de Saint Louis*, from Syria. It is a finely detailed piece of inlaid silver by an Ayyubid master who is known to have made other similar pieces. Musée du Louvre, Paris.

Opposite:
Frontispiece painting from the *Kitab al-Diryak*, Mosul, Iraq, 1199. The style is Seljuk. Bibliothèque Nationale, Paris.

within, and from the attacks of the Crusaders outside. The Sultan Sanjar (1118-57) managed to retain control of the eastern half of his empire, but he was unable to prevent the continued rise of various dynasties, related to the Seljuks, which were virtually independent in their various areas, and after his death even Iran was divided up by various Seljuk rulers. The most significant of the dynasties that, on the whole briefly, established sizeable empires in this period were the Atabeks in Iraq and Syria and the Ayyubids (the dynasty of Saladin), their successors in the late 12th century. On the whole, Seljuk artistic conditions were maintained. The Ayyubids brought the traditions of Seljuk Iran to Iraq and Syria, but there were certain innovations, associated particularly with the city of Mosul, in Iraq. The frontispiece of the *Kitab al-Diryak* (opposite) of 1199 displays many features of the pure Seljuk style – the central figure seated cross-legged, the Seljuk faces with aquiline noses and narrow eyes, and the costume detail. In metalwork, although that too followed the Seljuk style, Mosul was distinguished by particularly skilful craftsmen in the 13th century who forged a style of

their own in their brass vessels inlaid with silver, incorporating larger figures than those characteristic of the similar (but less accomplished) works of Seljuk Iran. Vessels of the same type, often indistinguishable, were also made in Syria.

The Mongols, who were not yet Muslims, began their conquests under the leadership of Genghis Khan early in the 13th century. By 1258 they had reached Baghdad, which they utterly destroyed, killing the last caliph. The initial effect of this violent pagan conquest on artistic life was naturally a negative one, but in the longer term the advent of the Mongols had a stimulating effect. Seljuk traditions were not abandoned, but the conquerors brought Islam into direct contact with the Far East, with important effects for the future of Islamic art in both East and West. By the end of the 13th century, Iran, despite the destruction of its cities, had recovered well, relative stability had been restored and the Mongols had embraced Islam.

The Mongol period is associated particularly with the beginning of the history of painting in eastern Islam, but it should be remembered that this is chiefly because while few paintings

147

Above:
The Phoenix, manuscript painting from a
work called *The Usefulness of Animals*,
made at Maragha, Iran, in the 1290s.

Pierpont Morgan Library, New York.
MS 500 folio 55.

وَكَادَ يَنْزِعُ الحَجَّا الشَّرَّ وَالنُّشَدَ

مَا الحَجُّ سَيْرَكَ تَأْوِيبًا وَإِدْلَاجًا وَلَا لِعَيْنِكَ إِجْمَالًا وَإِحْدَاجًا

الحَجُّ أَنْ تَقْصِدَ البَيْتَ الحَرَامَ عَلَى الحَجِّ سَبِيلَكَ لِلْحَجِّ لَا تَبْغِي بِهِ حَاجًا

وَنَطِّي كَأَهْلِ الإِنْصَافِ مُتَّخِذًا رَدْعَ الهَوَى هَادِيًا وَاحْتَنَّهَا جَا

149

have survived from the earlier period, many have from later times. Tracing the influence of various styles, though a subject of absorbing interest to historians of art, is not always very rewarding, and the paintings of early Mongol Iran are made up of so many traditional elements, emanating from Baghdad, China, and Seljuk sources, that it is easy to overlook the novel aspects. The painting of a phoenix (page 148), which illustrates a manuscript of 1297, *Manafi al-Hayawan* ('The Usefulness of Animals'), is one of the earliest known. The Far Eastern influence is immediately evident in the conventional representation of flowers and other natural features, which derive from Chinese painting, and the picture of this marvellous bird has a vigour and dash that gives it freshness and originality.

One of the largest works of the 14th century, a huge and profusely illustrated *Shah-nameh* ('Book of Kings'), displays a style so different, with its strong colours and realism, that it suggests it was made in some centre far removed from the Mongol capital of Tabriz; and yet another style is found in Shiras, where the preference was for strong linear effect and muted colours. The drawing is sometimes sketchy, and details of landscape or architecture indicated in a monotonously conventional way, though the sense of design is strong. Other paintings from a somewhat later date in the Mongol period show an increasing emphasis on space, with rudimentary perspective indicated by the depiction of groups of figures in a landscape setting on different levels, one above another, instead of being firmly anchored to the bottom line as in earlier paintings. What is most noticeable about Mongol painting in general is its inventiveness, characterized by the considerable differences in style in different localities, which appears to have been the result of the catalyzing force of Chinese culture.

The Far Eastern influence in painting introduced with the Mongol conquest also reached western Islam and contributed to the strange and

Right:
Persian miniature from a manuscript of the *Shah-nameh* of Firdawsi dated 1648. Victoria and Albert Museum, London.

150

powerful style that evolved in Mamluk Egypt. The Mamluks were descended from Turkish slaves of the Ayyubids, and came to power on the Ayyubids' fall in the middle of the 13th century. Soon afterwards they defeated the Mongols and gained control of part of Syria. Their accession represented no sudden cultural break, merely a gradual development growing out of the combination of Fatimid, Seljuk and Ayyubid art; but Mamluk painting did possess a degree of originality. The iconography is mainly Seljuk, and the style basically derives from the old Baghdad style, but with everything removed to a

setting of ornamental abstraction, on a glittering gold background. It is an art far removed from the affairs of everyday life.

Spain, after the fall of the Umayyad dynasty in the 11th century, was ruled by a series of local dynasties, and for a time by the Almoravides and Almohades of North Africa. It was under the Nasrids, who came to power in 1232 and lasted for almost a hundred and fifty years, that the country once more enjoyed the peace and stability in which great artistic works are usually produced. The Nasrids, at their capital of Granada, recaptured all the glory of the

Above:
The spectacular cupola of the Chamber of the Two Sisters in the Alhambra Palace. It is a brilliant honeycomb of pattern.

Below:
Paintings on silk from Herat, about 1400 – a fine example of the early Timurid style. The significance of the subject – rulers carried by grotesque monsters – is not clear. Topkaki Sarayi Museum, Istanbul.

Umayyad period, and on top of a hill overlooking the city they created perhaps the most famous of all the buildings of Islam, the palace of the Alhambra.

This great complex of buildings is plain on the outside but a blaze of decoration within. The upper walls are covered with plaster in which fine and intriguingly intricate patterns, abstract or semi-abstract, are made, while below run bands of ornamental tiles. The stalactite formations above make vaults appear like star-lit canopies (above), and the whole effect is

of a building floating above the ground – the effect that was so desirable a goal for Muslim builders. In this renaissance of Muslim Spain under the Nasrids, lustre-painting, possibly unknown before except through imports, reached new heights at Malaga and other centres. Tiles in red, brown, green and blue were made at Malaga for the Alhambra and other palaces, as well as tall vases decorated with abstract patterns or animals painted in a brilliant reddish lustre. Sometimes, coats of arms appear, not only those of the Nasrids but also those of foreign families from all over Christian Europe, where this type of ware became very popular. It seems that the Malaga potters eventually moved north, towards Valencia (a Christian city), to be nearer their export market.

In the east a new era began with the invasion of Iran by Timur (Tamurlane, or Tamburlaine) in the second half of the 14th century. He soon gained control of eastern Islam, and defeated the Ottoman Turks who had established a unified state in Asia Minor. By the early 15th century, styles in Iran and the Near East had changed sufficiently to warrant classification of a 'Timurid' style. In painting, early work consisted of deliberate copying of the Mongol miniatures illustrating historical manuscripts, but a new style developed in Herat under the patronage of a grandson of Timur, Baysunghur. The chief feature of the Herat style, from a compositional point of view,

Above:
Persian miniature painting by BIHZAD
illustrating Sadi's *Bustan*, school of
Herat, 1489. Egyptian National
Library, Cairo.

made in Herat, of two warriors in a
forest glade. Colours are characteristically bright but restrained. Beautiful blues and greens dominate the
composition in which the trees reach
steadily up towards the distant hori-
zon. In general, 15th-century
Timurid painting, and in particular
the work of the Herat school, set the
standard for all later paintings in
eastern Islam, and was never excelled.

At the end of the 13th century
Anatolia had come under the rule of a
number of local dynasties, among
whom dominance was eventually
achieved by the Ottoman, or Os-
manli, Turks. Osman I (1259-1326),
after whom the dynasty is named, was
assigned the duty of guarding the
frontier against the Christians, who
still held a small area in the north-
west of Asia Minor. Volunteers from
all over the Turkish world were
recruited by the Ottomans for their
war against the unbelievers, and in
1326, the Christian city of Bursa fell to
them; for a time, it was the Ottoman
capital. Victories over the Serbs and
the Hungarians spread Ottoman
power deep into the Balkans by the
end of the 14th century, and control
was asserted over virtually the whole
of Asia Minor. Disaster threatened
when Timur invaded in 1402, win-
ning a great victory over the Ottomans and capturing the sultan. However, Timur withdrew without con-
solidating his conquests, and after a
short but bloody period of strife,
central control was reasserted by
Muhammad I in the early 15th
century. Ottoman power began to
expand again, assisted by a highly
trained standing army, the Janis-
saries, and in 1453 Muhammad II
captured Constantinople, the ancient
capital of Byzantium, which became
henceforth the centre of western
Islamic civilization.

The most enduring works of the
Ottomans are the great mosques of
Constantinople built by the famous
architect Sinan in the 16th century.
The interior of these mosques brilliantly fulfills the goal of most Muslim
architecture by dissipating the
solidity of the building in a light, airy
space. This was achieved partly by
architectural innovations, especially

was a new concept of space. Horizons
were set high, and figures distanced
from them by descending from top to
bottom. As we have seen, some approach to this type of perspective had
been achieved in earlier Mongol
painting, but the Timurid style was
much more successful. A painting
(above) believed to be by Bihzad,
the leading master of the Herat
school, shows this accomplished new
use of space, not to mention the
greater realism of the figures and
other detail. Equally fine, and somewhat earlier in date, is the painting
from another manuscript, probably

Above:
An illuminated manuscript from Herat
in the 15th century, showing the rich
detail and assured composition of
Timurid painting. British Library,
London.

كردزواں مشغل كهستى فزور

نيم شبى كان ملك نيم روز

زهرہ و یہ مشعله داوریش کرد

خود فلک از دین عمار نیک کرد

معراج حضرت خير سالم على الله علىه

كرد رہا ہرم كانيات

منت خط و چار خد و شش جها

ديدہ انجار کر انجام کشت

زا مدنش آن شب درسماع

روزش در قدر و شش ر وواع

کوسک از خواب غفلتان كشت

Above:
A painting by ABD AL-RAZZAK of
Muhammad's Night Journey, Herat, 1495.
British Library, London.

Opposite:
Frontispiece painting from a copy of
FIRDUSI's *Sulayman-nameh* of about 1500,
from Bursa in Turkey. Sulayman

appears with attendants and angels and,
below, various monsters which recall the
earlier monsters of Herat painting.
Chester Beatty Library, Dublin.

155

وقال يا محمد ربك يقرءك السلام ويخصك بالتحية والإكرام

حق تعالى سنكا سلام قلدى ايتدى اشته جبرائيلى

سكا كوندردم كه سنوك أمروكه مطيع اولسنوك

دوشمنلروكى هلاك ايله كبسنك كوكلك ديلر

the positioning of the supporting columns of the dome close to the wall, so that their structural function is disguised and the dome appears to float above the building, and partly by the interior decoration. The ornamental tiles in Ottoman buildings give the impression of looking into a flower garden, or an endless abstract pattern, immensely complex, that stretches away to infinity.

Ottoman painting is sometimes regarded as an inferior imitation of Persian painting, which will be discussed below. However, the style, and indeed the object, of Ottoman painting is rather different. It has little of the lyrical, romantic ideals of Persian art, which was largely concerned with illustrating the classics of Persian literature according to long-established conventions. Ottoman painting is more immediate and down-to-earth. Current events, especially the affairs of the Sultan, form the main subject-matter, and the style is stiff and disciplined, as opposed to the sinuous quality of Persian art.

The frontispiece from a copy of the *Sulayman-nameh* (page 155), a historical text, is an early example of the Ottoman court school, about 1500. It shows Sulayman (Solomon) on his throne, under a dome, attended by courtiers and angels. Below him are rows of rather mysterious monsters; subservient creatures of more or less fantastic form had appeared in paintings from Herat about one hundred years earlier. The painting of the Prophet on his way to Mecca (opposite), attended by Abu Bakr and Ali, is almost a century later in date, and shows the Ottoman court style at its peak, basically hieratic in style, but with a strong infusion of popular realism, for instance in the faces (it was forbidden to represent the Prophet himself). The strong colours and stylized landscape are characteristic.

The most famous and most typically Turkish of Ottoman decorative arts is the knotted rug or carpet. As mentioned previously, rugs had been in use among the nomadic peoples of Central Asia at an early date. In the days of cities and stone buildings they had been retained as the principle item of furniture. They became popular in Christian Europe in the 16th century, and the most typical Turkish rug of this period is the 'Holbein' rug (left), so-called because that artist included them in his paintings (they were used primarily as table covers in Europe, not on the floor). The style is an abstract pattern of medallions, usually on a rich red background.

It has long been known that some of the finest pottery of the 16th century comes from the eastern Mediterranean region. It used to be ascribed to Syria or the island of Rhodes, but it is now thought to have come exclusively from the town of Isnik, some miles east of the Bosphorus. One reason for the mistaken attribution was that there appeared to be no great tradition of pottery in western Anatolia, though it now seems probable that there was such a tradition, merely that little trace of it has survived. Isnik ware (page 158) is divided by ceramicists into several types on a chronological basis, but its

157

Right:
A mosque lamp from the Dome of the
Rock. This fine piece of Isnik ware is
dated 1549. British Museum, London.

Above:
Portrait of a Turkoman, drawing by
SADIKI-BEG, showing the artist's
extraordinary mastery of line. Museum
of Fine Arts, Boston, Massachusetts.

Above:
Drawing of a tailor by RIZA-I ABASSI.
Smithsonian Institution, Freer Gallery
of Art, Washington, DC.

main characteristics can be defined
as a hard, white, porcellanous body,
with decorations painted under a very
thin, transparent glaze. The earlier
examples are blue and white; later,
green and sometimes purple were
added, and in the later period, which
lasted from the mid-16th to the late
17th century, a strong brick-red appeared. Brick-red tiles were used in
the mosque built by Sinan for Sulayman the Magnificent in Istanbul.
Besides tiles, large bowls, ewers, boxes
and mosque lamps, as well as the
pottery known as 'Golden Horn'
(because it was once thought to have
been made at the Golden Horn in
Istanbul) were made at Isnik.
'Golden Horn' pottery is painted
mainly in blue, and is characterized
by the restriction of the design to thin,
scrolled patterns studded with small
flowers.

After the death of Timur in 1405,
Persia went through troubled times,
marked by the rivalry of the tribal
groups known as the White Sheep and
the Black Sheep. The Islamic mystical movement known as Sufiism
had long kept alive religious culture
among the Persians and the Turkoman immigrants, stimulating a remarkable poetic literature. The
leader of one of these Sufi congrega-
tions founded the future Safavid
dynasty in the early 14th century. His
descendant, Ismail, was a successful
and precocious military leader who,
on occupying Tabriz in 1502 (when
he was fifteen), took the title of shah,
and in a few years united all Persia
under his rule. He was strong enough
to defeat the Uzbeks of Transoxiana,
but he was bloodily defeated by the
professional armies of the Ottoman
sultan. For roughly two hundred
years, intermittent conflict with the
Ottomans continued, and it seems
remarkable that the Safavids survived
at all. However, in the person of Shah
Abbas the Great (1586-1628), the
Persians gained a great ruler, who
defeated the Turks and Uzbeks, conquered Iraq, and transferred the

Above:
Interior of the mosque of Sultan Ahmet I, Istanbul.

capital to Isfahan, which remained the artistic centre of eastern Islam until the late 18th century. His death marked the end of the Safavid dynasty.

The Herat tradition in painting was perpetuated both in Tabriz, the Persian capital under Shah Ismail and his successor, Shah Tahmasp, and in Bukhara, the Uzbek capital. The Uzbeks had captured Herat at the beginning of the 16th century, and the master of the Herat school, Bihzad, seems to have gone to the Uzbek court at Bukhara before he went to Tabriz under Shah Tahmasp. At Bukhara the style continued virtually unchanged, but in the course of time it became more stylized and more lavishly coloured, in general more decorative, sacrificing the subtle naturalism of Herat art. In Tabriz, the true spirit of Herat lived on: the brilliant decorative effects never obliterate the artists' sharp observation of man and his affairs, and human figures, though never quite becoming true portraits, are nevertheless recognizably individuals. Tents, buildings, carpets and other incidental details are rendered with precision. Artists too emerged as individuals, with a personal style, and works were often signed. One of the masters who was for some years in Tabriz, Mir Sayyid Ali, later went to Kabul where, with others, he was instrumental in creating the Mughal style, the inheritor of this great achievement of Persian art. But the Herat tradition continued also in the paintings of Kasvin, where the Persian court moved later in the 16th century. Naturalism is particularly noticeable in drawing, which became for the first time a major art form in its own right at Kasvin. Perhaps the greatest master was Sadiki-beg, an artist of Turkish origin at the Persian court. His *Portrait of a Turkoman* (opposite) displays his strong and curving line and his ability to capture essentials with absolute economy. It is in such drawings that the greater realism of the Kasvin school is most evident.

Under Shah Abbas, the Kasvin style was transferred to Isfahan. The leading master there was Riza-i Abbasi, whose charming picture of a tailor (opposite) shows the same strong and economical line as in Sadiki-beg's drawings, and falls little short of true portraiture.

The minor arts also reached a high point under the Safavids. Lacquer bindings appeared in book-making, rivalling paintings with their creative design and fine colour. Richly patterned silks and brocades were made for covers and hangings and are often shown in contemporary paintings. In rug-making, exclusively abstract design was largely abandoned in Persia, motifs of animals and birds appearing among the medallions and scrolls; pictorial rugs were designed by artists, the actual rugmaker only making the rug itself. The main product of the potteries was the glazed tile for buildings. The great buildings of Isfahan are covered with polychrome tiles: often each tile contributes to a section of a larger pattern, and creates marvellous, dazzling effects in, for example, the famous Blue Mosque. Lustreware reappeared also, and Chinese fashions were brilliantly reinterpreted, often with the design, in low relief, following the shape of the vessel, with cobalt-blue and green the most common colours.

The Arabs had conquered part of

India in the 8th century and contact with Islam was never lost, but it was not until the 16th century when a large part of the country came under the rule of the Mughals that a unified Indian–Islamic civilization was created. The chief distinguishing feature of Mughal art was the fusion of Hindu and Muslim traditions: the extraordinary richness of architecture and the arts – the use of strong colours and gold in painting – owes much to Hindu tradition, and in some ways it would be equally appropriate to discuss Mughal culture in the chapter on Oriental Art as to include it in the world of Islam.

However, the Mughals were newcomers to India. The first Mughal emperor, Babur (1494-1530), a descendant of Timur, was a military adventurer driven to seek power in India by the Uzbeks; his cultural background was Turkish. After invading the Ganges valley, Babur and his successor Humayun built up a powerful empire which revived the political unity of India, but this first

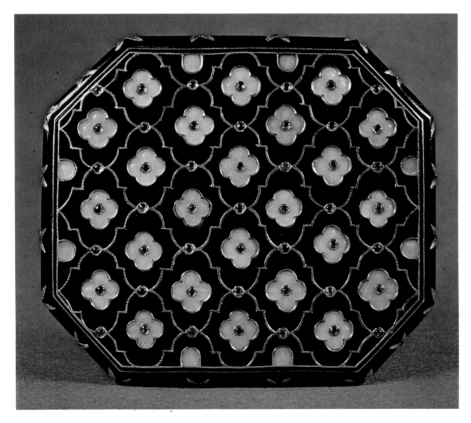

period of Mughal rule was troubled, and Humayun spent some time in exile in Kabul, also visiting Tabriz. He returned the year before his death (1555), bringing with him Mir Sayyid Ali and other Persian artists, to a still fragile realm. But his son Akbar (1555-1605) established the Mughal empire on firm foundations. He was a tolerant man who appreciated Hindu culture, and under him and his two successors, Jahangir and Shah Jahan, a refined Indo-Islamic culture developed, one of the greatest glories of which is its painting. In the later 17th century it declined, largely due to the intolerance of Aurengzeb, a fanatical Muslim who persecuted the Hindus, turned against artists, and banned the depiction of the human figure.

For their libraries, Mughal emperors maintained hundreds of calligraphers and painters, Hindus and Persians, who worked together copying scientific treatises, religious texts, court records and poetry, and illuminating them with paintings. Persian literature was the fashion at court, along with Persian decorative arts – calligraphy, illumination, bookmaking and leatherwork. An early example of Persian influence is the copy of the *Dastan-i Amir Hamza*, perhaps the greatest piece of book production ever undertaken in the Muslim east, which was probably begun in Kabul under Humayun and finished in India under Akbar some fifteen years later. The full-page paintings that survive (the work was later broken up) reflect Persian traditions in the settings, landscape or architectural, as well as in the painting of figures, but there is an intensity of emotion and a greater degree of realism than in Persian art. Both Akbar and his successors were keen collectors of Herat manuscripts, and their taste is reflected in some small manuscripts of Akbar's reign and later on fine, polished paper, in which the calligraphy and the paintings – gold landscapes with animals and flowers – are remarkably delicate.

One aspect of the trend towards realism in painting was that narrative painting of historical scenes, otherwise virtually absent from Islamic art except under the Ottoman Turks, began to appear. Scenes of battle, the hunt and court life, as well as pictures of the more domestic existence of the emperor and his wives, record Mughal life and times. Genuine portraiture was adopted, the most famous example being the painting by Abdul Hasan of Jahangir admiring a portrait of his father, Akbar (opposite) in the Musée Guimet, Paris. The inscription states that Jahangir was thirty years old when the portrait was painted, but he is shown as emperor though he did not accede until he was thirty-six. The probable explanation is that the imperial halo and the portrait of Akbar were added to the original picture after Jahangir had become emperor. Despite the obvious characterization of the portrait, the formal profile and the halo are signs of a stiffening attitude in court art, which eventually degenerated into mere ceremonial representation in which the emperor appeared more as an imperial symbol than an actual individual. The painting of bullocks dragging guns up a steep hillside (page 162) comes from the *Akbar-nameh* commissioned by the emperor, and illustrates an incident during the attack on a fort in Rajastan in 1568. Different artists were responsible for the masterly design and for the sparkling, realistic painting. (Sometimes a

Above:
The famous painting by ABDUL HASAN of Jahangir holding the portrait of his father, about 1600. It is now in the Musée Guimet, Paris.

whole team was employed, some specializing in portraits, some in landscape, and so on.) Persian influence may be detected particularly in the rendering of rocks, the camp (bottom right) and other details; the immediate realism of the scene belongs solely to Mughal art. Battles such as this were favourite subjects certainly, but the *Akbar-nameh* also

contained more intimate scenes, with greater concentration on individual figures, where realism is even stronger. Later Mughal painters delighted in such subjects as animals and birds, painted in dedicated detail, no doubt encouraged by the Emperor Jahangir's love of the world of nature.

Other influences besides Persian

Left:
Painting from the *Akbar-nameh*, about 1600. The scene depicted is a battle during Akbar's campaign in Rajastan, when guns were hauled up a mountainside. Victoria and Albert Museum, London.

were at work in Mughal painting, from local Hindu traditions, from the Rajput hills especially (one of Akbar's wives was a Rajput princess), from the older Muslim courts of the Deccan, and from Europe. European pictures were brought to the Mughal court by Jesuit missionaries, and something of the greater naturalism of Mughal landscapes and the use of perspective is due to this source. Mughal artists are known also to have copied contemporary European engravings (page 173).

A similar realism is characteristic of the floral forms of Mughal textiles, especially rugs, which were often made of silk – exquisite pieces emphasizing once more the tremendous richness of Mughal art and decoration. Beautiful objects were made of carved or inlaid jade (page 160), but above all, the refinement and flair of Mughal civilization was manifest in its glittering architecture – the best-known example, perhaps the best-known building in the world, being of course the brilliant white mausoleum built by Shah Jahan for his wife Mumtaz Mahal, the Taj Mahal at Agra. By comparison with the Taj Mahal, and Fatehpur Sikri, and the Red Fort at Delhi, contemporary European architecture, even the palace of Versailles itself, looks distinctly mundane.

Oriental Art

The ancient civilization of the Indus valley was destroyed quite suddenly in about 1500 BC, possibly by flood, possibly by the Aryan invaders who came through the north-west passes about that time. The Aryans brought with them the Sanskrit language and the Vedic religion and thus laid the basis for Indian civilization, which possesses to an unusual degree a continuity running from prehistoric times down to the modern age; change occurred gradually and the slow tempo of rural life contributed to a conservative outlook on life. That is not to say that the Aryans were the last people to invade northern India. In the 6th century BC the Achaemenians (Persians) overran the north-west and in the 4th century BC they were displaced by the armies of Alexander the Great. Both Achaemenid and Hellenic cultures contributed to the repertoire of Indian art. Moreover, Indian merchants and seamen travelled far away, to South-East Asia and the Near East, even to Africa, spreading Indian influence over a wide area

Right:
Sandstone group of a mother and child, 8th or 9th century, north India. Musée Guimet, Paris.

and bringing back new ideas from other lands. Persian attacks began again under the Sassanids in the 3rd to the 7th centuries, cutting off India from the West, and in the 5th century AD, when India was at last unified under the Gupta dynasty, there were further attacks from the White Huns, who were moving south from Bactria.

The essential element of the old Vedic religion was sacrifice. The Vedic gods were personifications of the forces of nature – sun and stars, water, wind, fire. The *Rig Veda*, the oldest religious text, consists of a thousand hymns in honour of Indra, god of war and storm, Vishnu, the sun, and so on. At some far distant time, commentaries were compiled – the *Brahmana*, *Upanishada* and *Aranyaka* – which gave rise to a new form of religion, Brahmanism, in which the concept of service replaced that of sacrifice, and the individual soul, based on the universal Self, gained a central importance. The whole system of thought was permeated by the doctrine of the transmigration of souls: the cycle of transmigration could only be broken by a life of obedience to moral rules and to asceticism. Brahmanism was a thoroughly 'Indian' religion in its tendency to universalism, its emphasis on order and a hierarchical social structure, and its élite caste of Brahmins.

In the 6th century BC a populist reaction to Brahmanism gave rise to two new religions: Jainism, which was ascetic, even harsh, and devoted to non-violence; and Buddhism which, though doomed to virtual extinction in most of India, was to have an immense and still-continuing influence on the world at large. The Buddha ('Enlightened One') was a minor prince from the foothills of the Himalayas, who preached charity to all creatures and moderation in all things. Certain aspects of Brahmanism, such as the caste system, were rejected; the concept of the transmigration of souls was retained and the Brahmanic gods were tolerated. It was thus possible to be a Buddhist without rejecting other beliefs, as long as they did not contradict the teachings of the Buddha. By a virtuous life, the Buddhist could improve his condition through various rebirths until he at last attained the state of permanent liberation, *nirvana*. Buddhism was a system of ethics as much as a religion.

Indian art was always a true expression of Indian civilization, adopting the forms of nature and man. Early Buddhist sanctuaries depicted the affairs of everyday life in their sculptures; in medieval Buddhist temples, the life of the gods imitates the life of the king. Buddhism was an egalitarian religion, which appealed to the downtrodden and to those classes, such as merchants, whose social status was inferior to their economic importance; in the course of time, however, in some respects at least, it became less democratic and less popular with the masses.

Meanwhile, around the beginning of the Christian era, Brahmanism itself was changing, becoming what we know as Hinduism. From the vast Brahmanic pantheon, a trinity of gods emerged – Brahma, the creator, Vishnu, the preserver, and Siva, the destroyer – representing the cycle of nature. In time, the latter two gained the largest followings, and many of the local deities became aspects of Vishnu and Siva. Eventually, the Buddha himself became in Indian thought at least an incarnation of Vishnu.

In all this religious conflict, interchange and mutual absorption, art and architecture played important parts. The followers of each religion bolstered their prestige by the construction of temples, but it was not until the Gupta period (4th-9th century AD) that a 'national' style evolved, and the general form of the Hindu temple, built now in stone rather than wood, was established. There was little difference in form between the temples of any of the Indian religions; the main difference

Left:
South Indian bronze of Siva as Lord of the Dance, 12th century. Rijksmuseum, Amsterdam.

was in the sculpture adorning them.

Sculpture has a highly important role in Indian art. It illustrates religious scenes and epics, as well as the mundane affairs of field and village. In slightly idealized style, it celebrates the beauty of life and of the human body. Sacred images were strictly governed by iconographical tradition, but they were meant to be aesthetically pleasing, and there was usually scope for creative genius. Paintings also played an important part, reflecting temple ritual and performing an educative function by illustrating the episodes in Buddhist legend or Hindu epic. Unfortunately, however, paintings are more vulner-

able to the depradations of time, and few survive that are more than about one thousand years old. Some secular art also existed, though again there is little trace of it except from comparatively recent times. It is very largely through religious carvings, reliefs and free-standing figures, that Indian art is to be studied.

Under the Emperor Asoka in the 3rd century BC the Maurya dynasty reached its peak in India, extending from the Indus valley to the northern Deccan. Asoka was a convert to Buddhism, and though he did not make it the religion of the state, he did a great deal to spread its social ideas – tolerance and non-violence – not only

in India herself but into the Hellenized territories of the north as well as south to Sri Lanka. In his reign sculpture began; undoubtedly, it did not start from scratch, but it seems that earlier sculpture must have been in less durable materials than stone. All over his empire Asoka had erected tall columns inscribed with moral instructions. They were surmounted by bell-shaped capitals, often with an animal on top (left) (the earliest evidence of the Indian delight in animals as subjects of art), and in style they owed much to Hellenistic Iran. Asoka was also influential in the emergence of temple architecture, notably in the development of the *stupa*, a dome-like structure surrounded by a barricade with four monumental gates (*torana*). It was based on the old funeral mound, and contained a relic of the Buddha or some other holy man. (At this period, the Buddha was not represented in person, but by a symbol, such as a pair of footprints, a throne, or the *chakra*,

Left:
Sandstone capital of one of the shafts on which the Emperor Asoka had moral codes inscribed. Maurya period, from Rāmpurua. Indian Museum, Calcutta.

Below:
Statue of the Buddha, in the Gupta style, 4th to 6th centuries. Sarnath Museum.

Below:
The north *torana* at Sanchi, 1st
century BC-1st century AD.

the wheel symbolizing Buddhist law.)
A Buddhist *stupa* was often placed on
the site of some pre-Buddhist shrine,
and that is probably why local deities
and female spirits *(yakshas)* often
appear as gatekeepers and servants of
the Buddha.

At Sanchi, the religious monuments represent a short history of the

Buddhist faith, from the cool ascetism
of the founders to the involvement of
an established, popular religion with
affairs of everyday life. Sanchi is also a
museum of the growth of sculpture.
The north gate of Stupa I (left)
betrays the influence of carving in
wood and is assembled on the
mortise-and-tenon principle. The
narrative reliefs offer instruction to
pilgrims in the virtues of Buddhism;
by this time (late 1st century BC – 1st
century AD) the Buddha appeared in
human as well as symbolic form. The
power and magnificence of the gate-
ways remind the pilgrim as he passes
underneath of his own insignificance,
though they also provide some reas-
surance in their depiction of a world
he knows – houses, villages, animals,
trees, and so on. There are no demons,
no sense of fear; the overall effect is of
sober joy. Not all the imagery is
strictly Buddhist. There are also
yakshi surviving from earlier cults and
now subordinate to the Buddha, and
there are early examples of frankly
erotic art which, in a land where there
was no guilt and horror of the 'sins of
the flesh', were not thought to be alien
to spiritual purposes, rather the opposite (early Western observers found
this aspect of Indian religious art hard
to take).

The monuments at Sanchi were
added to in succeeding centuries,
some of the most interesting in the
time of the Guptas, and it is still a
place of pilgrimage – though mainly
for tourists.

The Gupta dynasty reached its
height in the late 4th and early 5th
centuries AD, when India enjoyed one
of the most brilliant periods in her
cultural history. There was a flowering
of literature and philosophy, both
Buddhist and Hindu, fine music and
sculpture, and comparative tolerance
in religion, which was marked by a
mystical impulse evident in the refined
Gupta style in art. In architecture, two
traditional types of structure were
retained: the *stupa* and the cave-
temple, of which the finest examples
are those at Ajanta.

'Cave-temple' is the wrong word,
since it implies a temple made out of a
cave, whereas these sanctuaries were
entirely man-made, cut out of the
solid rock, and are therefore works of

Right:
The *Great Bodhisattva*, from the fresco in
Cave I at Ajanta, 6th century.

sculpture rather than architecture.
The earliest cave-temples reproduced
exactly the buildings of the time –
wooden structures with thatched
roofs which, naturally, have only
survived in these rock-cut imitations.
The origin of the tradition is a matter
of dispute; the tombs of the Achaemenid kings of Persia may have been
an influence, but there was in India a
tradition of caves as the dwelling
places of hermits, and Buddhism encouraged this tradition. An ad-
ditional advantage, in the troubled
period during the break-up of the
Maurya empire after the death of
Asoka, was that such places were
completely impregnable. The usual
method of construction was to cut out
the ceiling first, working down to the
floor – a method that made scaffold-
ing unnecessary. The stone was given
a high polish, probably with agate.

The twenty-nine caves at Ajanta, a
remote place in the north-west of the
Deccan, cover a period of about
eight hundred years. Although of
immense interest as sculptured 'buildings', their chief importance lies in the
fact that in this remote stronghold are
found many wall paintings of a date –
and distinction – not found elsewhere.
The earliest examples date from the
1st century BC, but they are in poor
condition. The Great Bodhisattva in
Cave I (above right) (a bodhisattva is
a being who has reached the desired
state of *nirvana* but refrains from
entering it in order to help others)
dates from the 6th century. It ema-
nates compassion and calm.

Though often described as frescoes,
the technique employed at Ajanta
was not the true fresco technique. The
wall was prepared with a mixture of
clay and some rough material such as
straw, with a coating of plaster on top.
On this the design was painted in red
ochre, over which a thin wash was
applied, allowing the red to show
through. The colours were added,
then certain points touched up with

Right:
Fresco, *Bodhisattva Padmapani* from
Cave I, Ajanta, 6th century.

Above:
Part of a stone frieze showing scenes from the life of the Buddha. This one depicts his birth, and is carved in high relief on dark grey-blue slate. Gandhara style, about 150 AD. Smithsonian Institution, Freer Gallery of Art, Washington, D.C.

Left:
Copy of fresco painting in the vimana of Tanjore, depicting three celestial musicians. Early 11th century.

Above:
Painting from the Kangara region of India showing the Hindu god, Krishna, approaching a princess. About 1820-25. Victoria and Albert Museum, London.

another, and landscape generally is indicated by conventional means. When a more naturalistic background was required, a single tree stood in for a forest.

The wall paintings and other details at Ajanta bear witness to changes in Buddhism, away from the austere simplicity of the early years and towards greater degree of ornamentation, with increasing Hindu influence. Ajanta in fact is the last great site of Buddhist art in India. Except in Bengal, Buddhism was to survive in its country of origin only in small areas. Nevertheless, the Gupta style, with its impressive combination of gentleness and power (page 167) was to prove pervasive, profoundly affecting Buddhist art throughout South-east Asia and spreading to China and Japan.

Changes appeared in the Gupta style from about 600 AD onwards, with less decorative detail and a more ornamental and impersonal quality appearing, though figures of the Buddha retain the same assured serenity. Narrative art, in spite of the continuing absence of obvious borders or divisions, shows a more sophisticated sense of composition. Two of the great centres of this post-Gupta style are Māmallapuram and Ellūrā.

Māmallapuram, south of Madras, was located near the centre of power of the Pallava dynasty, who ruled a large area from the late 6th to the mid 9th century. They were responsible for many free-standing buildings, but the temples at Māmallapuram (page 170) were carved from outcrops of rock above the white sand of the Coromandel Coast. There are ten excavated halls and eight monoliths commemorating several deities and rulers but principally dedicated to Siva and Vishnu, who appear in various aspects. It has been suggested that water-worship was important here, and if so the most famous single work of art at Māmallapuram would have had something to do with it. This work is an enormous relief (nearly 30 metres long), carved on two great boulders, which is known as The Descent of the Ganges (page 171). It is situated in the open air, in contrast with the sculpture in the excavated temples and halls, and the air of mystery that surrounds it is

gold and the outlines drawn in more strongly in brown or black. Large mirrors were set up to reflect sunlight into the dark caves so that the artists could see what they were doing.

Even the earliest paintings at Ajanta show a fully developed naturalistic style in the depiction of animals and to some extent in backgrounds of leaves and foliage. There is no perspective, distance being suggested by the common device of placing more distant figures above nearer ones. Mountains are built up from a collection of cubes piled one on top of more the result of our ignorance than the intention of the sculptors. The most generally accepted story goes like this. After the saint Agastya had swallowed the sea in order to catch some demons who had escaped into it, the earth was left without water. A virtuous king, Bhagiratha, was called upon to solve the problem, and he persuaded Brahma to let the Ganges come down to earth. However, to prevent the great weight of water destroying the earth, Siva was entreated to sit in the way, breaking the water's fall. The great rush of water, falling upon the head of the god, was diverted into streams which fell upon the Himalayas and thence flowed across the Indian plains. Only a section of this amazing relief is shown here, and we can see the river falling in the centre and various people and creatures converging upon the scene. Serpent-like deities indicate the river; Bhagiratha is seen to the left of the river meditating before a shrine. The overall impression is calm and peaceful, in spite of the extraordinary mass of incident and detail, all of it charged with meaning for those who contemplated the work. For example, to the bottom right is a cat, symbol of hypocrisy, surrounded by eager and adoring mice. This amusing vignette conveys a warning that not all sages and mystics are to be trusted.

At Ellūrā, where most of the sculpture is about one hundred years later, there is more power and intensity, but less of the elegant naturalism of Māmallapuram. There are thirty-four rock-cut caves, including some Buddhist sanctuaries contemporary with, but in workmanship inferior to, nearby Ajanta. The Hindu temples overlapped with the later Buddhist sanctuaries, but by the late 8th century Hindu toleration of the Buddhists was ebbing somewhat, and some of the Hindu work at Ellūrā violently appropriated earlier Buddhist monks' cells. The sculpture reproduces the gestures and poses of the style of dancing so important in Indian society (and still preserved), and also illustrates the various ways of making love, as listed in manuals of sex. The most impressive single 'building' at Ellūrā is the Kailāsanāth temple, which is 30 metres high (or

rather 'low', since it was carved from the top downwards) which represents the cosmic mountain inhabited by the god Siva. It was originally a single mass of stone, isolated by cutting trenches around it, then carved to form not only the main temple but also immense free-standing columns and a life-size elephant. Because of its situation, it cannot be photographed adequately, as everyone who has seen this, perhaps the greatest single object of art in all India, will confirm. A near-contemporary inscription says, 'When the gods saw [the Kaila-santha] they were struck with wonder and thought about it constantly, saying, "This temple of Siva must have constructed itself, for such beauty is not to be found in a work of art."'

During the Indian medieval period, from the 9th to the 16th century, the political map was in a constant state of fluctuation, mirroring the waxing and waning fortunes of

Above:
One of the temples at Māmallapuram with a standing elephant. 7th century.

Opposite:
Part of the great relief of the Descent of the Ganges at Māmallapuram. 7th century.

various political powers. Each dynasty hoped to outshine its rivals and predecessors by the magnificence of its temples, with results like the temple-city of Bhuvanesvar in Orissā, which represents the peak of the northern style just as Māmallapuram represents the peak of the southern Dravidian style. The Muktesvara temple at Bhuvanesvar, often described as the finest of all temples in the northern style, is, almost literally, a 'jewel', so encrusted is it with fine carving; but the most famous building of Orissā is the so-called Black Pagoda – the temple of the sun at Konārak – a name which stems not from Western disapproval of its erotic

170

sculpture (right) but from its appearance to sailors approaching from the sea.

Against the background of the rise and fall of local dynasties, regional differences in style grew more pronounced, not only between north and south but also within the smaller regions themselves. Sculpture and architecture remained integrated, with temple walls a mass of figures. Statues virtually in the round existed in plenty, but they were usually attached to the wall by a narrow section at the back. The variety of pose and gesture is apparently endless, giving the whole area great liveliness, in spite of a slight stylization of feature and exaggeration of form. In the south, temple sculpture was generally inferior to that in the north, but some splendid bronzes were made by the *cire perdue* ('lost wax') method, in which a model is made with a layer of wax over the core and clay packed around; the wax is then melted away, and the molten metal poured into the clay mould. These are mainly sacred images conforming to a fairly rigid iconography, though that does not detract from their sense of balance and movement. A fine example, now in Amsterdam, is the 1.5 metre bronze statue (page 164) of Siva (a common type in south India). Siva is shown with his flaming halo, his hair extending from either side of his head to join the halo. In his hair is a female figure, personification of the sacred River Ganges. His upper hands carry two of his attributes: *damaru* (the drum shaped like an hour glass) and *agni* (fire). His foot crushes the dwarf, symbol of ignorance.

The Muslim conquest of India began as early as the late 8th century AD when Muslim forces overran the Punjab, but the spread of Islam was gradual. The Delhi sultanate was established at the beginning of the 12th century, but did not become an imperial power until nearly a century later, when Gujarat, Rajasthan, and the principal Hindu states of south India were conquered. In the 14th century the Delhi sultanate began to break up, and early in the 16th century it was conquered by Babur, founder of the Mughal dynasty. The

Muslim invasions heralded a decline in traditional Indian art. The custom of ornamenting walls with sculpture continued, and wall paintings were still found in temples and palaces, but their quality was inferior: they became increasingly stylized and simplified and were often apparently rendered in a mechanical manner. The new Indo-Islamic style of the Mughals

Below:
Sculptured decoration at the temple of Khajuraho, 11th century.

(see Chapter Six) inherited the rich traditions of the past. European penetration also began under the Mughals, with Indian artists increasingly turning to European works for inspiration (right). (Copying was not all one-way; Rembrandt himself made some copies of Indian miniatures.) But after the 18th century, Indian painting went into a decline, with most artists content to reproduce mechanical copies of earlier works, European or Indian.

The countries of the Far East are a long way from Europe, not only in miles but also in cultural background. Relations between the two have always been smudged by misunderstanding, the result of making judgments based on premises that are simply not applicable. The first person to give a full account of China to the West was Marco Polo in the 13th century. He had lived there for twenty years and had seen much. Despite his penchant for exaggeration, he painted a remarkable picture of a civilization older and, in many respects, more advanced than that of Europe. He saw everything through European eyes, however, and the view would probably have been hardly recognizable to a contemporary Chinese. The Jesuit missionaries who entered China in the 17th and 18th centuries acquired a remarkable grasp of some aspects of Chinese civilization, but they too completely ignored other vital areas and saw things through the distorting lens of their own assumptions and beliefs. China had a profound influence on many educated people in 18th-century Europe, but their conception of it was at best partial, and at worst almost totally wrong. It was, for instance, the rational social ideas of Confucius, the Chinese sage who lived in the 6th century BC, who influenced the *philosophes* of the Enlightenment; but the influence of Taoism and Buddhism, which contributed much to Chinese thought and art, was disregarded. In the 19th century, European artists were inspired by the art of Japan, but the type of Japanese art they admired was a fairly recent style that had not been held in much esteem by the Japanese

themselves. Chinese and Japanese art had been known in Europe since the Renaissance, but it was not until the 20th century that the full range of Oriental art was appreciated.

This lack of comprehension and web of error was not confined to Western ideas of the Far East. Misunderstandings on a similar scale characterized Chinese or Japanese ideas about Europe. This was inevitable, in view of the slight contacts between the two over the centuries. Travel was always (and still is) difficult, because of barriers both geographical and political. The journeys of Italian merchants across the mountainous 'silk route' to China in the late Middle Ages had hardly begun when they were cut off, and there have been only brief intervals of comparatively easy contact since. China, in fact, has remained remarkably separate not only from distant countries but from much nearer neighbours. In the long period when Chinese civilization was formed, roughly between 1700 BC and the birth of Christ, the deserts and mountains of the north and west formed an unpassable obstacle to travel in those directions. The only contacts were the 'barbaric' nomadic peoples, enemies of the Chinese, whose hostility and relatively primitive culture served to heighten the Chinese impression of themselves as

the true vessel of civilization. To the east lay the sea, and at that time the Chinese were not a sea-going people. Throughout the centuries there has been a Chinese push to the south, where there was no comparable barrier, resulting in the predominant influence of Chinese culture in southeast Asia, and also in contacts with aspects of Indian civilization, creating interesting hybrid cultures in the region significantly called Indo-China.

There was nothing to contradict the Chinese belief, still current, that China represented the civilized hub of the universe; non-Chinese, like non-Romans in ancient Europe, were by definition 'barbarians'. This belief was encouraged by the influential thought of Confucius, with its emphasis on tradition. Unlike the Indians, who had little or no notion of history, the Chinese looked back on an ancient civilization, fundamentally unchanging, and possessed a clear view of their own history, which was marked by the reigns of succeeding emperors and dynasties. The emperor, the 'son of heaven', was the pivot of the state; in reality, he might have little power, but his symbolic importance was paramount. The feudal nobility owed their position to him; so too did the later class of bureaucratic officials – a cultural élite who gained power not through influence or military potential but through education and mental or artistic capacity. A situation in which the political and social élite is the same as the intellectual élite is unusual in any part of the world; it had an important effect on the development of Chinese civilization, not only in encouraging cultural hegemony – in a very large country – but also in determining the value put on the different arts by Chinese society. Thus painting and music, the arts of personal enjoyment and aesthetic satisfaction, were regarded more highly than the more craftsmanlike arts, such as architecture and the decorative arts (including pottery, in which China led the world by a vast distance). An art divorced from religion was common in China between the 5th and 9th centuries – when art in Europe and other places was almost always connected with religion in some way. There was an 'art market' catering for art collectors many centuries before such a development took place in Europe.

The first organized state in China arose about 1700 BC, according to traditional Chinese histories, under the Shang, an aristocratic, slave-owning people with an elaborate Bronze Age culture. They were remarkably able casters of bronze as is shown in the ritual vessel (right) of the 14th-12th centuries BC, in the form of a tiger protecting a man. The centre of Shang power lay in the valley of the Yellow River, but their influence spread much farther. The Shang also possessed a complex ideographic script, from which the Chinese absorption with the art of calligraphy may be traced.

In the 11th century BC the Shang were conquered by their eastern neighbours, the Chou, but the change in rulers was not marked by a significant cultural change, rather by the consolidation of the religious and political ideology of the Shang period

which was to be codified by Confucius (551-479 BC). Confucius taught the 'Three Universal Virtues of Wisdom, Love and Courage', roughly corresponding to the intellectual, spiritual and physical sides of man. The cultivation of perfect virtue was the supreme duty of the 'gentleman', by whom Confucius meant a gentleman by character, not by birth, a revolutionary concept which reduced the hold of feudalism and class distinction in China. The individual and society were to be perfected by 'eight steps': investigation of things, extension of knowledge, sincerity of the will, setting the heart right, cultivation of the self, family, harmony, national order and world

peace. Thus an ideal society starts with learning and culminates in peace. Despite the somewhat bookish nature of Confucius's teaching, the goal of a perfect society was never lost. Confucianism was adopted as the official creed under the Han dynasty (207 BC-220 AD), overcoming the more negative Taoism, and dominated Chinese government and society until the 20th century.

The founder of the Han dynasty was a soldier of peasant origin, and under his successors a centralized

174

Above:
An incense burner of the Han dynasty, probably about 100 AD. It is made of gilt bronze with inlaid stones, and has hunting scenes in low relief.
Smithsonian Institution, Freer Gallery of Art, Washington, DC.

bureaucracy was built up under Confucian influence, recruited from all classes according to ability. Applicants for official positions had to pass an examination from the 2nd century AD (some 1700 years before such a measure was adopted in England).

The Han empire stretched from the jungles of Indo-China to the deserts in the north, and from Tibet to the sea. The establishment of peace and firm government, the disappearance of the feudal aristocracy, and the introduction of a money economy led to rapid expansion and a new urban class of officials and merchants whose outlook was very different from the slave-owning nobility of the past. Caring little for noble lineage, warfare and grand ceremonial, they were more interested in material possessions and the comforts of life. The increase in trade brought contacts with the civilization of south and western Asia, and led to considerable cultural hegemony in China itself. Lacquer objects produced in the south of China were in use in the far north and in Korea.

Confucianism encouraged respect for the written word, not only as a means of communication but as an art; high officials were renowned for their calligraphic style in the same way as painters. The paintings which adorned the walls of palaces have mostly disappeared, but some frescoes have survived in tombs, which also contained stone engravings and sculpture and tiles, sometimes with scenes in relief of everyday life, often with a type of drawing that is close to calligraphy. The human sacrifices which had formerly accompanied burials were replaced by figures in terracotta, along with all manner of other objects – bowls, vases, spoons, ladles, boxes, jewellery, mirrors, cosmetic outfits; in fact, as one scholar remarked, the contents of Han tombs read like the catalogue of a department store. This sophisticated, bourgeois society, is best seen in the bronzes of the Han period. They include containers of various kinds and incense burners (left), in a sober style aeons removed from the strange magical bronzes of the Shang and Chou periods. These objects are both utilitarian and decorative, often with animals and landscapes in relief.

Towards the end of the 2nd century AD the Han dynasty was shaken by peasant revolts, and power slipped gradually into the hands of the generals who carved out their own little principalities as independent warlords. During the following four centuries China remained disunited as the invading Huns and other nomadic peoples streamed into the country. Despite the lack of central authority, however, Chinese civilization survived, proving stronger than the primitive cultures of the invaders thanks to its broad social basis, its more advanced agriculture, technology and social organization. Nevertheless, in some areas the social order was badly damaged, while Confucianism, always open to criticism for its excessive rationality, lost ground to Taoism among those who advocated a return to the simple, natural life, and to Buddhism, which was already making inroads under the Han dynasty and whose metaphysical dimension provided something lacking in Confucianism or Taoism. Buddhist monasticism, which had no parallel in Chinese society, possessed a strong appeal for those who had been uprooted by political upheavals.

These new developments naturally found expression in art. Buddhist images were made, at first close in style to Central Asia and India, but gradually assuming a thoroughly 'Chinese' form. As in India, Buddhist monks often lived in caves cut in a rocky mountainside, which became galleries of painting and sculpture as well as religious sanctuaries. The early Buddhas were usually small, but in the central region monumental figures were made. Chinese sculptors followed Indian iconography, but inevitably introduced indigenous ideas. For example, in nude figures, they abandoned the soft, smooth style of India in favour of a hard, muscular image, as in the 6th-century limestone figure (1 metre high) of a door guardian (right) from a famous cave sanctuary at Pei Hsiang-t'ang, on the northern border of Honan. The purpose of such formidable-looking creatures was to ward off demons and evil influences. The rather grotesque musculature can be ascribed to the lack of familiarity of Chinese sculptors with

the nude; they were more accustomed to draped figures, in which the folds of the drapery were represented in a manner suggesting calligraphy.

Alongside the new Buddhist influences, indigenous forms of art lingered on, for instance in the wall paintings of Manchuria. In the south, under the Eastern Chin dynasty (317-420), the characteristic Oriental scroll had appeared, offering new opportunities to painters who had hitherto been restricted to architectural decoration and to an educative purpose, according to Confucian ideas. Scrolls were made for the delight of courtly connoisseurs, who prided themselves on their accomplishments in poetry, music,

calligraphy and painting, and, by the 6th century, were developing a conscious theory of art criticism. The Taoist revival promoted an interest in landscape painting, in which landscape itself was the sole, or at least primary, subject – another example of Chinese taste a thousand years ahead of Europe.

At the end of the 6th century China was at last reunited under the Sui dynasty, soon replaced by the T'ang dynasty which lasted until 906. The early T'ang emperors were people of unusual ability (including the famous Empress Wu) who ruled over China at one of the most glorious periods of its history. In Ch'ang An, the cosmopolitan capital, Syrians, Persians, Tatars, Tibetans, Koreans, Japanese and people of other nations lived side by side. Trade and the arts flourished. Block printing was invented, and played an important part in advancing Buddhism, since its greatest practitioners were Buddhist monks. Paintings decorated the walls of buildings in China and beyond, as Chinese influence spread; stone sculptures in the cave sanctuaries gained a new maturity, becoming more mellow and less angular. Palaces were filled with wood carvings, lacquer and bronze works. Szechuan produced gold and silverware and brocades, Hsiangyang was a centre of wares in dry lacquer (lacquer is a type of gum which, applied in several coats, can be subsequently carved), Yangchou produced bronze mirrors, and fine porcelain was made in several centres. Something of the elegance and nobility of life in the early T'ang period can be seen in the ceramic figure of a court lady holding a mirror (opposite), which was made with numerous other such figures for tombs, symbolic companions for the dead in the life hereafter.

Left:
Dvarapala, one of a pair of door guardians in limestone, late 6th century, 109 cm high. Museum Rietberg, Zurich.

Opposite:
Seated Lady with a Mirror, a T'ang terracotta figure about 30 cm high. Such sophisticated and elegant figures were placed in tombs as company for the dead. Victoria and Albert Museum, London.

Above:
T'ang bird's-head ewer. British Museum, London.

The early T'ang emperors aimed at a homogeneous culture based on the unbroken traditions of the more refined south (their own origin was northern).

The Emperor T'ai-tsung (627-49) revitalized the Confucian tradition, which he commended to the nobility and the bureaucracy as an educational model, and he encouraged the development of the art of calligraphy, still regarded as a 'higher' art painting, though the characteristic Chinese artist as a man who belonged to the top class of society and was not obliged to earn his living by pen or brush was already appearing in the early T'ang period.

This remarkable and admirable society broke up in the 8th century. Arab attacks in the west cut China off from Central Asia and delivered a severe setback to Buddhism in that area. But a worse blow was the state persecution that began in the 9th century in reaction to the controlling grip that Buddhism was extending over the Confucian state. Though Buddhism was to be tolerated again, it never recaptured the vigour and liveliness of the early T'ang period. The golden age was already over. Ch'ang-an had been ransacked during a rebellion in the mid 8th century and never regained its former significance as a cosmopolitan capital. Like the Han before it, the T'ang empire split up into a number of successor states, accompanied by a general shift in the cultural centre of gravity towards the south. In 960 the Sung dynasty came to power, and endeavoured to restore the state of society under the T'ang, but with only partial success. The Sung never commanded so large an area; China was hemmed in by the Tartars, and in 1127 one of the least competent of the Sung emperors, Hui-tsung, more gifted as a poet, painter and calligrapher, was carried off into captivity with 3,000 members of his court, bringing to an end the Northern Sung dynasty. But the limited political success of the Sung did not impede cultural achievements. Cities like Hangchow possessed an elegance and comfort far beyond anything in Europe for many years. Mining of precious metals as well as iron was carried out on a large scale; silk manufacture, weaving, pottery and book printing were encouraged by the government; there were also important scientific advances, including the invention of gunpowder.

Sung culture was marked by the rise of the bourgeoisie, and the relative decline of the military aristocracy. Officials were often also artists, and the Academy of Painting was founded, which long attracted the finest painters in the land. Sung painting was never surpassed before or since. Well-known academicians, who held official titles and wore special dress, produced lovingly detailed pictures of plants, animals and landscapes on silk. Sometimes these illustrated a particular theme such as 'The hoofs of his horse returned heavily charged with the scent of the trampled flowers' – a difficult pic-

Above:
Liang K'ai, *Ch'an Patriarch Cutting a Bamboo Pole*, Sung period, early 13th century. Tokyo National Museum.

Opposite:
A rather horrifying scroll painting of the Late Sung period of a scene in hell, with sinners being tortured by devils. Museum für Ostasiatische Kunst, Berlin.

torial problem solved by showing a swarm of butterflies clustering around the horse's hoofs. There were also many schools of largely anonymous painters working in the same style, and guilds of artists who worked for Buddhist patrons. The Ch'an (Zen) sect of Buddhism was particularly influential, and a number of Ch'an monks became famous as artists. One of them, Liang K'ai, was originally an academician working at Hangchow, but when he was awarded a prize by the emperor, he left the palace and went to spend the rest of his life in the solitude of the Zen temples, painting in the simple, economical style of the monks (above).

七七泰山大王

179

Above:
TAO-TSI (CHE-TO'A), *Spring at Ngan-Tcheou*, painting in coloured ink, about 1700.

Opposite:
This exquisite and assured scroll painting (a detail only is shown) is a fine example of the work of professional landscape painters of the Ming period. National Gallery of Canada, Ottawa.

Sung pottery too is more varied in style, with a greater range of design than T'ang, thanks largely to court patronage. Here too the study of nature made its mark, with restrained colours, a smoother, more rounded line and much use of moulded leafy forms. Peonies and lotus flowers, fish and dragons were popular in the much admired Ting ware and the green-glazed 'celadon' ware.

During the 13th century all of China was finally conquered by the Mongols who, under the name of the Yuan dynasty, ruled the whole country for about one hundred years. The great Mongol Emperor Kubilai Khan fully recognized the superiority of Chinese culture, but in spite of his sincere attempts to preserve and encourage it, Chinese civilization under the Mongols went through a crisis from which, in some senses, it never quite recovered. Many cultural leaders were prepared to cooperate with the Mongols, 'barbarians' though they were, but others practised a kind of passive resistance. Huang Kung-wan, like one or two others, took refuge in Taoist communion with nature; his slightly mannered landscapes, with their tendency to reduce natural forms to a series of small repetitive devices, set the style for much later landscape painting.

When the country was again united under a native dynasty, the Ming, in the 14th century, there was a reaction against the cosmopolitan spirit of the Mongol period (when Europeans had found a welcome in China), and an attempt to return to the old Chinese ways. The Ming dynasty, after some initial forays, put a virtual ban on foreign travel, though by the 16th century European merchants had re-established themselves on the South China coast, and Chinese exports, particularly porcelain, reached Europe in increasing quantity. The central Chinese city of Ching-tê-chên turned out porcelain by the ton, mainly the well-known blue-and-white ware, while the city of Nanking had something like 50,000 looms producing silk. In spite of this mass production, the standard remained high, and the conservatism of the times did not prevent all originality.

However, the attitude of the early Ming rulers towards artists was harsh and oppressive. The old, aristocratic academy was abolished; imperial artists now worked in conditions little better than slave labour, with eunuch overseers and the possibility of execution for unsatisfactory work. The old traditions continued in southern cities such as Suchou, where the so-called 'Wu' school practised the arts of poetry, calligraphy and painting. By the 16th century there was much variation in individual technique. Ch'iu Ying's picture of a Ming emperor crossing a river (opposite), from a hanging scroll of the early 16th century, shows the characteristic Chinese subordination of figures to landscape. The landscape is slightly idealized, Chinese artists always being concerned with inner truth rather than outward appearance, and though the palette is limited the

colours are strong. This was a common feature of the paintings of professional artists like Ch'iu Ying; Chinese taste has generally preferred the work of the well-born literary élite who, though often holding official positions, were not obliged to earn a living.

The growing weakness of the Ming dynasty in the early 17th century led to a takeover by the Manchu, or Ch'ing. They were Tartars, like the Mongols, but were more successful in acquiring Chinese culture and fostering traditional Chinese arts. Under the Manchu there was a revival of the arts, though a strain of self-conscious rigidity appeared in court art particularly. In the old tradition, some of the Manchu emperors were artists themselves and took an interest in the output of the palace workshops, but under this patronage court art became increasingly conservative and mechanical.

The centres of creation were, as had happened before in Chinese history, the provinces, where several schools of painters, some holding official positions, others jealously guarding their independence, flourished. The Buddhist monasteries were

Opposite:
A Buddhist guardian deity of the Nara period in Japan. This fragile life-size figure in terracotta has been preserved thanks to its location for centuries in a closed shrine. Hokke-dō, Tōdai-ji, Nara.

Below:
Detail from the *Animal Scrolls*, Heian period, 12th century, ink on paper. Kozan-ji, Kyoto.

again among the chief contributors, and a man like Chu Ta, a member of the former Ming dynasty, preferred to live his eccentric life among them, remote from the influences of the court. He was alleged to be mad, though his madness may well have been feigned, and his paintings breached most of the ancient traditions. Under the influence of wine (a common stimulant among Chinese artists) he made strikingly expressive sketches with an illusion of spontaneity, of birds, flowers, rocks and fish.

The expansion of Europe brought a rapid growth of trade with China in the 19th century, and Chinese exports, particularly porcelain and lacquer work, increased enormously. Many a Chinese merchant made his fortune out of this trade, but European customers were undiscriminating, and the existence of a vast and uncritical market abroad led inevitably to a decline in standards. The influx of cheap Western articles also dealt a severe blow to many traditional Chinese handicrafts. Chinese scholars increasingly looked to the past, and the eventual result of centuries of foreign occupation, rigid conservatism, and Western imperialism was the collapse of the Chinese empire in 1912.

The culture of Japan was strongly influenced by China, at first percolating through Korea. In the 6th century AD Buddhism triumphed in Japan; the ideas of Confucius stimulated the creation of a real apparatus of government, and Japan adopted the Chinese script. During the Nara period (710-84), T'ang culture exerted a powerful attraction; Nara, the capital, was modelled on the T'ang capital, and the treasure amassed by the Emperor Shomu in the 8th century included many T'ang works, as well as native objects and some from as far away as Persia. The sculptors working in the imperial temple at Nara made, among other things, a bronze Buddha 17 metres high, which may still be seen in its original location. Smaller sculptures were usually modelled in terracotta (opposite) or carved in lacquer.

The Heian period (784-1192) was a time of relative peace and prosperity, at least in Honshū, and the Japanese had the time and the inclination to follow their own ideas. Chinese influence remained strong, but the decline of the T'ang dynasty demonstrated that the Chinese too were mortal; formal relations with China were broken off for nearly two hundred years. One aspect of the nationalistic spirit was the development of a new script, cultivated especially by the ladies of the court (among whom were many of the chief writers of the time), and therefore sometimes called the 'Women's Style'. The use of coloured paper emphasized the delicacy of the new script.

During the Heian period the struggle between the nobles, who retained more of their traditional rights than the corresponding class in China, culminated in the dominance of the Fujiwara clan, who gained the chief positions in the state and also produced the greater part of the cultural élite. Less successful noble

183

families withdrew to the provinces where they built up autonomous principalities of their own in the course of time, founding the various families of war lords who ultimately came to dictate events in Japan.

Later Heian culture was essentially aristocratic, urban, and sophisticated; beauty was almost worshipped, as a kind of cult, and aristocratic ladies dictated fashion. One of the most famous literary works was the *Tale of Genji*, an immensely long novel by the Lady Murasaki, which describes contemporary court life. It was illustrated in the Japanese style *Yamato-e* (Yamato being the tra-

ditional homeland of Japanese culture), which had originated in painted panels and sliding doors. On horizontal scrolls, text and illustration became one; they show wonderful command of space and colour relationships. Besides this highly decorative, courtly form of art, painters also depicted scenes of everyday life, sometimes humorously. The 12th-century animal scroll (page 183) which is unique in Japanese art, comes from a temple, and is probably a satire on contemporary abuses among the Buddhist priests. The *Adventures of Kibi in China* comes from a slightly later scroll, and illustrates in a lively

and colourful way the adventures of a Japanese emissary in T'ang China who was asked to perform a series of problematic intellectual tasks by the Chinese court. The total length of this scroll is about 25 metres.

A new Buddhist sect which gained some influence in the 9th century was the school of Kukai, mystical in tendency and owing something to Hinduism. Images played an important part in its secret rites, and were often rather frightening figures of many-headed supernatural beings. Another Buddhist cult was founded in the late 10th century by the priest Genshin, which promised to even the humblest believer a rebirth in the Paradise of Amida. Despite its rather simple appeal, the Amida cult had a strong following among the aristocracy, who founded many Amida temples. Buddhism was often rather militant in character in Japan, but overall it retained sufficent tolerance to absorb aspects of the old Japanese religion of Shintoism. Some Buddhist sculpture of the later Heian period has Shinto subjects; the same sculptors apparently worked on Buddhist and Shinto sculptures rather indiscriminately. Buddhist sculptors worked mainly in wood, at first from single tree trunks, later from blocks of

Opposite:
The great Amida Buddha of Kamakura, about 13 metres high, mid-13th century.

Right:
A Shinto goddess in painted wood, about 25 cm high, Heian period, Nara. It is clear that the same artists were responsible for both Shinto and Buddhist works. Yakushi-ji, Nara.

Below:
One of a pair of wooden statues by UNKEI, Nara, 12th to 13th centuries.

wood joined together.

During the Kamakura period (1192-1338) Japan had two centres of artistic life: the old capital of Kyoto and the new one at Kamakura in the north-east, where fashions were dictated by the war lords. Buddhism continued to be the main repository of literary traditions, and some important new sculpture was produced by the Amida sect, including the vast figure of cast bronze at Kamakura (opposite) dating from the 12th to 13th centuries. Originally, it was commissioned in conscious imitation of the giant Buddha at Nara, mentioned above, and it was situated in a temple hall; the building has since been destroyed, and the Amida Buddha, nearly 14 metres high, now sits beneath the sky. The immense

cost of this bronze was met by voluntary subscriptions, and the style suggest a famous contemporary sculptor, Kaikei. It represents the peak of Japanese Buddhist monumental art, which went into a decline soon after.

Of the other Buddhist sects, far the most important was Zen Buddhism, which reached Japan from Sung China in the 14th century. Its simplicity and emphasis on meditation appealed to the warrior class, and it had the advantage over other sects of Buddhism of being thoroughly unadaptable for possible political ends. The influence of Sung China was much increased by the monks who travelled to China to study Zen; contemporary buildings are in a style termed 'Chinese', and the Chinese art of monochrome ink painting took

185

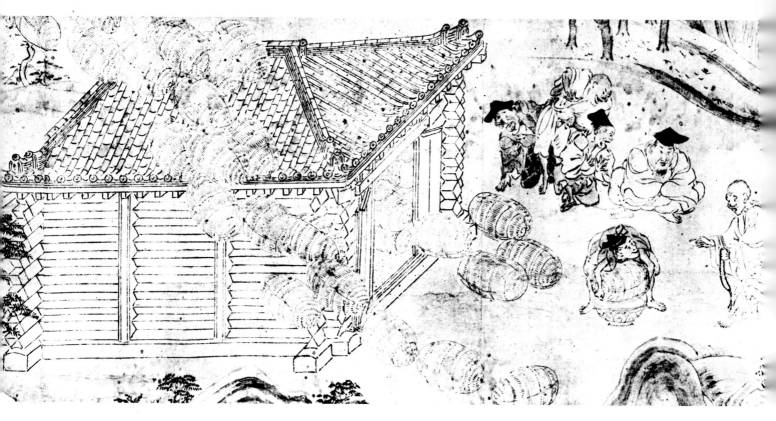

hold in Japan at this time. Especially
notable are the many portraits of
priests, which were often given to
students as an aid in meditation.
Scroll paintings were also in favour
during the Kamakura period. The
Amida monasteries produced horrifying pictures of torments and suffering,
comparable with the grisly works of
the guilds of painters in the region of
Ning-p'o in Sung China (above), in
order to impress upon people the
desirability of the Paradise of Amida.
Court painters illustrated poetry and
novels with scenes of everyday life and
there was an increasing tendency
towards objective reality which, in
the 14th century, often degenerated
into cliché.

The Kamakura period is notable
also for advances in pottery. As
before, the technique came from
China, but Japanese potters used
Chinese methods to produce a powerful style of their own, more rugged
and austere. The ceremonial practice
of tea drinking, particularly associated with Zen Buddhism, created a
demand for the wide variety of vessels

used in this ritual. The most celebrated tea bowls are perhaps those in
the ware known as Raku, deceptively
coarse-looking, with a soft glaze in
red, black or yellow. These, however,
date from the Muromachi period
(1338-1578).

With the emperor powerless and
the shogunate (supreme military gov-
ernors) weak, Japan in the Muromachi period was plunged into civil
wars caused by the struggle for power
of the various feudal lords who commanded the warrior clans of the
provinces. But in spite of these dis-
couraging conditions, the arts continued to flourish, and the political
incapacity of the Ashikaga shoguns
did not prevent them extending generous patronage to artists. Cultural
life remained, as in the Heian period,
centred on the Ashikaga court in
Kyoto; the tea ceremony, associated
with the art of flower arrangement,
was fully evolved, and the Nō drama,
with its masks which reduce characters to types, became popular.
Connoisseurship was developed until
it was almost an art in itself; special
areas were created in rooms for
displaying works of art. The spirit of
Zen had a strong influence on society,
among ordinary people as well as the
aristocratic and military élite, and the
Zen monasteries were primarily res-

ponsible for the evolution of yet
another characteristic Japanese art
form, landscape gardening, which
included 'dry' gardens made only of
varicoloured stones and gravel.

The art of painting in ink, with
little or no colour, remained the art
most deeply affected by Zen. It
reached its peak with the work of
Sesshū (1420-1506) who, like many
others, spent some time in China but
derived his greatest inspiration from
the landscape itself, and the work of
earlier, Sung artists. He typifies the
successful combination in this art
form of a number of apparently
disparate elements – a precise, calligraphic style and a free, expressive
spirit; an academic manner and a
profound understanding of nature
(opposite). Many of the artists patronized by the shoguns came from the
Kanō family, whose paintings on
sliding doors and screens, combining
precision of line with a sophisticated
composition of broad, open surfaces,
led to the decorative painting of the
17th century.

In the late 16th century Japan was
reunified under Toyotomi Hideyoshi,
and the period from 1573 to 1615 is
called the Momoyama period after
the site of one of Hideyoshi's palaces
near Kyōto. The Momoyama period
saw the building of great castles,

inspired by European example though Chinese and Japanese in style, with formidable stone bastions. The large castles and palaces of the period created new opportunities for the painting of screens and sliding partitions. The style of the Kanō masters was heightened by stronger colours and gilt backgrounds, but the tendency towards lavish decorative display was modified by the needs of the tea ceremony and its controlled ritual.

The first contacts with Europeans had been made some years earlier; St Francis Xavier reached Japan in 1549 and by his saintly example converted many people to Christianity. European merchants brought in scientific instruments and guns, but in spite of these sensational innovations, life for ordinary people in the rigidly organized society of Japan changed comparatively little. Social status was controlled by law, making it theoretically impossible for a man to rise in the world. Nevertheless, the arrival of the Europeans caused great excitement in Japan, manifest in certain paintings, especially the so-called *Namban Byōbu* ('screens of the southern barbarians') made in the late 16th and early 17th centuries (below), and betraying the usual exaggeration of features (note the baggy breeches) that appears to be an inevitable result when one people confronts another hitherto unfamiliar.

Above:
Landscape painting, from a scroll of the school of SESSHU, ink and pale colour.

Below:
A painted screen with six divisions painted with the popular subject of the arrival of Europeans in Japan. Early 17th century. Musée Guimet, Paris.

Hideyoshi was succeeded as regent by the equally formidable Tokugawa Leyasu, who gave his name to the long period (about two hundred and fifty years) of peace which he inaugurated. The emperor remained a figurehead, the feudal lords were held in check by a strong central government, and the capital was moved to Edo, the modern Tokyo. Leyasu banned Christianity in 1612, and cut off virtually all contact with the outside world, thus buying stability at the price of technological stagnation. This situation prevailed until the famous visit of Commodore Perry of the United States in 1853, which reopened Japan to world trade and led indirectly to the deposition of the Tokugawa Shogunate, and the restoration of the emperor in the enlightened person of Meiji (1867).

During the Tokugawa, or Edo, period, a prosperous, mercantile middle class arose in the cities and provided the patronage for decorative artists like Honnami Kōetsu (1558-1637), member of a well-known family of fencing masters, who was the leader of a revived form of the traditional art of poetry on a painted background. Kōetsu himself was primarily a calligrapher; the background design was usually executed by another artist. Artistic co-opera-

tion of this kind was encouraged by the school of artists in various styles which Kōetsu founded near Kyōto. It was a period of rich costume for women and in the theatre, and some of the finest screen paintings show the influence of textile design. Other artists worked in a more naturalistic vein, in the tradition of Chinese literary painting, while by the late 18th century European techniques such as oil-painting and copper engraving were arousing interest.

Porcelain manufacture began in the 17th century following the discovery of kaolin (china clay) at Arita. The Kakiemon family of potters gave their name to a highly original group with over-glaze enamels in soft red, turquoise, yellow and blue and subtly assymetrical designs. Japanese porcelain was frequently copied in Europe, while European subjects were sometimes depicted in Japan, giving rise to much later confusion. During the late 17th and 18th centuries there were a large number of notable individual potters at work, such as Ninsei (opposite), in various centres, but from the mid 19th century the European export market absorbed vast quantities of rather tasteless, over-enamelled wares and provoked a general decline in artistic standards.

Popular literature and the drama

provided the subject-matter for coloured woodcuts, and in the 17th century there was a fashion for scrolls with portraits of beautiful courtesans, the most famous name in this field being that of Suzuki Harunobu (1725-70). Another print-maker, Sharaku, is most famous for his portraits of actors, of which he completed rather a large number in a very short period (1794-95). Later masters, portraying the colourful life of the prosperous middle class, influenced French painters in the 19th century, but with the reopening of Japan, most of the cultural traffic flowed in the opposite direction, and Japanese artists copied Western techniques with the same assiduity that engineers were to show in the 20th century.

The Renaissance

In 15th-century Italy a civilization developed that was in many ways markedly different from that of medieval Europe. The name 'Renaissance' applied to it later means 're-birth' or 'revival', and the ideas and attitudes of the time were, or were thought to be, a deliberate return to those of the classical world. There was tremendous interest in Greek art and literature: builders studied the ruins of Greek temples; princes and merchants rushed to buy the ancient works that were dug up in the fields. Men believed that they were bringing about a revival of the culture which had passed away with the Roman empire, and to some extent they were; but men looked forward as well as backwards, and the innovative side of the Renaissance was equally important. People were not merely interested in reviving the past, even if they thought that was what they were doing; their interest in classical culture spread much more widely, over the whole field of man's experience. A spirit of inquiry, never dead but on the whole quiescent during the Middle Ages, was born; it was no coincidence that the great age of discovery, when European man set out to discover the world, took place during the Renaissance.

Contemporary social and political changes were also significant. Rulers made themselves more powerful and many countries threw off their allegiance to the Roman Catholic Church in the interests, partly at least, of national autonomy. The growth of trade created a richer and therefore more powerful merchant class. The invention of printing vastly speeded up the spread of ideas. Towns grew larger, and city life became the norm for an increasing proportion of the population. In Italy, city life was more advanced than anywhere else in Europe, and Italian society was largely organized in 'city states'. It was there, most notably in Florence, that the Renaissance began.

Without denying the revolutionary aspects of the Renaissance, it must be said that the division of history into periods can lead to misunderstanding. Human history has no sharp breaks, only more or less gradual evolvement, and there is no sharp line to be drawn between the Middle Ages and the Renaissance. Moreover, since the Renaissance is associated with a classical revival, forms of art that do not conform to the model tend to be disregarded. It would be easy to

Above:
BRUNELLESCHI's version of *The Sacrifice of Isaac*. It was submitted along with Ghiberti's for the competition for design of the doors for the Baptistry, Florence. Museo Nazionale del Bargello, Florence.

190

suppose, from the evidence of books, that artistically Florence was worth the rest of Europe put together during the 15th and early 16th centuries, but extraordinary though the Florentine output was, that is of course untrue. Nor were Florentine artists in the early 15th century setting out simply to revive the classical style. The truth is more complex.

At the beginning of the 15th century, there was an international Gothic style which, with comparatively minor exceptions, was found in most of Europe. Its main sources were France and Bohemia, but it was also found in northern Italy, where the Florentine Lorenzo Ghiberti (c. 1378-1455) submitted his *Sacrifice of Isaac* (below) as his entry for a competition to design the bronze doors of the baptistry in Florence in 1401. The elegant refinement of this work, which won the competition, shows its connection with the decorative Late Gothic style of northern Europe (though the figure of Isaac displays classical influence). But already there

Above:
Pietà by a little-known artist at the court of Burgundy, about 1400. Musée du Louvre, Paris.

was a reaction evident, a revolt against the decorative, passionless Gothic in favour of some more dramatic and meaningful style, and artists were searching for new sources. Some found it in the work of an earlier generation, in Giovanni Pisano, or in the paintings of Giotto. Others found it in the remains of the classical world which, in 15th-century Italy, lay all about. This was not a new inspiration, for we have seen that medieval Italian artists sometimes turned to the same

source. This time, however, the revival of antiquity was associated with the new learning, the study of man and his works, and with historical circumstances that seemed to parallel those of the ancient world. Florentine republicans identified with the republicanism of ancient Rome in their struggle against the Visconti dukes of Milan. The antique became fashionable, in the same way that there is a taste for primitive art among modern 'progressives'.

Florentine sculptors borrowed freely from many sources, and classical art was only one of them (there was little surviving classical painting to exert a comparable influence on painters). Yet Florentine scholars quickly seized on it to reinforce their own powerful predeliction for the ancient world, and to some extent at least it was these writers, most notably Vasari in the 16th century, who created the idea of a 'renaissance' of antique art. Ghiberti himself wrote three 'Commentaries' in about 1450, when he was an old man, in which he divided the history of art into three parts, the classical period, the Middle Ages (very short), and the 'revival' of art, which, according to him, began about 1300 and culminated, naturally enough, with his own work. Even Ghiberti did not think in terms of a revival of classical art in the strict sense of the word.

Another artist whose work illustrates the relatively eclectic nature of

Above:
ROGER VAN DER WEYDEN, *Entombment*, about 1450. A large step has been taken since the restrained, rather formal court art of the previous subject. Musée du Louvre, Paris.

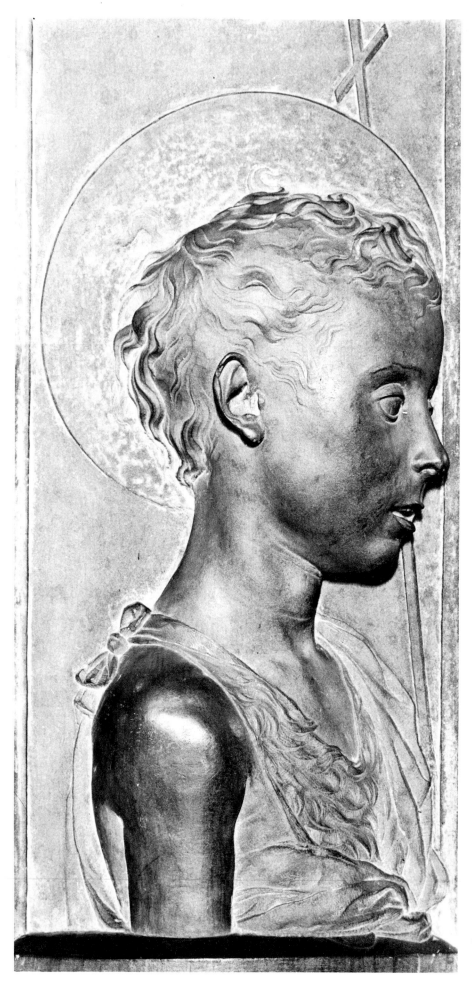

Above:
DONATELLO, *Lo Zuccone*, marble statue of King David, 1427-36, life-size. Museo dell'Opera del Duomo, Florence.

Left:
A delicate bronze relief by DESIDERIO DA SETTIGNANO. Museo Nazionale del Bargello, Florence.

Opposite, left:
DONATELLO's bronze relief of the head of John the Baptist being presented to Herod, from the font of the Siena Baptistry, 1427. It shows how the device of linear perspective developed by painters was adopted by sculptors also.

Opposite, right:
MASACCIO, *The Trinity*, fresco from Sta Maria Novella, Florence, 1426-27.

Florentine art in this period is Donatello (*c*. 1386-1466) whose powerful imagination encompassed both the classical tradition and the Gothic style of the Pisanos. Donatello's gilded bronze relief for the font of the Siena Baptistry (above) depicts a scene full of drama in a classical architectural perspective. Some of Donatello's sculptured figures were placed in niches of perfect classical form, showing that somebody had been studying classical remains very closely. It may be that the sculptor owned something here to his friend Brunelleschi, the architect of the dome of Florence cathedral, who is known to have studied Roman ruins.

A younger contemporary of Donatello was the painter Masaccio (1401-28?). He rejected the Late Gothic style but owed much to Giotto, to contemporary sculptors, and to the study of perspective as demonstrated in Donatello's font relief. His fresco *The Trinity* (right) in Sta Maria Novella, Florence, also shows his knowledge of classical architecture. Masaccio died at twenty-seven and little of his work survives. His solid figures and austere style, and his complete rejection of all idea of decorativeness or even beauty, represent a complete break with the Late Gothic style. His ability to render the mass and volume of objects and their relation to space have led some to call him the father of modern painting.

Renaissance Italy was a country in political turmoil. Although there was a period of comparative peace and stability between 1460 and 1490 which was later to be regarded as something of a 'golden age', even that was not as peaceful as it seemed in retrospect. The Medici rulers of Florence survived until 1494, but they escaped disaster only by the skin of their teeth in the Pazzi conspiracy of 1478. Virtually no Italian ruling dynasty survived the 15th century unscathed. The Visconti family was replaced by the Sforzas in Milan, and different members of the Sforza family struggled among themselves for possession of the dukedom. The Papacy changed at unpredictable intervals, sometimes falling into the hands of one princely family, sometimes another. This eventful, often violent political background had its effect on the lives of artists, partly because they depended on patrons. Benvenuto Cellini spent some time in a papal prison; Michelangelo fled from Florence to Rome when the Medici dynasty fell; Leonardo was atracted to Milan by the Sforzas and left again when Duke Ludovico Sforza fell in 1499. And it is said that the sombre piety of the later works of Botticelli stemmed from the effect upon the artist of the preachings of the puritanical friar, Savonarola. Generally, however, style was not affected by circumstances. Subjects might vary according to the commissions artists were offered, but that was a

superficial matter.

Later in the 15th century Italian artists, who had long been accustomed to look to the classical world for certain details, began to appreciate the art and architecture of the ancient world as a whole. They came to a more profound understanding of classical art, whereas before they had simply raided it for ideas. At first, however, this trend was less obvious in Florence than in other cities, largely because Florentine art of the early 15th century offered such a rich mixture of styles and ideas that naturally preoccupied the next generation. Artists in Florence were concerned with the achievements of Masaccio and Donatello, and with the correct

Above:
Madonna and Child by LORENZO MONACO, Florence, about 1410. The centre panel of a wooden altarpiece, this is an essentially ornamental painting, a long way in feeling from the work of Masaccio. Palazzo Davanzati, Florence.

Right:
VERROCCHIO, *David with the Head of Goliath*, bronze, about 1476. Museo Nazionale del Bargello, Florence.

representation of perspective. The sculptor Andrea del Verrocchio, who was born in Florence in the early 1530s, may have been a pupil of Donatello. At any rate, much of his work, mostly in bronze, reflects Donatello's interests, almost suggesting a sense of rivalry. Like Donatello, Verrocchio produced a figure of *David*, an equestrian figure (the famous bronze statue in the piazza of SS Giovanni e Paolo in Venice) and *putti* (cherubs, rather a speciality of Donatello). A contemporary of Verrocchio, Desiderio da Settignano, may also have been a pupil of Donatello. He did not have Verrocchio's great range and dynamic creativity, but no artist excelled him in his sensitive finish; never has a sculptor more skilfully evoked the softness of skin in marble.

The extraordinary diversity of style and talents in late 15th-century Florentine sculpture was mirrored in painting. The legacy of Donatello and Masaccio included a new variety of faces (the lynx-eyed Gothic look disappeared) and a more studied placing of figures in their environment and in relation to one another. The traditional restraint and refinement of Florentine painting was not abandoned – Donatello's more dramatic later works found less favour in Florence – as in the works of an artist like Fra Angelico, a Dominican friar who became prior of the monastery of Fiesole. He was in fact older than Masaccio, but lived much longer (he died in 1455). Nothing is known of his early training as a painter, and in many respects his work is more closely allied with the Gothic than the Renaissance. He was a brilliant colourist whose paintings, mainly devotional works, are as 'angelic' as his character and have an extraordinary gentle quality. Late in life he was summoned to Rome by the Pope to decorate a Vatican chapel with scenes from the lives of St Stephen (page 198) and St Lawrence, where his style, no doubt influenced by his surroundings,

Left:
VERROCCHIO, *Christ and the Doubting Thomas*, 1465-83. Verrocchio's training as a goldsmith is evident in the care with which every detail is conveyed in this bronze group in Florence. Or San Michele, Florence.

Above:
FRA ANGELICO, *Scenes from the Life of St Stephen*, about 1448. This painting is in the Vatican, where the painter had been summoned from Florence by the Pope.

Left:
FRA FILIPPO LIPPI, *Annunciation with Donors*, about 1455. The painter's interest in interior detail has led him to place the scene in what could be either a chapel or a bedroom. Palazzo Venezia, Rome.

became more elaborate, and markedly divorced from other Florentine painting of the time. His pictures of St Stephen preaching do not follow the conception of perspective outlined by the influential scholar and architect, Leone Battista Alberti, and there is clearly a debt to Giotto and his school (see page 134). The richness of the vestments reflects a personal taste shared with several contemporaries, including Fra Filippo Lippi (died 1469), another monk and a member of the Carmelite order. Fra Filippo Lippi was a less saintly character than Fra Angelico, getting into trouble with his Medici patrons when he was convicted of forgery and later, when he had been rehabititated and made chaplain of a convent, running off with a nun, by whom he had a son, the equally famous painter, Filippino Lippi. His work shows an impressive synthesis of contemporary styles, with the influence of Masaccio paramount in the solidity of the figures in his early paintings. Fra Lippi's work is more human than that of most of his contemporaries. In his famous fresco of the death of St Stephen in Prato cathedral, he included among the figures in the background a number of portraits of contemporaries, includ-

ing himself. He painted many panel pictures of the Virgin (opposite), and succeeded in capturing an expression of serene wistfulness which was to set the style for the numerous *Madonnas* of the following half century.

The leading fresco painter in the period 1470-90 was Domenico Ghirlandaio (1449-94; the name means 'garland-maker', he was one of many Renaissance artists who adopted nicknames). His work was influenced by Masaccio and Verrocchio, among others. He was a prolific painter with a large studio, his pupils including Michelangelo, and his most famous

works are the frescoes he painted for Sta Trinità and Sta Maria Novella in Florence. His *Adoration of the Shepherds* (below) is in tempera, the technique used by Duccio and the Siena school (see page 133). This painting is a good example of the multiple influences at work in late 15th-century Florence. The marble sarcophagus and other features are taken directly from classical art, while the landscape in the background, and possibly the figures

Below:
Domenico Ghirlandaio, *Adoration of the Shepherds*, Florence, 1485. S. Trinità, Florence.

of the shepherds to the right, owe something to Flemish painting, which had recently become popular in Florence. The procession in the background recalls French court painting of the Late Gothic period, and the face of the Madonna suggests the influence of Fra Lippi.

Ghirlandaio was primarily a fresco painter. His even more famous contemporary, Sandro Botticelli (*c.* 1445-1510), painted mainly on panels, and though the two have some characteristics in common – a taste for classical ruins and colourful costumes, for instance – Botticelli's style was rather different. Botticelli was a highly poetic painter, whose mood often appears faintly melancholy, an impression heightened by the very strong curving line with which he drew his figures. A precocious artist, with a flourishing studio of his own by the age of twenty, he may have studied under Fra Lippi; his early works certainly bear a strong resemblance to the painting of Fra Lippi's son, Filippino Lippi, some of which were at one time thought to be by Botticelli. Nearly everyone must be familiar with at least two of Botticelli's paintings, the famous allegory, *Primavera* ('Spring') and *The Birth of Venus*, both now in the Uffizi Gallery and reproduced a thousand times. This is ironic in a way, for in later life Botticelli turned away from pagan subjects – he is said to have burned some of his paintings – and devoted himself to deeply sincere, very troubled religious paintings; he seems to have undergone a grim religious crisis in his own life after the burning of Savonarola. His *St Sebastian* (opposite) belongs to an earlier period: it was painted in 1474. There is very little

classical feeling in this painting: note, for example, that the saint is tied to a tree rather than the classical column preferred by most of the many other painters of this much-favoured subject, and the background suggests a Flemish landscape. The saint himself is represented as a beautiful youth; there is no attempt to represent pain in his face, and he is serenely untroubled by the arrows piercing him.

A powerful linear quality was not unique to Botticelli, but was a common feature of Florentine painting in this period, possibly deriving from the fact that so many painters, including Ghirlandaio and Botticelli, began their apprenticeship in a goldsmith's workshop. This was so common a practice that it cannot have been coincidence, and the explanation seems to be that drawing, which was becoming a more important part of an artist's training, could most easily be learned in a goldsmith's shop than in a painter's studio. Painters – and sculptors too – now frequently made a series of studies before beginning a painting. Take for example the preliminary sketches made by Antonio Pollaiuolo (*c.* 1432-98) for his *Battle of Nude Men* (opposite), about 1470, which is basically a study in the male nude. Pollaiuolo, incidentally, was a goldsmith himself, and this painting shows how close this linear draughtsmanship is to the craft of the goldsmith. This tradition was to reach its apotheosis in the work of Michelangelo. There was, of course, nothing new in drawing, but drawing now had a wider purpose. Instead of concentrating merely on outline and surface, artists like Leonardo sought to capture the structure of the figure or object. He made drawing a method of experiment, and this was a new, characteristically Florentine development.

Pollaiuolo, also a reputable sculptor, was a good example of the

Left:
BOTTICELLI, *St Sebastian*, 1474. This was a very popular subject, and it is interesting to see how different painters treated it. Botticelli was interested in painting a beautiful youth; the picture has virtually no emotional content and the arrows appear superfluous. Gemäldegalerie, Dahlem, Berlin.

201

'Renaissance Man', by which we mean someone talented in many fields, but the supreme example of this phenomenon is Leonardo da Vinci, who was born near Florence in 1452 and died in 1519. The illegitimate son of a lawyer, Leonardo showed his gifts for the arts early. His father placed him in Verrocchio's studio, where Botticelli was one of his fellow-pupils. He probably painted the angel in Verrocchio's *Baptism* in the Uffizi and, according to an old story, it was on that occasion that Verrocchio acknowledged the superior mastery of his pupil. At the age of twenty, when Florence was entering the period of its greatest glory, Leonardo was ready to set up his own studio. Florence did not suit him, however. He was not entirely sympathetic to the classical revival then in full swing; he was more of a searcher and an inventor, and he could not speak Greek. When he was about thirty he left Florence to enter the service of the Duke of Milan, where there were fewer rival artists and where scholarly fashion was less directed towards classical studies and more towards such subjects as mathematics, an interest that Leonardo shared.

Leonardo's chief commission at Milan was to make an enormous statue in bronze, though at the end of twenty years the work remained unfinished, a characteristic failing of Leonardo (only the model was completed, and that was later used by soldiers for target practice). He also amused the court with ingenious amusements, such as a mechanical lion for a play, and filled his notebooks with drawings of human muscles, flowing water and leaves, as well as designs for a vast and bewildering assortment of machinery – a vehicle driven by springs, a parachute, even a primitive kind of flying machine. He designed enormous siege guns and a dam for a river; he invented a kind of alarm clock to wake himself up. Very few of the machines that Leonardo designed were ever built or would have worked if they had been, but the scope of his imagination and the fertility of his invention remains staggering.

In his painting too Leonardo, unfortunately, was always experimenting. One reason why so little of his work remains, or is in poor condition, is that he could not resist the constant temptation to experiment with his media, often with dire results. His famous painting of the *Last Supper* is one example: he devised an experimental oil medium which, painted on damp plaster, soon deteriorated. Other experiments, however, were more fruitful. His most famous painting, and probably the most famous painting ever made, the *Mona Lisa*, was unlike any portrait painted before. The mysterious half-smile fascinated his contemporaries as it has fascinated posterity. According to the art historian Vasari, Leonardo was commissioned to paint La Gioconda, as the painting is also known, by the subject's husband (whose name was Giocondo), and one explanation for the famous smile is that Leonardo employed musicians to play and joke while he was painting. The effect of a smile is actually achieved by the deft use of the painter's brush, for example the delicate shadings around the lips. Similar subtle expressions occur in other paintings, such as the *Virgin of the Rocks* (opposite) of which two versions exist, one in the National Gallery in London and one in the Louvre in Paris, which also owns the *Mona Lisa*, bought by Leonardo's last patron, Francis I of France, for 4,000 gold florins (it has remained in the Louvre ever since except for a brief interval when an ingenious thief stole it in 1911). The *Virgin of the Rocks*, which was painted as the central panel of an altar, is in some ways a finer example of Leonardo's genius. The gentle grace of the figures, and the brilliant use of light and shadow, enthralled younger painters of the time.

At the end of the 15th century the political situation in Italy became even more disturbed with, as had so often happened in the past, the invasion of foreign armies. It began with the attempt of Charles VIII of France to conquer the Spanish-ruled kingdom of Naples, an unsuccessful and comparatively brief sortie, but it became more serious when Italy, and Milan in particular, became a central issue in the power struggle between the Valois dynasty of France and the Habsburgs, represented respectively by Francis I and the Emperor Charles V. This conflict, which lasted until 1529, saw armies marching across Italy, Rome sacked by mutinous imperial troops (to the grief of the Emperor) and a second brief expulsion of the Medici from Florence.

Rome never produced native artists to compare with those of Florence. Nevertheless, Rome played an even more vital part in the art of the High Renaissance (*c.* 1490-1520) because of its importance as a centre of patronage. The great days of the Investiture Contest (11th and 12th centuries), when a Pope had humbled an emperor, were far in the past, and in the 15th century the Papacy was politically feeble, unable even to impose order in the city of Rome herself, which was disturbed by the struggles of rival aristocratic factions. Alexander VI (1492-1503) was the first of the Renaissance popes who attempted to make the Papacy a real political force again, his chief instrument being his nephew Cesare Borgia, who by cunning and force (he was the inspiration for Machiavelli's political treatise, *The Prince*) subdued central Italy. The premature death of Alexander ended the Borgia supremacy, but his successor, Julius II, a member of a rival family, pursued similar policies. It was largely Julius, also, who made Rome the centre of artistic patronage. This was not accomplished simply by force of personality, though no more forceful individual has ever sat on the throne of St Peter, but was rather largely the result of fortuitous political conditions. It so happened that Florence was undergoing a short and fragile existence as a republic, and it was easier to lure away artists who, in the days of the Medici, would probably have remained in their native city. Julius lasted only ten years (1503-13) but by another stroke of luck his two successors, Leo X (1513-21) and Clement VII (1523-24), separated only by the brief reign of a Dutch

Opposite:
LEONARDO, *The Virgin of the Rocks*, about 1507. Raphael learned much from the grace and charm that Leonardo imparted to the human figure. National Gallery, London.

pope, Adrian VI, were Medici. Thus the head of the Medici family during that period resided not in Florence but in Rome, and Florentine artists who might have otherwise returned home remained in Rome. In the first twenty years of the 16th century Rome was the centre of the art sometimes defined as 'High Renaissance', though since this term embraces artists as different as Raphael and Michelangelo, it is not an easy one to define. It really amounted to a series of developments and of new ideas, which were worked on in different ways by a number of different artists, all of them men of outstanding capacity and at least one, Michelangelo, a genius without peer.

For the origins of the High Renaissance we must look again at Florence. We have seen how 14th-century Florentine artists were strongly affected by classical art, but that this was by no means the only source of their inspiration and that to talk about a 'classical revival' is a generalization in need of strong qualifications. At the end of the century, however, Florentine sculptors finally embraced classical art in a profound and comprehensive way. The young Michelangelo carved a *putto* which was mistaken for a genuine antique and his marble figure of *Bacchus*, now in the Bargello, Florence, was copied (not precisely of course; perhaps 'reinterpreted' is a better word) from a classical Greek figure, possibly by Praxiteles, though the original has disappeared, and was designed to stand in a garden among other genuine Greek sculpture. The *Bacchus* is not a complete success, but a few years later, after a visit to Rome, Michelangelo made, from an old marble block previously worked on by another sculptor, his famous figure of *David* (right), which has been called the 'greatest sculptural monument to the "classical revival"' in Florence. In this enormously influential work, Michelangelo deliberately challenged the great men of ancient Greece, and did so successfully. The figure, over five metres high, stood in the main square, and was seen as a political gesture; the struggling Florentine republic identified with David, a successful underdog in his battle with Goliath, which

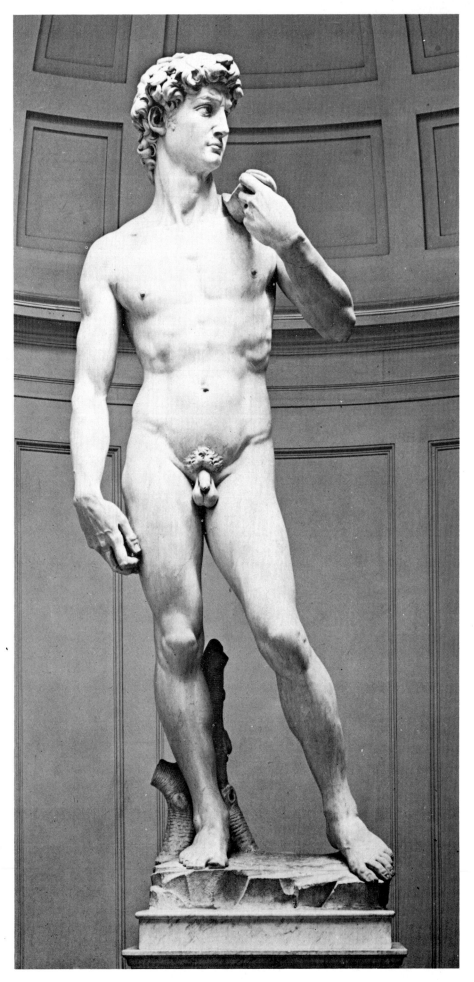

Above:

MICHELANGELO admired the work of
Signorelli (page 206), but as this figure
of Jonah, 1511, from the ceiling of the
Sistine chapel demonstrates, he lifted the
art of figure painting on to a new plane.

Opposite:

MICHELANGELO, *David*, marble, 1501-4.
Galleria dell'Accademia, Florence.

represented the victory of freedom
over tyranny.

Michelangelo (1475-1564) was a
young man when he made the *David*
and his style was to mature considerably later. A gifted poet as well as a
painter and architect he was above all
a sculptor, and his paintings, which
are probably even better known than
his sculptures, have the same quality
of monumentality displayed in the
Florence *David*. In 1504 the Florentine Republic commissioned him to
paint one of a pair of frescoes of battle
scenes, the other being undertaken by
Leonardo. Since neither artist, characteristically, finished the work, this
interesting contrast in styles can only

be judged from the preliminary drawings.

In 1505 Michelangelo was summoned to Rome to build a tomb for
Pope Julius II. He worked out an
elaborate plan which included about
fifty life-size figures, though the
grandiose plan was subsequently altered on several occasions. Indeed, the
work became something of a night-
mare for the artist: he worked on it for
forty years, long after Julius himself
was dead, and almost everything that
could go wrong did so. When at last it
was finished Michelangelo was bit-
terly disappointed with it. One reason
why the work was so interminable was
that Michelangelo left it at various

205

Above:
LUCA SIGNORELLI, *The Damned*, about 1503. This painting is an example of the way in which Renaissance artists sought new and unconventional poses for the human body. Chapel of S. Brizio, Orvieto Cathedral.

Left:
MICHELANGELO's *The Last Judgement* in the Sistine Chapel, 1534-41.

times for other works. He had hardly begun when Julius took him away from it in order to paint the vault of the Pope's private chapel, known as the Sistine Chapel. It was said that he was recommended for this enormous task by the architect Bramante, who was jealous of him and felt confident that so challenging a project would be beyond him. The total area covered is over 500 square metres. In an amazingly short time, and without assistants, Michelangelo completed his nine huge paintings of scenes from the Old Testament, surrounded by Prophets and other figures (page 205). He stood on a wooden platform 20 metres above the floor, bending over backwards; paint dripped on his face and he suffered pain in his back and shoulders ever afterwards. The impetuous Pope sometimes came to inspect progress. Climbing to the platform he would ask, 'How much longer?' Michelangelo would grimly reply, 'As soon as I can'. The result is an extraordinary Biblical symphony, in which everything is conveyed in terms of the human figure: the scene of The Creation, for instance has a sky-born Yahweh reaching out to touch the fingertip of the newly created Adam. Years later, under Pope Paul III, Michelangelo returned to the Sistine Chapel to paint on the wall behind the altar his *Last Judgment*, perhaps his greatest masterpiece, a majestic but grim scene, recalling the recent Sack of Rome in 1527. Some people regarded the writhing nude figures as inappropriate for the situation, and for a time parts of the painting were hidden from view by discreet touches of drapery.

Michelangelo, a withdrawn and rather tortured man, was often on poor terms with his fellow artists. He found Leonardo uncongenial, he suffered a broken nose in a scuffle with the sculptor Torrigiano (who later worked in England), and he had no sympathy for his great contemporary in Rome, Raphael (1483-1520). The two men well represent the diversity of art in the High Renaissance. They could hardly have been less alike. Michelangelo, inward-looking and prickly, unable to tolerate assistants for long, had the utmost difficulty in

finishing any work of art, not because he was a slow worker – he was notoriously fast, as the Sistine vault confirmed – but because he was never satisfied. Raphael, good-natured and sociable, kept a vast studio and with the aid of numerous assistants completed, despite dying at the age of thirty-seven, a vast quantity of work. Their styles were equally different: Michelangelo was serious, passionate, monumental; Raphael was more flexible, graceful, elegant, 'painterly'.

Raphael was born in Urbino, the

Above:
RAPHAEL treated the nude quite differently. Whereas Michelangelo's *Jonah* is grand and powerful, the figures of Raphael's *Triumph of Galatea*, a fresco of 1511, are lithe and graceful. A great deal of later European art can be placed in one of these two traditions. Villa Farnesina, Rome.

son of a painter. He came under the influence of Leonardo and Michelangelo during a four-year stay in Florence as a young man, but it was Rome, where he lived from 1508 to 1520, that saw the full flowering of his genius. The Pope was but one of many patrons, and some of the most famous works of his prodigious output are the decorations he did for grand private houses such as the Villa Farnesina (above). *The Triumph of Galatea* was painted in the same year as Michelangelo's figure of *Jonah* (page 205), and the two works well illustrate the contrast in style between the two greatest artists of the Roman school. But for all the lithe elegance of Raphael's figures of gods and goddesses, so different from the monumental grandeur of Michelangelo's figures, there are signs of the latter's influence in Raphael's figures of the Tritons, while the pose of the central figure, elegantly turning from the hip, was derived from a painting by Leonardo which is now lost.

Raphael was a court painter of the best kind. His patrons were educated,

cultured men, and the artist was not compelled to restrict the creativity of his fertile and well-stocked mind for fear of being misunderstood, a common fate of 'court' artists in other periods. They would have understood, for example, that his 'painted tapestries' in the Villa Farnesina were a recollection of the awnings used to cover the open-air theatres in Roman times.

Raphael's style lived on after his early death in the work of his numerous students and followers. They included some artists of high standing in their own right, though perhaps the finest of Raphael's followers in Rome was a man who only arrived there after his death (and, incidentally, died at the same age – thirty seven), Girolamo Parmigiano, or Parmigianino (1503-40).

Meanwhile, Florentine art had been somewhat impoverished by the activities of Pope Julius II, who lured the best artists to Rome, but such was the extraordinary fertility of the city, that a number of fine painters, though fewer sculptors or architects, were

Above:
RAPHAEL, ceiling fresco in the Villa Farnesina, Rome, 1518. The story illustrated is the classical tale of Cupid and Psyche, and here we see that despite their differences Raphael learned from Michelangelo too.

Opposite:
PARMIGIANINO, *La Madonna dal Collo Lungo*, about 1535. Parmigianino was an admirer of Raphael. The composition, like that of many Mannerist paintings, may strike us as contrived, with the deliberately contrasted straight and curving forms and children's faces crowded together in one corner, but the charm and elegance of the work cannot be denied. Palazzo Pitti, Florence.

Above:
PONTORMO's *Descent from the Cross*, oil on wood, 1526-28 in S. Felicità, Florence.

Human figures occupy virtually the entire space available but without overcrowding; they are linked to each other by glance and gesture and at the same time draw in the spectator, strongly engaging his emotions.

There were of course many fine artists in early 16th-century Italy who belonged neither to Florence or Rome. Patrons like Duke Federico Gonzaga at Mantua were anxious to attract the best artists to their courts. Correggio (1489-1534) was born in the small town from which he took his name, near Modena, and did much work in Parma, including the magnificent *Assumption of the Virgin* (opposite) inside the dome of the cathedral (a photograph cannot do it justice). He was strongly influenced by Leonardo, and to a less extent by his slightly older contemporary, Raphael. The bold and theatrical grouping of his figures is almost baroque in spirit, though his smaller scale works with non-Christian subject-matter, like the delightful picture of Mercury instructing Cupid with Venus in attendance in the National Gallery, London, have a soft and delicate charm, while excelling in expressions of love and joy – another indication of future artistic developments. Correggio was advanced also in his technique, since his preferred medium was oil. Oil painting, in which the pigments are bound in oil and diluted with linseed oil or turpentine, was a Flemish invention which reached Italy in the last quarter of the 15th century and eventually replaced tempera. Oil is more versatile, equally capable of rendering the most fine and delicate detail and of great depth and richness. The technique used by Michelangelo, among others, was to paint first in tempera on gesso, then add a glaze of oil colours, a kind of hybrid technique. A later development, brought to perfection in Venice (see below) was to paint first in one colour, fill in the light parts with thick, opaque colour, and then add a series of glazes which gave ever-deepening richness: thus the picture was built up in stages. It was not until the 19th century that a more direct method became common, resulting from the custom of painting direct from nature, a method requiring

around to fill the vacant spaces. The most outstanding were Andrea del Sarto (1486-1530) and his pupil Jacopa da Pontormo (1494-1557). Sarto, influenced by the work of both Leonardo and Michelangelo, painted in rich colours. He was renowned in his day for his precise drawing, and is best known nowadays for his religious frescoes. It was said that when rioting Protestant soldiers entered the church of San Salvi in 1529, they were so struck with awe at the sight of Sarto's *Last Judgment* that they left again quietly without committing violence.

Pontormo was a more complicated artist, belonging rather to the movement called Mannerism (to be explained later on) than to the High Renaissance. His style varied considerably according to the type of commission he was engaged on, and it is the more difficult to follow his development now since so many of his church frescoes have been destroyed. He was powerfully affected by Michelangelo, and not the smallest of his achievements was that he got on well with that uncomfortable genius. His *Descent From The Cross*, probably his most famous work, reflects Michelangelo's absorption with the human figure. Despite some distortion, this is a brilliantly worked-out composition.

greater speed than the picture produced mainly, if not entirely, in a studio.

As we have seen, the style of the High Renaissance was not uniform but diverse, and its diversity was most obvious in the contrast between Raphael and his successors on the one hand and Michelangelo on the other. This lack of unity makes it even more difficult to distinguish between the High Renaissance and the phase known as Mannerism, which forms a link with the later, Baroque period. The word 'mannerist' or 'mannered' is sometimes applied to the art of many different periods and places, and when used like that it means a certain deliberate exaggeration or affectation of style. Mannerism as a term defining Italian painting in the generation after 1520 is also used in that sense. More specifically, it refers to a trend based on an admiration for the art of Michelangelo, and with a consequent exaggeration of certain features derived from him (the later works of Michelangelo himself are usually classed as 'Mannerist'). Typical features were the elongation of the human figure or exaggeration of the muscular contours of the body; gestures were often violent, even distorted; compositions were tense and crowded and colours vivid. Social and

political conditions are sometimes suggested as the cause of this style – religious and political unrest, the sack of Rome – while others have noted the neurotic personalities of a high proportion of Mannerist artists. These explanations tend however to emphasize the aspect of Mannerism as a reaction against the High Renaissance, whereas it should rather be seen as the result of a new generation of artists working out new ideas based on the achievements of the immediate past.

So far, no mention has been made of Venice which, like Florence, was a relatively self-contained centre of artistic creation during the Renaissance and, indeed, excelled even Florence in the continuity of its artistic tradition. Standing on the eastern edge of Christendom, Venice was a powerful state, its prosperity based on trade, and its government, dominated by a small aristocratic class under the Doge, strong and stable. In certain respects it would not be an exaggeration to describe Venice as an efficient police state, but as long as the political and economic security of the state was not threatened, the atmosphere was comparatively liberal; for artists, at any rate, it was a good place to live, and many artists attracted to Venice from other places showed no particular desire to go home again. The state was an eager patron, and many opportunities were offered by the religious guilds of Venice; private patronage was less important than in Rome, but still provided a market for smaller religious works and portraits.

The Gothic tradition remained influential in Venice into the late 15th century. The classical revival was introduced mainly by artists from Padua and other places who settled in Venice, such as the Lombardi family of masons and sculptors. Tullio Lombardi's marble figure of *Adam* (right), about 1490, brilliantly captures the sleek texture of Athenian sculpture. The model for this figure is said to have been the lost *Bacchus* of Praxiteles which was also imitated by Michelangelo, as mentioned above; on the whole, Lombardi's figure is the more successful work. Another influential innovator of the classicizing

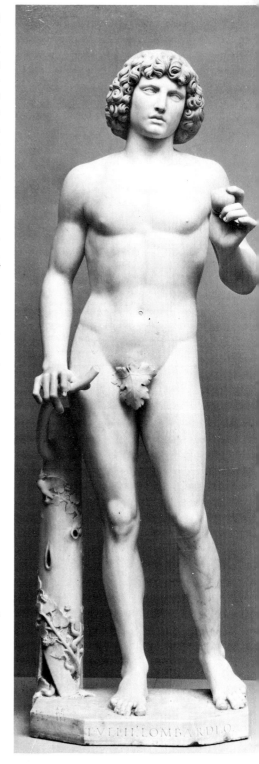

Above:
Lorenzo Lotto, *Portrait of a Man*, about
1507. Kunsthistorisches Museum,
Vienna.

style was the Padua-trained painter Andrea Mantegna (1431-1506), whose figures derive mainly from an expert appreciation of antique sculpture and whose paintings are filled with lovingly observed classical remains.

Mantegna married a member of one of the most talented families in Venice, the Bellini, and his influence can be seen in the work of the most famous of them, Giovanni Bellini (c. 1430-1516), who contributed more than any artist of his time to the creation of the great Venetian school. The hard sculptural quality of his *Madonna* of about 1465 clearly derives from Mantegna, though Bellini's best remembered qualities of brilliant colours and effects of light, evident in a *Madonna* painted fifteen years later

(below), can be traced to another influence, that of the Sicilian painter Antonello da Messina, who was in Venice in the 1470s. It was probably from Messina that Venetian painters learnt to define form and detail in painting by their handling of light; it was this blending of light and dark tones, allied with a sure eye for colour, that gave Venetian painting its extraordinary richness. Antonello had another important effect on painting in Venice: he encouraged the change from tempera to oils. The use of canvas stretched on a frame was becoming common also, even for large narrative paintings which in other parts of Italy at the time would have been normally painted in fresco, on the spot. In the damp and salty air of Venice, it was found that paintings

on canvas lasted better than frescoes.

Another feature of Venetian painting evident in many works of Giovanni Bellini is a strong feeling for landscape. No one exemplifies it better than that enigmatic genius, Giorgione (a name, incidentally, that seems to have been bestowed upon him after his death), who is thought to have been a pupil of Bellini. Very little is known of Giorgione except that he died of the plague in 1510, when he was in his early thirties. The works definitely ascribed to him can be numbered on the fingers of one hand, though there are several others thought to be by him, including some that appear to have been finished by Titian, a fellow-pupil of Bellini but slightly younger, probably after Giorgione's death. *The Tempest* (page 216),

Above:
TITIAN, *Assumption of the Virgin*, 1516-18. Sta Maria Gloriosa dei Frari, Venice.

Right:
GIOVANNI BELLINI, *Madonna and Child*, about 1480. Burrell Collection, Glasgow Art Gallery and Museum.

in Venice, is probably the most famous of the handful of undisputed Giorgiones. The subject of this painting is a mystery – it appears to have been changed during the course of composition – and the mystery is enhanced by the calm and peaceful figures set in a landscape in which a violent storm is turning the sky black and brilliantly lighting up the buildings in the background.

The outstanding master of the Venetian school and one of the greatest painters who ever lived was Titian (*c*. 1477-1576) who owes at least some of his great reputation to his long life (he died in his eighties) and to the fact that he retained his powers until his death. As a young man he collaborated with Giorgione, and the extent of their collaboration is one of the great problems of Renaissance studies. Titian's early work signalled a number of important innovations in Venetian painting, in particular an increased emphasis on the human figure and greater vigour and excitement. Painters like Giovanni Bellini had generally painted small figures in an expansive setting; their pictures were refined and restrained. In Titian's *Assumption of the Virgin* (opposite), an enormous work (seven metres high) painted for a church in Venice about 1517, the figures take up so much of the space that the background is excluded, and the scene has a vivid drama and energy quite foreign to Venetian traditions. Though there is not much evidence of Michelangelo's influence in the figures, the inspiration of this work is more Roman than Venetian (a number of fine Venetian artists, including Lorenzo Lotto (page 213) had been lured to the Rome of Raphael and Michelangelo).

Below:
Tintoretto, *The Finding of the Body of St Mark*, about 1562. The artist gave great drama to his picture of this famous incident in Venetian legend by his handling of light and dark. Pinacoteca di Brera, Milan.

GIORGIONE, *The Tempest*, about 1503.
Gallerie dell'Accademia, Venice.

With the *Assumption*, together with a number of other works of about this period, Titian formed his personal style and established his international reputation. He became court painter to the Holy Roman Emperor, Charles V, of whom he painted several marvellous and sympathetic portraits. There is a well-known story that on one occasion when Charles V, the greatest ruler in the world, was sitting for his portrait, Titian dropped his brush, whereupon the Emperor, in a gesture heavy with significance, bent down and picked it up for him. Titian was in such great demand that he worked in many different places – in Milan with the Emperor, in Rome with the Pope, in Augsburg with Philip II (son of Charles V), and of course in Venice. Not only portraits were required; equally admired were Titian's mythological scenes, like the famous *Sacred and Profane Love*, the most famous study of women in the Venetian High Renaissance, or the *Perseus and Andromeda* (opposite), a

much later work (about 1560) now in the Wallace Collection, London, and an almost equally famous example of Titian's superb handling of the female nude, in which he had no peer. His portraits, particularly those of Charles V, were humane but realistic, the painter's admiration for his sitter being no less evident than his awareness of his great difficulties. The famous portrait of *Pope Paul III with his Nephews* (page 218) is a truly astonishing work in its total lack of sycophancy: the Pope appears as a mean and ancient autocrat with rheumaticky hands, and his nephews as calculating obsequious parasites. The painting is unfinished; it seems a reasonable guess that the family did not like it. It was probably painted in 1546 and soon after this, Titian, now getting on in years and working mainly in Venice, evolved the remarkably different style of his late period.

Though he appears comparatively prolific, Titian worked in a slow and

deliberate way. He first laid a solid foundation in an earthy, reddish colour, and on top of that he applied the lighter tones, then a series of thin, transparent glazes of colour, leaving an interval between each application. In this way he achieved the depth and richness of colour for which he is famous. In his later period, two important changes are evident. The first is a tendency towards more subdued colouring, with dominant tones of blue, brown and grey and a greater preoccupation with tone rather than colour; the second is a distinct change in technique. His method of painting becomes freer, and the paint is applied in a way that might be called 'impressionist'; increasingly, he used a finger instead of the brush to soften details. This development, the causes for which have been endlessly disputed, was to be enormously important for the future of European painting, not least because Titian had come to think in terms of *paint*. Earlier painters had

216

followed a drawn outline and it is always easy to see, even in the later work of Bellini, for instance, how painting could be translated into sculpture: every fold of the dress, each strand of the hair, is precise. But Titian's later paintings could be nothing but paintings. It is, said Cecil Gould, 'paint for paint's sake', and that made Titian the most important individual influence in European painting before the Cubists arrived on the scene.

Of Titian's most notable younger contemporaries in 16th-century Venice, the most remarkable were Tintoretto and Veronese. Tintoretto (a nickname derived from his father's trade of dyer, *tintore*) is said to have written on the wall of his studio, 'The drawing of Michelangelo, the colour of Titian', those being the examples

he wished to follow. He is known to have made drawings based on Michelangelo's sculptures, and he also made experiments with small human figures of clay or wax suspended in a box at odd angles and lit by a candle shining through a hole. His style is bold, emotional, theatrical, these effects being heightened by his virtuoso manipulation of light and shadow, as in his famous *Finding of the Body of St Mark* (page 215), painted for the guild of St Mark in Venice (St Mark was, of course, the patron saint of Venice, which is why he figures so often in Venetian art. The incident portrayed here is the alleged discovery of the saint's body in Alexandria, whence it is supposed to have been brought to Venice in the 9th century.) Like Titian, Tintoretto was more interested in making a pattern

Above:
Titian, *Perseus and Andromeda*, about 1560. The use of a consistent colour tone gives unity to all parts of this picture by the greatest master of the Venetian school. Wallace Collection, London.

217

Above:
TITIAN, *Pope Paul III with his Nephews Alessandro and Ottavio*, about 1546, one of the most striking group portraits in Western art, and largely accomplished in shades of red. Museo e Galleria Nazionali di Capodimonte, Naples.

Opposite:
VAN EYCK's great picture of *The Madonna with the Chancellor Rolin*, about 1435, a technical *tour de force* by one of the most accomplished painters of the 15th century. Musée du Louvre, Paris.

Left:
VERONESE, *The Marriage at Cana*, 1563. Musée du Louvre, Paris.

of figures, less in the setting or background which formed so important a part of early Venetian painting. Again like Titian, he had a long and productive life, dying in 1594 at the age of seventy-five.

Veronese (1528-88) is an artist of a very different kind. He is most famous for his large decorative pictures in magnificent and highly detailed architectural settings (he often worked in collaboration with architects, including Palladio). He delighted in painting luxurious trap-

pings and colourful clothes, but avoided scenes with high emotional content or dramatic incident, as favoured by Tintoretto, preferring set pieces such as *The Last Supper* or his *Marriage at Cana* (opposite) now in the Louvre, which contains no less than a hundred and thirty meticulously painted figures.

The work of Titian and his younger contemporaries has taken us a long way from the early Renaissance. Italian art had always been influential in northern Europe and this

influence was to become almost overpowering after the Renaissance, but there were of course other traditions alive and flourishing elsewhere, some of them, in the beginning at any rate, owing little to Italy. In the Low Countries particularly, there was a 'renaissance' of a kind in 14th-century painting which is above all associated with the names of two artists, Jan van Eyck and Roger van der Weyden.

Van Eyck (1390-1441) was court painter to the duke of Burgundy and worked for much of his life in Bruges,

detail of costume and architecture, the powerful gift for portraiture, and the grasp of perspective, in which he excelled contemporary Italian artists. The infant does not appear satisfactory to modern eyes, but no Renaissance infants do, since people at that time did not regard them as babies, but rather as potential adults, and painted them accordingly. Another area in which Jan van Eyck was ahead of Italian contemporaries was in his use of oils. He did not invent the medium, but improved it (probably with his less-famous brother, Hubert) though it is hard to say how much the crystal-like quality of his painting is due to the clearer quality of the paint and how much to the artist's unique ability in handling the medium.

Roger van der Weyden (1399-1464) worked most of his life in Brussels, and was official painter to the city; he visited Italy in 1450, where his work was greatly admired. He did not employ the brilliant detail of van Eyck, but took a great step forward in depicting human feeling: he managed to represent the emotion of grief, which earlier Gothic artists had often stumbled badly over, with sympathetic conviction, as in his *Entombment* (page 193). It was this expressiveness, plus his well-ordered composition, that made him so powerful an influence in northern Europe for half a century after his death. His warm humanity is also evident in his portraits, such as that of Francesco d'Este in the Metropolitan Museum of Art, New York (left).

Later Flemish artists found it hard to live up to the examples of Jan van Eyck and Roger van der Weyden. The finest of them, Hugo van der Goes (*c.* 1440-82) made a strong impression on Ghirlandaio and other Florentine artists. The powerful effect of his paintings is partly due to the viewpoint adopted by van der Goes, who abandoned the convention almost universally accepted in 15th-century Flemish painting where the artist 'looks down' on the scene (as, for example, in van der Weyden's *Entombment*), and places his subjects so that they are slightly higher than the spectator, and therefore more dominant. Van der Goes is said to have had some mental trouble later in life, and

Above:
ROGER VAN DER WEYDEN, *Portrait of Francesco d'Este*, about 1450. Metropolitan Museum of Art, New York. The Michael Friedsam Collection, 1931.

where he also found patrons among the prosperous burghers of the cloth trade. His paintings have an exceptional clarity, and his brilliant detail is clearly derived from illuminated manuscripts. His grasp of pictorial structure, however, owes nothing to this tradition, but derives from his awareness of contemporary Italian painting. With all this, however, he combined remarkable talents of his own. In his portrait of the duke of Burgundy's chancellor with the Virgin and Child (page 219) all van Eyck's extraordinary virtues are displayed – the meticulous painting of the distant landscape, the exquisite

another Flemish artist who, to modern eyes anyway, shows signs of mental disturbance is that unique individual, Hieronymous Bosch (above). The fact is that his fantastic paintings, full of grotesque and sometimes ghastly incident, would have meant much more to his contemporaries than they do to us; the folklore symbolically exploited by Bosch is now mostly lost. One theory to explain the unique art of Bosch is that he was a member of an obscure heretical religious sect, though if that is true it is surprising that he was admired by, among others, Philip II of Spain, a monarch with a decidedly short way with heretics.

Above:
BOSCH, *The Temptation of St Anthony*, about 1505. Museu Nacional de Arte Antiga, Lisbon.

NE RVMPE QVIESCO.

During the second half of the 15th century the Flemish style of painting spread throughout Europe north of the Alps (and, as we have seen, also had some influence south of the Alps). It was thoroughly assimilated, for example in the work of a number of German painters and sculptors of that period, though perhaps the most notable of them, Michael Pacher (*c.* 1435-98) worked in a rather difficult style. His masterpiece, the wood altarpiece for St Wolfgang in Austria (opposite), is in the German Late Gothic tradition but owes a good deal to Italian influence, seen, for example, in the skilful use of depth to increase the dramatic effect. Pacher came from the Tyrol, not far from the Italian border, and may have visited Padua about 1470, shortly before this altarpiece, the most magnificent example of a type that was fairly common in Germany, was begun.

Northern European artists did not, of course, forsake their own long-established traditions the moment

they were confronted by the Italian Renaissance. One outstanding problem was the almost total disparity in style between the Late Gothic of the north and the classical revival of the south. A painter who was remarkably successful in assimilating Italian influence while not forsaking the German tradition was Lucas Cranach (1472-1553). He was court painter to the Elector of Saxony at Wittenberg, and often took his subjects, notably the female nude (above), from Italian art, with which he was obviously familiar. Cranach's alluring nudes, however, are completely unclassical; they are Germanic in every feature. They are also unashamedly erotic.

An artist far less successful in assimilating classical influences was the Dutch painter, Jan Gossaert, known as Mabuse, who visited Italy in 1508 and so saw his models at first hand. The unfortunate result was a rather ludicrous and undignified combination of Flemish and Italian styles. Mabuse belonged to a group of artists known as the 'Romanists' for their devotion to Roman art in the early 16th century, a devotion which had some unfortunate results of wider

Above:
Lucas Cranach, *Nymph*, about 1530. In his unabashedly erotic nudes, Cranach combined the Gothic and Italian traditions with outstanding success. Thyssen–Bornemisza Gallery, Lugano. Collection Countess Margit Batthyany-Thyssen.

Below:
Mabuse, *Neptune and Amphitrite*, about 1516. Gemäldegalerie, Berlin–Dahlem.

Opposite:
Michael Pacher, *Coronation of the Virgin*, completed 1481, one of the most magnificent wooden altarpieces in Germany. St Wolfgang.

223

significance than the odd graceless painting. What happened towards the end of the 15th century in northern Europe was that Italian art became not merely admirable, but fashionable and correct. It was no longer a matter of assimilating certain Italian influences, as Cranach did, but rather of copying, in a somewhat slavish way, the art of Renaissance Italy. Northern courts imported artists from Italy such as Pietro Torrigiano, who executed the tomb of Henry VII in London's Westminster Abbey. France in particular was closely connected with Italy after Charles VIII's invasion of 1494, and Francis I was the most eager importer of Italian artists, including Leonardo and Andrea del Sarto (though he did not stay long), giving rise to a new school of French court art, mentioned below. Clearly, northern patrons – and northern artists – were impressed by Italian art, but there was more to it than that. In Italy the Renaissance included not merely a great blossoming of the arts, but a parallel literary tradition including sophisticated theories of art criticism. There were rules by which a work of art could be judged to be 'good' or 'bad', as well as a whole vocabulary of art-critical terms. The criteria of 'good' and 'bad' were, as we have seen, dependent upon an adherence to antique models. It therefore followed that art in the classical tradition was 'good' and art not in that tradition, including all Gothic art, was 'bad'. This is of course too sweeping a generalization: not all Gothic art received unqualified condemnation, at least not from discerning critics; nevertheless, the overall tendency was powerfully in favour of Italian art, and that tendency was to continue for a long time. It had a distinctly depressing effect on much northern art.

Yet it was possible for a great artist like Albrecht Dürer (1471-1528) to accept the Italian idea that 'good' art has rules, and can be subjected to academic analysis while remaining fundamentally faithful to the German tradition. The outstanding figure of the so-called 'Northern Renaissance', Dürer was born in Nuremberg, the son of a goldsmith in whose workshop he received his early training. He is

remembered for his engravings even more than his paintings, and early examples show the influence of the detailed realism of Roger van der Weyden and the Flemish school. In 1494 he made the first of his journeys to Italy, where he made a thorough study of the basis of Italian art. For a time at least he seems to have believed that the Italians had discovered some golden rule of proportion that was the secret of beauty in art. His ideas later became much more complex, but he remained interested in academic theories and wrote books on human proportion and on measurement and perspective. Inventive and perceptive, he also wrote on fortifications and the building of towns; he was, in short, something of a northern Leonardo. In his art, however, he managed to maintain a rewarding balance between the spirit of Gothic art and German craftsmanship on the one hand and the intellectual outlook of

Above:
DÜRER, *Self-portrait*, 1498. Dürer was perhaps the most accomplished artist of the Northern Renaissance. This self-assured portrait was painted soon after his first visit to Italy. Museo del Prado, Madrid.

the Renaissance on the other. Although he was pre-eminently a master of line, in his pen-and-water-colour studies (opposite) as well as his impassioned engravings, painting, including several self-portraits (above), was hardly less important in his work as a whole.

It was in France that Italian ideas on art were most eagerly embraced. Francis I employed Italians in the building of his palace at Fontainebleau where a Franco–Italian Mannerist style was developed by artists known as the Fontainebleau School. In the decorations of the palace painting was richly combined with moulded stucco work, with soft and

Above:
DÜRER, *The Hare*, watercolour and
gouache, dated 1502. Graphische
Sammlung Albertina, Vienna.

elegant figures and much 'strapwork' (curling scrolls) and garlands (below). Another remarkable Italian who spent some years at the French court was Benvenuto Cellini (1500-71), one of the most entertaining characters (thanks to his flamboyant autobiography) of the Renaissance period. Trained as a goldsmith, the young Cellini was twice thrown out of Florence for brawling, and once escaped a sentence of death. In 1540 he arrived at Fontainebleau, bringing with him a gold salt cellar, which he finished a year or two later and presented to Francis I (opposite). It is the only undisputed surviving example of Cellini's work in precious metal, and a triumph of the Renaissance goldsmith's art. The iconography of the piece is complicated (Cellini explains it in his writings); the two figures represent Earth and Ocean, and in style accord well with the decorations at Fontainebleau. Back in Italy, Cellini, when not fleeing from various places to escape his just desserts, was much admired as a sculptor. His most famous work, a bronze figure of Perseus, may still be

seen in Florence.

The School of Fontainebleau was itself influential throughout Europe, and it is increasingly difficult to trace the influence of the Italian Renaissance, through such more or less indirect means, throughout Europe in the 16th century. At the court of the Holy Roman Emperor, for instance, in spite of the presence of Titian and other Italians at various times, the classical tradition was established largely through the works of travelling Dutch artists such as Bartholomaus Spranger, whose *Hercules and Omphale* (opposite) displays his highly individual version of the revived classical style. Much of the work of 16th-century artists in France, Germany and the Low Countries came somewhere between the two poles represented by Cranach, with his assimilation of Italian ideas into the German tradition, and Spranger, with his unreservedly Italianate, though individual, style, and as in the work of Mabuse (page 223), it often came to a rather uncomfortable compromise. The best paintings belong to genres least affected by Italian ideas,

namely portraiture and landscape.

Without doubt the finest portraitist was a German-Swiss painter, Hans Holbein (1497/8-1543), best-known, at least in England, for his portraits of Henry VIII. In such a work as the late (1542) portrait of that formidable monarch at Castle Howard (page 228) he conveyed the importance of the subject by his brilliantly detailed treatment of costume; but his most remarkable gift was for capturing some aspect of the sitter's character by subtle expression or gesture, a gift still more evident in his portraits of less powerful subjects.

By the end of the 15th century, landscape was coming to be seen as a subject in its own right, and not just a scene glimpsed through a window or filling a vacant space behind a group of figures. Discounting a drawing of the Arno valley by Leonardo in 1473, the Flemish painter Joachim Patenier (1485-1524), an acquaintance of Dürer, is sometimes regarded as the first landscape painter in this sense (first in the West, that is; we have seen that in China landscape painting was many centuries older). A better

known landscape artist is his near contemporary, Albrecht Altdorfer (*c.* 1480-1538), a native of Bavaria who was deeply impressed by the scenery of the Austrian Alps during a journey down the Danube in 1511 (page 229). His landscapes still tend towards fantasy, though less so than Patenier's, and he also liked to include buildings of elaborate architecture in his pictures.

The greatest landscape artist of the 16th century, however, was Pieter Brueghel the Elder (1529-69), founder of a distinguished family of painters of whom the best known, after himself, are his sons Jan and Pieter Brueghel the Younger (1568-1625 and 1564-1638 respectively). The elder Brueghel, born near Bruges, paid the now customary visit to Italy as a young man, but was more impressed by the scenery on the way than he was by Italian painting. The greatest artistic influence on him was probably Bosch, and the element of satire, though not always of a particularly savage kind, is usually evident in his well-known pictures of peasant life which earned him the nickname 'Peasant' Brueghel. Like Bosch, Brueghel is sometimes hard to interpret, though a fruitful source of study for social historians. His *Landscape with Gallows* (page 230) combines a scene of apparently carefree country life in idyllic scenery with the ominous

Above:
BARTHOLOMAUS SPRANGER, *Hercules and Omphale*, 1575-80. Kunsthistorisches Museum, Vienna.

Right:
BENVENUTO CELLINI, *The Royal Salt*, completed 1543, probably the most famous surviving example of the Renaissance goldsmith's art. Kunsthistorisches Museum, Vienna.

Opposite:
PRIMATICCIO, *Detail from the Chambre de la Duchesse d'Etampes*, Fontainebleau, about 1541-45, paint and stucco.

presence of the gallows, reminder of violence and death. Experts have argued at length concerning the significance, if any, of the magpie perched on the gallows, and over whether the wayside cross, apparently pointing towards the village church in the middle distance, is intended to convey a religious message. These details, fascinating though they may be, need not detain us. More important to note is the brilliance of the painting of the summery countryside – not, as it happens, very typical of Brueghel's landscapes, in which Nature is usually more remote, or harsher, as in his many well-known scenes in the snow.

In spite of the peasant jollities, Brueghel's work carries pessimistic undertones, a reflection, perhaps, of the troubled times he lived in, when religious and political strife was tearing the Netherlands apart. Though he was successful in his own day, he was rated less highly than other artists painting in the Italian style, who today are almost completely forgotten, and admirers like Rubens notwithstanding, he continued to be

underrated until comparatively recent times. As late as 1916, a great expert on Dutch painting remarked that he hardly dared to suggest that Brueghel might be mentioned in the same breath as Jan van Eyck, for fear of sounding provocative. But Brueghel's rescue is now complete, and he stands among the greatest of the Dutch masters.

The Age of Baroque

'The age of Baroque' is a convenient term to describe European art from the late 16th to the late 18th century – the period dividing the Renaissance from the Modern period. The word 'baroque', however, in a stricter sense describes a style of art, and not all art in Europe during the two centuries of the Baroque period was in the Baroque style. A feature of the period is the growing variety of artistic styles and the increasing importance of regional styles and schools of artists.

One reason for the proliferation of regional centres of art was political, and stemmed from the changes in the European system caused by the Reformation. The monopoly of power enjoyed by the Roman Catholic Church in Europe until the 16th century had ended, and with the rise of Protestantism came the rise of powerful nation-states, acknowledging no authority, political or religious, beyond their own frontiers. Power remained in the hands of the traditional ruling classes, and governments like that of Louis XIV in France were strong (if not necessarily efficient) and authoritarian. The overthrow of the old regime in the French Revolution of 1789 marks a convenient end to the period. It did not, of course, mark the end of powerful, authoritarian governments in Europe, but cracks were already appearing in the system long before 1789. The rise of modern science in the 17th century prepared the way for a sceptical, rational age in the 18th century, in which religious influences were in decline and the doctrine of political freedom was in the ascendant.

All these developments had their effect on artists. Nevertheless, in some important respects the situation for artists was little changed. They still worked for the same kind of patrons – the court, the Church and the aristocracy – and they still made the same kind of works of art and took their subjects from the same sources – the Bible and classical literature. Antique art remained the foundation on which most contemporary art rested, although artists of the Baroque period viewed classical Rome to a large extent through the eyes of Renaissance Rome.

The beginning of the most significant developments in the age of Baroque can be seen in the Renaissance period. One of these was the rise of *genre* painting – scenes from everyday life. We have already seen examples of it in the work of Brueghel, and it was in the Netherlands especially that this development took place. In that country, the traditional patrons of art scarcely existed since the Dutch had formed an independent, Protestant republic, and therefore the taste of the middle classes, a rising influence elsewhere too, had a vital role to play. Other, traditionally humbler categories of art, such as portrait-painting and still-life (inanimate natural objects, most typically flowers and fruits, painted at close range), came into their own. The decorative arts such as furniture and porcelain (not made in Europe until the 18th century) were brought into the mainstream of stylistic developments.

The Baroque period is so called because the Baroque style, although only one of the art styles of the 17th and 18th centuries, was the predominant one in European art of that time. The characteristics of Baroque style are greater emotion and movement. Almost everything is pitched in a higher key, the tone is more florid and colourful, textures are richer, there is more decoration, more contrasts between light and shadow, more freedom, and occasionally an evident

conscious striving for effect, which was for a long time to give Baroque a bad name. The style originated in Italy in the late 16th century and spread to most of Europe, taking on slightly different forms in different countries. It is sometimes said that there is no Baroque in England, and it is true that there was nothing quite like the work of, for example, Bernini, but it is more helpful to say that Baroque in England was rather different from Baroque in Italy or in Germany.

There were styles in the Baroque period that were in no sense 'Baroque', and this was a time of increasing divergence of style. There was a more strictly classical tradition which in the second half of the 18th century merged into what is called the Neoclassical style, superseding Baroque and opening the way to Modern art. There was also Naturalism, or Realism, associated in particular with the powerful influence of Caravaggio on much 17th-century European paint-

ing and with the Dutch school of which Rembrandt was the outstanding master. Finally, there was a fourth style which was a direct offshoot of Baroque in the 18th century – Rococo.

Although it would hardly be possible to discuss any kind of art without recourse to the labels that are appended to styles, it is important to remember that there was hardly any such creature as a pure 'Baroque' painter. The name, like most other art-historical labels, was invented later. The existence of these labels can lead to almost as much misunderstanding as clarification, because it is easy to lose sight of the fact that every great artist has his or her own style, not made to fit into the categories of later art historians, and even to fall into the error of making aesthetic judgments based on some generally accepted convention that may be of only limited relevance to the work of art concerned.

The word 'baroque' is thought to

come from a Portuguese word meaning a misshapen pearl. In 16th-century France and Italy it was applied in a metaphorical sense to any idea or thought process that was very involved or contorted. It was not until the late 18th century, when Neoclassicism held sway, that it came to be applied to art, and then in a wholly derogatory sense, meaning a picture or sculpture that ignored classical rules of proportion. Later it was used to refer to 17th-century Italian architecture in particular, then to all forms of art in similar style, but still in a

derogatory sense. It was only very slowly that 'Baroque', like 'Victorian' somewhat later, ceased to be a term of disapproval. Throughout the 19th century, Baroque art was seen by most people as merely a degenerate continuation of the style of the Renaissance, and in countries like England where the Baroque style in the Italian or the German sense never found much sympathy this prejudice continued into very recent times; perhaps it has not entirely disappeared yet.

The offshoot of Baroque known as 'Rococo' also originally meant something much more restricted than it does now. The word comes from the French *rocaille*, which described the motifs of rock and shell work in 16th-century decoration. Just as we connect the word 'baroque' with architecture, so 'rococo' is typically associated with decoration – decoration of a fanciful, flamboyant kind with lots of swirling scrolls and garlands, in which symmetry is deliberately abandoned. Thus Rococo was both a development from and a reaction against Baroque, in much the same way as Mannerism was both a reaction and development of the style of the Renaissance.

Baroque art in the narrower sense of the word was characteristic of the more conservative countries in Europe – Italy, Spain, and parts of southern Germany which remained loyal to the Roman Catholic Church and retained a semi-feudal, rural society. It was less evident in a country like England, which was Protestant and economically advanced. To some extent, therefore, Baroque art represented the Roman Church, and large religious works – churches, altars, devotional sculptures, and so on – are the most typical products, though not, of course, the only ones of the Baroque style. One negative aspect of the Protestant Reformation as far as art is concerned was that religious images were no longer made for churches – indeed, at certain times and in certain places Protestant iconoclasts destroyed magnificent medieval religious works.

It is in religious art that the direct emotional appeal which is so marked a feature of Baroque art makes its most dramatic appearance. We have seen how artists in the Renaissance became concerned with representing emotion, and this concern became much greater in the Baroque period. One of the most famous examples is a marble sculpture by Bernini in Rome, *The Ecstasy of St Teresa* (page 233). The incident represented is the Saint's vision of the love of God which she experienced as a flaming arrow thrust into her by an angel. Bernini wished to present the feelings of the saint in visual terms, and it would be hard to imagine a more remarkable attempt: the work is charged with a kind of mystical energy. But besides its almost overpowering emotionalism, *The Ecstasy of St Teresa* demonstrates many other features of the Baroque – its sensation of upward movement, the striking use of light (natural light comes from a concealed source to augment the effect of the golden metal rays), and the use of illusionism to heighten the emotional appeal.

Giovanni Lorenzo Bernini (1598-1680) studied sculpture with his father and was fortunate in acquiring as an early patron a man who was subsequently elected Pope as Urban VIII (who remarked at the time that the world was fortunate to have him for Pope but even more fortunate to have Bernini to decorate his pontificate). His earliest sculptures show Bernini's extraordinary ability to make marble look like any other material, however unlikely – flesh, cloth, bark, even feathers. He delighted in overcoming the physical qualities of his medium, annihilating the solidity of marble, a notion that would have been anathema to Michelangelo (and to most modern artists). But still more remarkable was his arrangement. His dynamic, swirling figures make gestures that lead the eye off in diagonals suggesting a focus-point outside the work itself; everything is momentary, instantaneous. Bernini was immensely popular in his own lifetime. Summoned to Paris by Louis XIV, who wanted him to work on the Louvre, his journey was like the progress of royalty, with city corporations turning out to honour him and triumphal arches erected along his route.

Spectacular illusionism, of which Bernini was so great a master, was not a simple matter of realistic reproduction. The *St Teresa* is hardly 'realistic'; on the contrary, it is highly imaginative; but it is certainly convincing in the sense that the incident almost seems to be actually happening before the eyes of the spectator. No one was more keenly aware than Bernini that, as he put it while working on a bust of Louis XIV (the outstanding result of his visit to France; the Louvre project came to nothing), in order to imitate the model faithfully, it is sometimes necessary to put in something that does not exist in the model. As an example, he cited the case of the darkness some people have around the eyes, an effect created in sculpture by hollowing out the marble in that place. Another illusionistic device which Bernini was one of the first to use was to place the focus outside the work, where the spectator is standing. An example of this in painting was the equestrian portrait, in which the rider is pictured head-on and appears to be about to ride out of the frame. (This device was invented as early as 1590 by El Greco, a Spanish artist whose very varied background and extraordinary personal style make him particularly difficult to fit into any category; his powerful rhythm and movement, however, have something of the Baroque spirit.) This form of illusionism, designed to startle, was another characteristic feature of Baroque art, in which the reaction of the spectator is more carefully considered than in the art of almost any other style.

Bernini is the central figure of Baroque, and exemplifies the tendency for the different art forms to come together at that time. Architecture moved closer to sculpture, and sculpture to painting. Painting, however, became more strictly visual, representing what the eye actually sees, rather than what the spectator knows he is looking at. It did this by a

Opposite:
BERNINI, *Angel with Superscription*, 1668. Bernini started with a classical statue as model for this more than life-size marble but transformed it into an extreme form of Baroque. San Andrea delle Fratte, Rome.

234

greater concern with colour and tone rather than form and outline, a development we have already seen beginning in Venetian painting. Bernini had studied painting and stage design as a young man and his sculptures, like the *St Teresa*, which is framed like a picture by columns and pediment, make use of effects of architecture and painting. As with some Hindu temples, it is a moot point whether a work such as the *Baldacchino* (a canopy over a throne or, in this case, altar) in St Peter's, Rome (partly executed by Francesco Borromini) is architecture or sculpture, while the use of coloured marbles and bronze in the work suggests the effects of painting.

Coloured marbles and gilded wood carvings were aspects of the Baroque artists' effort to enchant the spectator by sheer visual splendour – rich colours, gorgeous tapestries, lavish furniture. Even the interior of a

church could become a brilliantly dazzling decorative set-piece (opposite). There was a new emphasis on sensuous beauty, as in Rubens's paintings of healthy, glowing flesh and rich, deeply textured clothes.

Peter Paul Rubens (1577-1640), the supreme master of Baroque painting in northern Europe, though born in Germany, came from a lawyer's family in Antwerp, where he grew up. Belgium, or more properly the Spanish Netherlands, remained part of the old order in Europe, under the rule of Spain, loyal to the Roman Catholic Church, and with an aristocratic class who patronized the arts. The young Rubens was educated by the Jesuits and prepared for the courtly life as a page to a countess. His early training as an artist was in the Flemish 'Romanist' tradition, and in 1600 he went to Italy, where he was court painter to the duke of Mantua. He remained mainly in Italy for the next

237

eight years, studying the Italian masters and being particularly influenced by Titian and the Venetians. On his return to Flanders, to take up a court position in Brussels, his prodigious career blossomed. He opened a studio that did enormous business and where prices were scaled according to the amount of work put in by Rubens himself, paintings by Rubens alone being naturally the most expensive. Quite apart from his artistic achievements, he made a large fortune, but unlike many artistic geniuses, he was a good administrator, and the products of his studio were of consistently high quality. One of the by-products of his remarkable output was a whole school of engravers busily occupied reproducing the works of his studio. Rubens was also a considerable scholar, a collector of art, books and manuscripts and an able diplomat who spoke five languages fluently. His total output of paintings was said to have exceeded 3,000, besides some 400 drawings.

Rubens's prodigal genius is difficult to approach if only because it was so many-sided. He created masterpieces in every field of painting: religious, allegorical, classical, landscape, portraiture, and so on. He was the first painter to develop the techniques of true Baroque movement, building his compositions around a dynamic spiral line, starting in the foreground, usually near one corner, and swirling upwards and inwards, giving a tremendous vitality to the picture. This device can be seen in *The Assumption of the Virgin* (page 237). The sharp foreshortening of figures, a means of gaining greater depth and dramatic emphasis, is also characteristic of Baroque painting, as are the swirling draperies, which are not quite realistic but charged with inner energy, the strong highlights, and the way in which figures merge into one another, making it difficult for the eye to separate one and consider it in isolation from the whole.

Rubens's first wife was Isabella Brant. The affection and happiness apparent in his portrait of himself with his wife at about the time of their marriage (opposite) continued until her early death. A few years later, when he was approaching fifty, Rubens married a girl of sixteen, who appears in many of his paintings, either as herself or as a model in religious and mythological works. He visited Spain twice, meeting Velasquez, and London, where King Charles I, the greatest art patron of his day, commissioned him to paint a self-portrait, a remarkable honour; he also painted the ceiling of the Banqueting Hall, Whitehall, recently restored to its original splendour.

Another Flemish painter who spent some time in England was Anthony van Dyck (1599-1641). He was Rubens's favourite pupil, and was like him in style, though less exuberant, following the more courtly side of Rubens's art. Like his master, he was influenced by the great Italian painters, especially Titian. By the late 1620s he had a studio in Antwerp which rivalled that of Rubens, but in 1632 he went to England, where he remained until his early death, and it is for his portraits of the royal family and other English notables, especially

the king himself (above), that he is chiefly remembered. Charles II gave him a knighthood and married him off to an English lady. Van Dyck's portraits are court portraiture at its best, though we may be sure that the ladies of the Stuart court were rather less beautiful than van Dyck makes them appear. He lacked the acute accuracy of Holbein as well as the pulsing energy of Rubens, but his gift for conveying humane aristocratic distinction was unrivalled, and more than anyone else he deserves the

credit for founding the tradition of English portraiture which was to reach its peak in the work of Gainsborough and Reynolds over a century later.

The divergence of political and social developments in Holland resulted in the rise of the Dutch school of painting as something quite separate from Flemish painting. Flanders (the southern Netherlands) remained under Spanish domination in the early 17th century, loyal to the Roman Catholic Church and with

Above:
Van Dyck, *Charles I on Horseback*, 1649. Royal Collection.

Opposite:
Van Dyck, *Marchesa Balbi*, about 1625. This portrait of an aristocratic lady from Genoa is a superb example of Baroque portraiture. National Gallery of Art, Washington, DC. Andrew Mellon Collection.

240

241

the aristocracy playing an important role. Holland (the northern Netherlands) had broken away, established its independence, after a long struggle in which a vigorous tradition of nationalism was formed, and eventually became a predominantly Protestant, republican state. One result was the virtual elimination of religious painting, which still remained one of the strongest traditions in Flanders and other Catholic countries (many Dutch painters, notably Rembrandt, did sometimes paint religious subjects, but there was no great ecclesiastical art, serving Catholic doctrine). Another type of painting that found little favour in Holland was historical painting. The confident and prosperous Dutch merchants who had successfully rebelled against Habsburg rule, created the most thriving state in Europe and even succeeded, for a time, in wresting control of the seas from the English, wanted – and were well able to pay for – art that reflected their own society as faithfully as possible. That meant portraits, but not only portraits; the ordinary affairs of everyday life, their homes, their towns and their social institutions became fit subjects for art. Portraits, however, were most important, and some artists, notably Frans Hals, painted scarcely anything else.

Frans Hals (1580-1666) was actually of Flemish descent, though he lived most of his life in Haarlem (dying in the building that is now the Frans Hals Museum). He was a member of a remarkable family of artists, of whom the best known after himself is his brother, Dirck. All seven of his sons became painters, striking evidence of the extent of artistic patronage in 17th-century Holland. Hals is remembered especially for his ability to render a lively expression, as in his famous *The Laughing Cavalier*, or his group portraits, in which he overcame the difficult problem (in a sense more successfully than Rembrandt in similar circumstances) of

Above:
Jan Steen, *The World Upside-Down*, about 1663. Steen concentrated on *genre* pictures, and though this example is ostensibly a warning to behave oneself, it is clear that Steen privately cherished some affection for a rather anarchical domestic life. Kunsthistorisches Museum, Vienna.

Opposite:
Detail from *The Merry Toper* by Frans Hals (1580-1666). Rijksmuseum, Amsterdam.

showing a group of faces in which none were emphasized at the expense of the others, while avoiding a stiff composition of rows of figures. Hals used colours with restraint but adopted a lively technique, frequently dispensing with any background detail and indicating the less important parts of the painting with broad, fluent brushstrokes that could be said to anticipate French impressionism, over two hundred years later.

The Dutch school of the 17th century sought a new kind of realism

Left:
FRANS HALS (1580-1666), *Portrait of Zaffius*. Frans Halsmuseum, Haarlem.

– a faithful record of the way of life of the Dutch people. Realism in art is of course always to some extent relative, and perhaps what the Dutch painters recorded was not so much the Dutch way of life but their way of life as the

Left:
FRANS HALS (1580-1666), *Portrait of Zaffius*. Frans Halsmuseum, Haarlem.

Dutch people liked to see it – not by any means the same thing. Moreover, as a picture is an artificial thing, limited by purely physical considerations such as the fact that it occupies a precisely defined space, there is – even in the most determinedly realistic painting – more artifice than may at first appear. Nevertheless, no society before, and possibly none since, has been so faithfully recorded by its painters. Nearly every type of environment was pictured – the Dutch countryside with its windmills, canals and farms, the coast and its shipping, people of all classes, old and young (some of Hals's most impressive portraits are of the old people in the almshouse where he spent his declining years), the furniture, objects and food of Dutch households, street and market scenes, clothes and uniforms,

and so on. And all were treated in realistic terms: each part of the composition was painted with the same attention, in natural light, and from direct observation. However, there were stylistic conventions of one kind or another, which can be observed, as time went on, going in and out of fashion and becoming less obtrusive and more flexible. Early landscapes, for example, show every leaf painted in careful, painstaking detail, but are often somewhat artificial in composition. A closer approach to realism is signalled by the adoption of an eye-level view, instead of one artificially raised; by more sober colours; then by a growing grasp of form, so that the landscape acquires greater depth. But besides this subtle evolution of style individual painters had, of course, their own style; a certain golden glow of sunlight is associated with Albrecht Cuyp (below), a grander, heavier, more Baroque style with Jacob

Opposite:
ALBRECHT CUYP, *Cattle and Figures*,
about 1660, a fine example of Cuyp's
fondness for lighting his pictures with
what seem to be the rays of the setting
sun. The National Gallery, London.

Above:
CARAVAGGIO, *David with the Head of
Goliath*, about 1605. Caravaggio is one of
those artists who is no less important for
his influence on other painters than for
his own extraordinary work. He
modelled Goliath's features on his own.
Galleria Borghese, Rome.

Ruisdael, and so on. The greater the master, the more important are the personal characteristics of his style.

The greater master of the Dutch school and one of the greatest painters who ever lived was Rembrandt van Rijn (1606-69). He was born in Leyden into a well-to-do miller's family, and studied under Pieter Lastman, a painter of some contemporary popularity in Amsterdam. Though he never visited Italy himself, the young Rembrandt was influenced at second or third hand by Italian artists, especially Michelangelo Caravaggio (1573-1610). Indeed, Caravaggio's influence on Rembrandt and

Opposite:
CARAVAGGIO, *The Conversion of St Paul*, 1600-01. Santa Maria del Popolo, Rome.

Below:
CARAVAGGIO, *Bacchus*, about 1590. Uffizi Gallery, Florence.

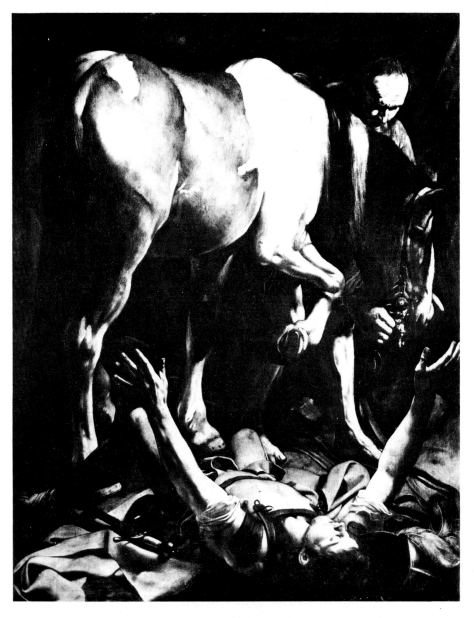

on the Dutch school as a whole would be hard to exaggerate. At a very early age Caravaggio developed a naturalistic style in reaction against the prevailing Mannerism of Rome in the late 16th century, delighting in the faces of ordinary folk instead of the idealized figures that appeared in the canvases of his contemporaries. Even more important than his naturalism, however, was his dramatic use of light and shade to define form and provide emotional intensity; this technique is known as *chiaroscuro*. We have seen how some Renaissance artists, notably Correggio, were interested in such effects (which the development of oil painting made possible), but Caravaggio was far more forceful, sometimes almost melodramatic; his *Conversion of St Paul* (left) is a good example.

At first in Leyden, and later in the wider environment of Amsterdam, Rembrandt established himself as a painter with considerable success. He married a girl called Saskia, with whom he was very happy, and whom he painted almost as often as he painted himself. One of his first major commissions, from the Company of Surgeons, was to paint a certain Doctor Tulp giving a lesson in anatomy. This somewhat macabre subject was a fairly common one in contemporary painting, but Rembrandt brought fresh ideas to a hackneyed theme, exploiting to the full the contrast between the lively expressions on the faces of the students and the still, white form of the corpse. In some respects, though, this was the work of a young artist who has not quite found his feet. The strong focus at the centre, achieved by brilliant light, makes some of the outer faces lose impact, and there is something not quite right in the handling of space. The heads are very well arranged, but some are clearly posed – the artist could not get them all concentrating equally on the lesson – and would there be room for the lower limbs of the bodies to which the heads are attached? In spite of these slight

Left:
REMBRANDT, *The Anatomy Lesson*, a later painting than his *Anatomy Lesson of Doctor Tulp*. Rijksmuseum, Amsterdam.

247

imperfections, the painting was a notable success and marked an important stage in Rembrandt's rise to fame.

Another famous group portrait, popularly known as *The Night Watch* (above), was painted in 1642, about ten years later, and was rather less popular at the time. Again, Rembrandt sacrificed some of the portraits of individual members of this company of the civic guard in the interests of the composition as a whole; their faces are almost lost in the encompassing darkness, and it is not surprising that they expressed some dissatisfaction with the finished painting. This picture, in fact, is sometimes regarded as a turning point in Rembrandt's career. It coincided with the death of his wife (leaving him with a small son, Titus) which must have been a severe blow. He hired a young woman, Geertge Dircx, as a nurse, who became his mistress, an irregularity frowned on by the puritanical Dutch. This, together with the relative failure of *The Night Watch*. on top of severe financial worries, marked a change in his fortunes. Rembrandt gradually sank deeper into debt, and in 1656 was declared bankrupt; his house and paintings were sold off to pay his debts. His son and his mistress both died before him. He was never without patrons, and in his last years he became a figure of respect, though remaining poor. Like many great artists, Rembrandt was not properly appreciated by his contemporaries,

who preferred less talented but more fashionable men. Yet it was in his later years, when his personal circumstances must have been far from happy, that his greatest work was produced. Some people believe that personal hardship is actually a catalyst in the work of artistic creation. Whether or not this is true, what is certain is that really great artists do not, as a rule, suffer any dimunution of their creative spirit in face of personal difficulties of the kind which Rembrandt experienced. His famous

painting of *Bathsheba* (above), now
in the Louvre, was painted in 1654,
not long before all his possessions had
to be sold.

It is difficult to sum up Rembrandt's achievement in a few words.
He took the method of Caravaggio
and his disciples and added to it two
unique gifts of his own: his profound,
loving and ever-growing insight into
human nature, and his extraordinary
technical ability. Although he had
much in common with the Dutch
school from whom he emerged – his
interest in portraiture, his concern

with light – he transcended any art
movement of his time. His development can be followed through the
numerous self-portraits, from youth
to extreme old age; no painter delighted more in himself as a subject,
and no painter showed less signs of
egotism in self-portrayal: these paintings are the record of his urgent search
into human character. His studies of
women display equally penetrating
analysis. The *Bathsheba* has been
called one of the noblest, most poig-
nant and psychologically most realistic treatments of sex in the history of

Above:
REMBRANDT, *Bathsheba*, 1654. Musée du
Louvre, Paris.

art. (Bathsheba was the woman
whom King David saw bathing in
Jerusalem, and for whom he had her
husband, Uriah, sent into a battle
where he was certain to be killed,
allowing David to marry Bathsheba,
who became the mother of Solomon.)
Rembrandt's female nudes are not, in
general, physically attractive in a
superficial sense; this is an exception,
perhaps because the model was not

his wife or his mistress but an engraving of a classical relief, though the work is, of course, with its deep human realism, worlds away from classical art. The artist has brilliantly captured the conflict of emotions in the woman who has just read David's letter expressing his desire for her.

Rembrandt's was a prodigal genius. Though portraits formed the major part of his output, he also painted religious and mythological scenes, still-lifes, genre pictures and landscapes. He even experimented with painting in the Mughal style (see Chapters Six and Seven), which was

Right:
An etching of his mother by REMBRANDT (1606-69).

Below:
VERMEER, *A Lady and Gentleman at the Virginals*, about 1660. The virginals were keyboard instruments, forerunners of the piano. Royal Collection.

then becoming known in Europe. He made thousands of drawings, searching and experimenting with different possibilities, and retained a lifelong interest in etching (opposite). This technique was known since the beginning of the 16th century and is similar to engraving, except that the incisions are made in the metal plate not by cutting but with acid. The plate is covered with a wax ground, on which the artist draws with a needle, cutting through the wax but not marking the plate, and the plate is then immersed in acid, which bites into the exposed parts of the metal.

Rembrandt towers over Dutch painting in the 17th century like a giant, but a little below his level there were a host of fine painters known, perhaps a little unfairly, as the 'Little Masters', who specialized in genre painting – the recording of the prosperous, satisfying and unpretentious life of the country. Each artist tended to have his own speciality, which could be the unruly characters to be seen enjoying themselves at the inn, or the class which paid them – the merchants and tradesmen with their wives and daughters, pictured in some quiet domestic occupation, often playing musical instruments as in Vermeer's *A Lady and Gentleman at the Virginals* (opposite). Although Vermeer belongs to this group, he stands a little apart. His pictures share their characteristics of subject matter, small size, and highly realistic treatment, but are distinctive in their sense of quiet intimacy; typically there are only one or two figures in his interiors, quietly concentrating on what they are doing and, unlike the group portraits of Hals or Rembrandt, oblivious of the attentive eye of the artist. The contemplative stillness of Vermeer and his assured composition is quietly satisfying (perhaps it is this quality which makes Vermeer prints so common in doctors' and dentists' waiting rooms).

A realist of a very different kind from the Dutch school was the Spaniard Diego de Silva y Velasquez (1599-1660). Although there were no Spanish painters of international reputation before El Greco (1541-1614), there was a popular tradition in Spain of carved and painted

Above:
VELASQUEZ, *Philip IV of Spain*, 1635. This painting consciously echoes an equestrian portrait of Charles V by Titian. Museo del Prado, Madrid.

Top:
EL GRECO, *Christ Driving the Traders from the Temple*. About 1600. National Gallery, London.

251

wooden sculpture, particularly religious images, of startling realism (eyelashes of real hair, for example) for altars or for carrying in processions, which had its effect on the style of Velasquez. Although he visited Italy, Italian art, with the exception of Caravaggio, seems to have had little influence on him. He was appointed court painter at Madrid in 1625, and he is best known for his portraits of the Spanish court. They are, however, portraits of a different kind from those produced about the same time by Van Dyck in England. He conveyed all the stiffness and grandeur of the Spanish court, as in his famous equestrian portrait of Philip IV (page 251), but his portraits give the impression of frail human creatures inside the majestic trappings, people rather less grand than their clothes. They are somehow not quite as dignified as they are trying to appear.

In his court paintings, Velasquez never lost the sympathetic, rather pessimistic view of human frailty which also appeared in his paintings of humbler folk – peasants, water-sellers, dwarfs and clowns. This quality, together with his gift for conveying mysterious, suppressed feelings in his sitters struggling to the surface (but not quite reaching it) is perhaps most evident in a late group portrait, *Las Meninas*, 'The Maids of Honour', (opposite), in which the painter has portrayed himself, together with the lady attendants, pets and dwarfs which surround the figure of the little princess. They are looking at the Spanish king and queen, whose portrait is being painted and who are seen reflected in a mirror at the back of the room. A servant, who has brought a drink for the princess while she watches, is just going out of the door. This uniquely intimate painting, a genre scene rather than a courtly group portrait, is interesting in many ways, not the least being that it shows the painter at work, indicating a new self-consciousness entering painting and the artist's interest in his medium.

Few painters except Rembrandt were so original in their use of paint, which Velasquez applied less to reveal and define forms than to veil

them slightly, drawing attention to the paint itself. Examining his treatment of a richly brocaded dress, we feel that it is the paint rather than the material which is of interest. Thus, in details, Velasquez is no realist at all, though the picture considered as a whole offers a perfect example of the artist's zeal for optical realism: the sense of space in the room, for example, is perfectly conveyed (and is one of the qualities which link Velasquez with the Baroque).

So far in this chapter on the Baroque period in European art we have considered the 'pure' Baroque style of Bernini in Italy and the school of realism as typified by the masters of the Dutch school, and in a different style, by Velasquez. Turning to a third stream in 17th-century art, we encounter the classicism of France in the reign of Louis XIV, which lasted from 1643 to 1715. During the second half of the 16th century France experienced troubled, miserable times; the country was torn by religious wars, marked by the savagery of the notorious Massacre of St Batholomew (1572). Henry IV reunited the country at the beginning of the 17th century and laid the basis for the authoritarian state of Louis XIV, the grandest, most powerful, and most pretentious monarch of the age. Under Louis, the 'Sun King', French society was fashioned in his image, and his reign coincided with the Classic period of French art. 'Classic', rather than 'classical', for although the influence of antiquity was important, 'Classicism' implies more general qualities: a sense of restraint, and a belief that intellectual qualities are more important than emotional ones. To some extent Classicism was a conscious reaction against the Baroque, but although artists were more respectful towards classical traditions than were Baroque artists, Classicism was not merely reactionary; it was in its way no less creative than Baroque; classical principles of clarity, harmony, balance, were followed, but not slavishly. As time went on, in fact, Classicists became less classical, which eventually resulted, in the late 18th century, in a renewed effort to return to purer classical principles known to us as the Neo-classical

movement.

One of the first, and perhaps most purely classical, painters was Nicolas Poussin (1594-1665), who came from a poor Norman family. Not until the age of thirty did he achieve his long-cherished ambition to go to Rome, where his genius flourished. Besides the ancient sculpture of Greece and Rome, the strongest influence on him was that of Raphael, the great exemplar for 17th-century Classicists. He also learned much from Titian, especially his warmth and colour, but his later works sacrifice much of these qualities in the interests of greater clarity and calm logic. 'My nature leads me to seek out and cherish things which are well ordered, shunning confusion which is as contrary and menacing to me as dark shadows are to the light of day,' he wrote, and his paintings took on a mood of austere gravity, in which movement is restrained, the figures are generally comparatively small in relation to landscape, there are no oblique lines and all is composed with logical exactness. His paintings are remote, though beautiful, with outlines precisely indicated, as, for example, in *The Burial of Phocion*. (The incident pictured here is the burial of an Athenian statesman, whose ashes were scattered outside the city because of his refusal to abandon an unpopular policy under pressure from the mob.)

In Claude Lorrain (1600-82), the supremacy of mind over emotion is less marked. He was also humbly born and orphaned young, but a stroke of luck brought him to Italy in the company of some travelling merchants when he was still a youth, and he worked in artists' studios in Naples and Rome. Like Poussin, he found Rome more congenial than his native country, and apart from one short trip never returned. The landscapes of Claude (as he is often known), unlike those of the Dutch school, are not painted from life, but are idealized – and a good deal tidier than any actual landscape. The figures in the landscape are even less important than they are in Poussin, and were in fact sometimes painted by somebody else when Claude was turning out commissions for his Italian patrons. It is

Above:
VELASQUEZ, *Las Meninas* (The Maids of
Honour), 1656, a very unconventional
group which includes a self-portrait.
Museo del Prado, Madrid.

perhaps curious that two artists, friends, both French, both living in Italy, both primarily concerned with landscape (Claude especially), and both inspired by the same traditions, should have had such different styles. In Claude it is the subject-matter rather than the style which is classical. His sense of poetry and wonder, his bewitching soft light, qualities which grew more pronounced as he grew older, made his paintings picturesque, in the best sense of the word. It is perhaps not so surprising that Poussin, with his cool logic, should have been very popular in his native France (and perhaps more attractive to later artists than to people generally), while Claude should have enjoyed such a vogue in England. The great 19th-century English landscape

Left:
CLAUDE LORRAIN, *Landscape with the Nymph Egeria*, 1669. Museo e Galleria Nazionali di Capodimonte, Naples.

Below:
WATTEAU, *Fête in a Park*, 1720-21. Wallace Collection, London.

painter, Turner, another master of luminous effects of sunlight, wanted his paintings to hang beside those of Claude in the National Gallery in London.

In France during the early 18th century there was a reaction against the repression of the last, dark years of Louis XIV which found its expression in the gay frivolous style of the Rococo in architecture and decoration. The outstanding painter of this period, however, was not in every respect characteristic of the new spirit. Jean Antoine Watteau (1684-1721) was apprenticed to a painter of arabesques – decorative panels carved as well as painted which included flowing patterns of foliage – as well as being connected with an artist who painted pictures of the Italian *Commedia dell' Arte* (Harlequin, Columbine, and so on). These were important influences in his work. Like the arabesques of the interior decorators, his own paintings are graceful and flowing. By the time he arrived in Paris in 1702 Rubens was beginning to replace Poussin as the most fashionable artistic influence, and in some ways Watteau resembled Rubens, but without the grandeur, energy and large scale. Another influence perhaps was the type of open-air party given by an early, wealthy patron, from which Watteau may have taken the idea for his *fêtes galantes* (opposite) – scenes of fashionable people in a rural setting – which became such a prominent feature of his output. But there is much more to Watteau than graceful little pictures of elegant people swanning about in parks and on terraces. He had an intense poetic vision, and his *fêtes galantes* are at once gay and sad, real and fantastic. There is no Baroque grandeur and little use of the antique, except in playful allusions. His drawings in chalk show a beautiful sensitivity and precision, though it is his silvery, sparkling landscapes that best reveal his poetic imagination as well as his command of colour.

Watteau had a difficult life and was a rather difficult man. He was poor most of the time, and had tuberculosis which killed him at the age of thirty-six. He was, even more than most painters, a spectator rather than a

participant in the society he portrayed so sharply. His figures seldom look straight out of the canvas (his famous portrait of the clown Gilles is one of the exceptions, though even he has an inward-looking gaze). They appear most frequently in pairs, intent on each other.

Watteau left no great successors, though he was certainly an influence on painters such as Gainsborough (1727-88), and to some extent on François Boucher (1703-70), the most successful artist of the mid-18th century and the great favourite (no wonder, considering the charm of his portraits of her) of Madame de Pompadour, the attractive and influential mistress of Louis XV. Boucher represents the triumph of the Rococo in France. Like Watteau he bene-

fitted from the new, less respectful attitude towards antiquity: his Venuses and Dianas are decidedly sexual creatures, scarcely less so than his portraits of another royal mistress, Louise O'Murphy. Venus, indeed, was a particularly appropriate subject for the art of Boucher, the goddess of love who moved in a world of shells and corals, nymphs and foaming waves – the very subject-matter of so much Rococo decoration. Boucher's sinuous lines and clear colours have much in common with the new art of porcelain making, of which the most notable centre was the factory at Sèvres; his flesh tints have a lustre like fine china, as in his painting of *Cupid a Captive* (right), which was one of three pictures painted for the boudoir of Madame de Pompadour. It is easy to see why Boucher should have been admired by Renoir (page 281).

Boucher's chief successor was his former pupil Jean-Honoré Fragonard (1732-1806), the great virtuoso of French Rococo landscape painting in whom all the charm of Watteau reappeared without the underlying melancholy; the influence of Tiepolo (see below) is also evident in his fluffy skies and mellow light (opposite). He was born a little too late, or lived a little too long, since the French Revolution made his art anachronistic at a stroke; yet Fragonard, a seriously underrated painter until quite recent times, was much more than the elegant entertainer of the fashionable world of the old regime in France. His range was extraordinary, and the more sources of inspiration for his art that can be tracked down, the more extraordinary appears Fragonard's ability to transform them into something uniquely personal. He was a master of drawing, etching, *gouache* (a type of water-colour in which the paint is opaque, not transparent) as well as oils, and in his later life particularly he showed himself to be an astonishingly able painter of children and childhood. And though Fragonard was untouched by the Neo-classical movement, the triumph of which in revolutionary France made him appear redundant, in some ways his painting anticipates the Romanticism of the late 18th and early 19th centuries.

The Rococo never developed in Italy as it did in France, but there were trends in later Italian Baroque, and even in Classicism, which veered in its direction. These trends were most noticeable in Venetian painting, which, after a rather dull spell during the 17th century, recaptured its former splendour in the 18th. The style of Giovanni Battista Tiepolo (1696-1770) was largely based on the legacy of Veronese combined with late Baroque influences. Tiepolo, the last of the great fresco painters, is

256

surpassed in the brilliance of his decorations, such as the scene painted in the palace at Würzburg (page 232), in which a serious subject, the Betrothal of Beatrice of Burgundy to Frederick Barbarossa, is treated with effervescent lightness and grace, and brilliant command of space. An earlier work, showing the Holy Trinity (Father, Son and Holy Spirit) appearing to a saint (below), has the rich colour, steep fore-shortening and strong diagonals of the Baroque, as well as an airy lightness and a luminous quality that harks back to Veronese. Incidentally, this picture was merely a study for an altarpiece, demonstrating the enormous pains that Tiepolo would go to in order to achieve his unequalled brilliance of effect. Tiepolo's immense virtuosity was displayed on walls and ceilings of

Above:
FRAGONARD is known chiefly for his pictures of frolicsome courtiers, but in this dramatic painting of the *High Priest Coresus sacrificing his life to save Callirrhoë*, 1765, he is in a more heroic mood. Musée du Louvre, Paris.

Right:
TIEPOLO, *The Trinity Appearing to St Clement*, about 1735. The spaciousness of this brilliant picture would make one suppose that it is much larger than it is – 69 by 56 cm. It is actually a study for a larger work, which testifies to the immensely elaborate preparations of the artist. The National Gallery, London.

Opposite:
BOUCHER, *Cupid a Captive*, 1754, painted for Madame de Pompadour's boudoir; a typically frolicsome picture. The Wallace Collection, London.

palaces in Venice and elsewhere in northern Italy and other countries of Europe. He went to Spain to carry out a scheme of decoration for the royal palace in Madrid and also painted altarpieces for a church there, which were subsequently replaced by another painter, a Neo-classicist, totally contrary in style to Tiepolo (and inferior in talent).

A Venetian painter of another kind, almost exactly contemporary with Tiepolo, was Giovanni Antonia Canal, better known as Canaletto (1697-1768), whose bright, sharply detailed views of his native city (above), and of London, were especially popular in England. It is not surprising to learn that Canaletto worked as a scene painter in his early years; his paintings have something of the quality of a stage set, bathed as they are in a steady, even light. Sometimes brushed aside as a 'picture-postcard' painter, Canaletto was actually no less skilful at figures than he was at architectural views, as his fine drawings demonstrate. However, his views did become rather mundane after years of repetition, and though his scenes of London are justly popular, he never quite came to terms with the English countryside.

It would be wrong to say simply that Baroque and Rococo disappeared in the late 18th century owing to the rise of Neo-classicism – the strict imitation of Greek or Roman models. There were too many other things going on. There was, for example, a small but startling revival of the Gothic, manifested in Horace Walpole's villa at Strawberry Hill near London where fireplaces were modelled after altar screens in Gothic cathedrals. More important, Neo-classicism roughly coincided, and at many points mingled with, the rise of the Romantic movement, to be discussed in the next chapter.

In architecture, one aspect of the return to classical principles was English Palladianism (named after the Italian architect Palladio), which firmly rejected Baroque ornament and drama in favour of a clean classical style. The movement had some parallels in sculpture also, though it had little direct connection with the best of English painting in the 18th century.

Most of the best painting in England before the 18th century was done by foreigners, such as Holbein in the early 16th century and van Dyck a hundred years later. Godfrey Kneller

Above:

CANALETTO, *Venice: the 'Bucintoro' returning to the Molo*, about 1730. His beautiful prospects of Venice and London are some of the most-often reproduced paintings in the whole of 18th-century art. Royal Collection.

Opposite:

POMPEO BATONI, *John, Marquis of Monthermer*, about 1760. Batoni painted many of the visitors from the British Isles in Rome on their Grand Tour, and that is why he is well represented in British collections. The Duke of Buccleuch and Queensberry, K.T.

carried on the court portrait tradition
of van Dyck but at a rather less distinguished level. When viewed in bulk,
as at Hampton Court, his portraits
look dull and routine. The first great
English painter of international re-
pute was William Hogarth (1697-
1764), best known for his vivid and
satirical pictures of contemporary life,
which were made with popular engravings (sold cheaply in large numbers) in mind. Critics often express
regret that Hogarth spent so much
time on these works. His rarer portraits show an incisive grasp of character, and his ideas, if not his pictures
themselves, were somewhat ahead of
the time. Hogarth insisted, for instance, that the proper study of
painters was not earlier works of art
but nature itself, still a rather novel
idea, at any rate outside Holland.

Perhaps Hogarth's portraits were

his finest work, and portraiture was the dominant feature of English art in the second half of the 18th century. The leading painter in this school was Sir Joshua Reynolds (1723-92), first president of the Royal Academy, who had studied for a long time in Italy, and shows a Venetian influence particularly in his use of colour. A great many members of English society are commemorated in his portraits, of which the most successful, perhaps, are of literary men like Laurence Sterne or Dr Johnson, characters who fully exercised Reynolds's sympathy for intellectual qualities. Unfortunately, Reynolds often adopted a common device of the time, the use of bitumen, a medium made from pitch, to bring added richness to his colours. Bitumen has a radioactive ingredient which causes deterioration, and that is why many of Reynolds's paintings have become so cracked and blackened.

Reynolds's chief rival, and, in the eyes of posterity though not of most contemporaries, a superior artist, was Thomas Gainsborough (1727-88). Gainsborough was one of the first great masters of English landscape, a subject he preferred though he was compelled to spend most of his time on portraits. Some of his finest works, such as the portrait, apparently unfinished, though worked on for ten years, of Mrs Sheridan (opposite), wife of the playwright, combine the two. His brilliant technique, fluent colours and flowing rhythm never deviated into mere charm, nor did his highly eclectic tastes and love of experiment ever degenerate into the bizarre. His famous *Blue Boy* is a frank tribute to van Dyck, and in his last years he painted a number of arresting imaginary compositions which he called 'fancy pictures', such as *Diana and Actaeon*, in the National Gallery, London.

Left:
A self-portrait by SIR JOSHUA REYNOLDS (1723-92).

Opposite:
GAINSBOROUGH, *Mrs R. B. Sheridan*, about 1783, a brilliant Romantic portrait in which Gainsborough displayed his appreciation of landscape. National Gallery of Art, Washington, D.C Andrew Mellon Collection.

Above:
DAVID, *Madame Récamier*, 1800. Musée
du Louvre, Paris.

Opposite:
Opposite:
GEORGE STUBBS, *Horses in a Landscape*, about 1765. Long dismissed as a 'mere' painter of horses, Stubbs in recent years has found his place among the greatest of English artists. The National Trust, Ascott, Wing.

George Stubbs (1724-1806) was a contemporary of Reynolds and Gainsborough. Less highly regarded than these two in his day and for a long time afterwards, he is increasingly seen as one of the very greatest of English painters. As an artist he was self-taught, and he painted a number of portraits in the north of England as a young man before visiting Italy and, subsequently, settling in London where he wrote his *The Anatomy of the Horse*. It is indeed as a painter of horses that Stubbs is best known (opposite); he made a fair living from painting the racehorses of aristocratic owners, and he has few equals as a painter of animals in general.

While it would be rather odd to call Stubbs's beautiful paintings of horses 'Neo-classical', they do share one of the distinctive qualities of Neo-classical painting: clarity of line. The conflict, or state of tension, between the Baroque and Classicism had been going on, in France particularly, throughout the 17th and early 18th centuries. The apparent triumph of the Classicists in the last twenty years of the 18th century, though it stopped poor Fragonard dead in his tracks, was not, any more than any other change in style, a sudden and definitive break. In French sculpture, unlike German, the Baroque had never made a very strong appeal, and though the Rococo ushered in a period of greater sensuality and lightness, sculptors on the whole found it too indisciplined. Nevertheless, the attitude towards the human body of a sculptor such as Etienne Falconet (1716-91) was rather different from that of the ancient Greeks and Romans. His figures of bathing girls (page 255), while perfectly respectable, are sexually alluring. Claud Michel, called Clodion (1738-1814), and J. A. Houdon (1741-1828) were somewhat closer to the classical tradition.

Early French Neo-classical paintings were rather uninspired imitations of the antique. The style reached

its climax in 1784 with the *Oath of the Horatii* of Jacques-Louis David (1748-1825), the great master of the style in France. It is a political painting, advocating the sacrifice of personal ends in the cause of revolutionary republicanism, like the later painting of the *Lictors Bringing Back the Bodies of his Sons to Brutus* (above), which was exhibited in Paris soon after the outbreak of the Revolution. The youths had been executed for treason to the state, according to Roman legend, on the orders of their father, who is shown sternly looking away from the corpses which strike horror and grief into the women of the family. David himself played an active political part in the Revolution, representing Paris in the Convention and serving on the Committee of Public Safety. He harnessed the arts to the Revolutionary cause, abolishing the old Academy, reorganizing the palace of the Louvre as a public gallery, planning the revolutionary fêtes, and even designing the costumes of the deputies. He was imprisoned after the fall of Robespierre, and thereafter his style changed somewhat. To this period belong his beautiful portraits of women, of which the most famous is of Madame Récamier (opposite), now in the Louvre. He became more or less official court painter to Napoleon, and in his portraits of the Emperor his

Above:
DAVID, *Lictors Bring Back the Bodies of His Sons to Brutus*, 1789. This is a political painting, with a message: the consul Brutus ordered his sons' execution as traitors to the state. Musée du Louvre, Paris.

earlier, severe style has almost vanished; there is even a suggestion of Romanticism. David had a great influence on later artists and Ingres among others was his pupil.

265

The Modern Age

In the 18th century, art was largely ruled by the academies, which set out certain rules and conventions. Classical principles were widely advocated, and a tradition of painting that basically derived from Raphael was upheld. This is not to say that some artists did not practise a rather different sort of art from what the academies preached, and obviously the work of a Boucher or a Fragonard was in a very different style from that of Raphael. This does not mean that there were no divergencies; as we have seen, there was plenty to disagree about, and the different legacies of, on the one hand, Poussin, and on the other, Rubens, provoked spirited rivalry. But the arguments took place within an area that seems very small by comparison with that created by art today, when artists are constantly seeking to extend its boundaries. From the Renaissance to the Rococo, the most esteemed artists were chiefly those who stood at the centre of this relatively narrow European artistic tradition, but since the 19th century the greatest artists have usually been those who step farthest outside, or beyond that central tradition.

Already in the 18th century, there was a reaction evident against the stable, ordered world of the 'age of reason'. One of the forms it took was the desire for a more natural existence: the strait-jacket of civilization was rejected and people looked back with nostalgia to a largely imaginary, simple golden age of the past. Alongside the growing interest in and enjoyment of nature was a curiosity about other, non-European societies. The explorer Captain Cook wondered if the simple society of Tahiti was not, in many respects at least, better than that of late 18th-century England. The old order was apparently collapsing fast, not merely through violent political change as in France in 1789, but also through the economic changes of the Industrial Revolution, through the loosening grip of religion on many minds, and through the growing conception of man as essentially a lonely individual. Other developments in the 18th century led towards the conflicts and changes of the 19th: the scientific study of classical remains, and especially an interest in ancient Greece (as distinct from Rome) which was stimulated by the writings of the archaeologist and scholar of art, Johann Joachim Winckelmann, a revival of interest in the Middle Ages, which were at last recognized as very far from the cultural vacuum to which Renaissance writers had tended to confine them, and a growing fascination with Egypt, following Napoleon's expedition there (when French furniture began to sprout sphinxes' heads and lions' feet), with India and with the Far East. Besides the classic tradition (itself shown to be far more diversified than most people had assumed), there were a host of new artistic models, and this development was encouraged by the growth of the academic discipline of art history, of which Winckelmann was one of the earliest, and most influential, exponents. Thus the 19th-century artist was much freer, less bound by generally accepted conventions, than his predecessors.

One effect of the austere Neo-classical style of David at the end of the 18th century was to banish the lavish decorativeness and colourfulness of contemporary art which, except in the hands of a genius like Fragonard, was tending to degenerate into frivolous prettiness. The most notable of David's pupils, Jean Auguste Dominique Ingres (1780-1867), upheld the Neo-classical ideal throughout his long life and had an

even greater influence on French painting. Clarity of line was Ingres's watchword. Drawing was everything: 'a thing well enough drawn is always well enough painted', he said. Colour accordingly was a snare, liable to destroy purity of outline and form, and David's delicate drawings have an absolute minimum of the modelling characteristic of all drawing since the High Renaissance. He aimed to eradicate all Romantic tendencies in his pupils, and forbade them even to look at Rubens with his seductive colouring and Baroque dynamics.

Nevertheless, in spite of Ingres's status as the defender of classical standards, there were elements in his own work which had much in common with Romanticism – a taste for the exotic and the bizarre, for instance – while his appeal to the viewer's emotions is in the tradition of Rubens rather than Poussin. He is best remembered for his senuous paintings of women, who are beautiful, lyrically delineated oriental houris with glowing skin, such as those of *The Turkish Bath* (above), a late work which summarizes all

267

Ingres's vast knowledge of the female form assembled in a masterly design.

In view of his brilliant draughtsmanship and his basic realism, it would be absurd to class Ingres as a reactionary, and his inhibiting influence on French academic art of the 19th century is more due to his towering talent.

If Ingres can stand as the great representative of classicism in early 19th-century French art, and he would be glad to do so, Delacroix is the exemplar of Romanticism, although he would be much less pleased to be so labelled. The Romantic movement is hard to define exactly. Romanticism implies personal, emotional expression rather than the pursuit of formal beauty, and Romantic elements can therefore be found in the art of almost any period. Its chief manifestations in the art of the late 18th and early 19th centuries

are a love of the exotic and the strange, of wild landscapes, of freedom and energy; it is not a 'style' in any technical sense, and its subject-matter varied in different countries.

Eugène Delacroix (1798-1863) was ultimately, since he had more influence on the modern, a greater force in 19th-century art even than Ingres. Nevertheless, he regarded himself as belonging to the classic tradition and admired Poussin and Raphael, in his early years at any rate. He was influenced in his youth by Théodore Géricault (1791-1824), and acquired from him his love of English literature and English art. Titian, Rubens and Rembrandt were at various times his greatest favourites, but he also learned something from Constable, particularly the technique of enlivening large areas of colour with vivid flicks of paint; it is said, rightly or wrongly, that he repainted some

details of an early masterpiece, *The Massacre of Scio*, after seeing Constable's *The Haywain*. The subject of the former was an incident in the Greek struggle for independence from the Turks, and Delacroix painted a number of other pictures with similar themes, for example his famous *Liberty Leading the People*, a celebration of the revolution of 1830. His subject-matter was very varied; much of it was drawn from contemporary literature, including his famous *The Death of Sardanapalus* (above), from a tragedy by Byron, though the massacre of the concubines along with the destruction of the rest of the king's possessions before he dies comes not from Byron but (probably) from Delacroix's own interest in scenes of bloody violence. Despite the frantic violence on the periphery, the scene is dominated by the still, impassive figure of Sardanapalus in his heavy

Opposite:
DELACROIX, *The Death of Sardanapalus*, 1827. Musée du Louvre, Paris.

Below:
Etching from GOYA's *Los Caprichos*, about 1796.

white robes. The studies that Delacroix made for this picture show that he was interested in expressive movement, heightened by colour and *chiaroscuro*, not in anatomical accuracy.

Delacroix visited Morocco in 1832, where the colour and exoticism of life exhilerated him. The brilliant light offered new opportunities for studying colours and shadows. He filled his fascinating notebooks – the source of many striking comments on the arts in general – with perceptive technical notes, such as that a man with a yellow complexion will have violet shadows while one with a reddish complexion will have green shadows. He found also in North Africa amplification for both the Romantic and the classical tendencies in his art. He was surrounded by the strange and the picturesque, but the tall and dignified Arabs reminded him of the ancient Greeks and Romans. 'Rome is no longer in Rome', he remarked in Algiers. Delacroix also painted a number of very large murals, work which was congenial to him since he was always more interested in the larger unity than in detail, but, much of the work being completed by assistants, his vigorous designs are sometimes slightly marred by poor workmanship.

The Spanish painter Francisco de Goya (1746-1828) might have been expected to be more of a 'public' artist than either Ingres or Delacroix, since he was court painter to Charles III and Charles IV of Spain, but in fact this extraordinary genius was an artist of a peculiarly personal kind. He owed something to Tiepolo and Rembrandt, especially in his early work, but like many really great artists of the modern period, he did not fit easily into any school or movement. It is not only Goya's highly individual style which makes it surprising that he was so popular in court circles, but also his subject-matter. He lived in a gruesome time, when a decadent state was torn by civil war of a particularly brutal kind, and Goya's great contribution to art and human society was to display, in a startlingly dramatic and often horrifying way, the ghastly pointlessness of man's inhumanity to man. His first work of this kind was a set of etchings called *Los Caprichos* (literally, 'Caprices'), in which he satirized the corruption of the court and the Church. Goya's satire, however, was unlike that of Hogarth, or the political lampoonists whose audience was the same kind of people as those being satirized. Goya was more universal, and his satire was rooted in his intense compassion for humankind; he was not interested in political parties or factions. His grief at the evils he saw around him was perhaps accentuated by his own troubled nature, poor health, and deafness, which may have heightened his sensitivity to the stranger side of the human race, a striking feature of many of his etchings.

Between 1808 and 1815 Goya worked on a famous series of etchings called the *Disasters of War*, and it is to this period that his *Execution of the Rebels on 3 May 1808* (above) belongs. As the title of the painting, a large work (266 × 345 cm), suggests, a specific event is depicted, though the result is a universal condemnation of war. This intensely dramatic picture owes something to the Baroque tradition, while its clarity of design relates it to the Neo-classical, and the bleak landscape and the deliberate sacrifice of detail for dramatic effect belong to the Romantic movement. In short, this painting draws from most of the chief traditions in European art and, in its turn, influenced a host of later artists, including Manet and Picasso.

Goya's passionate pursuit of truth made even his court portraits rather unflattering, but he was quite capable of portraying human beauty, as in his famous picture *The Nude Maja*, in the Prado, Madrid.

An artist even farther removed from the main trends of art in his time was the English visionary, William Blake (1757-1827), who is as well known for his poetry as for his paintings and engravings (his preferred medium). Blake reacted furiously against the dictates of the influential first president of the Royal Academy, Sir Joshua Reynolds, who demanded great historical and religious works in the classical tradition. Blake, passionate, imaginative, and highly sensitive to medieval art, rejected the Neoclassical establishment root and branch. He took his artistic ideas from a variety of sources, notably Michel-

Above:
GOYA, *The Execution of the Rebels on 3 May 1808*, 1814, a terrifying indictment of the cruelties of civil war. Museo del Prado, Madrid.

Opposite:
SAMUEL PALMER, *The Harvest Moon*. Tate Gallery, London.

angelo, but his pictures embody literary ideas, chiefly his own, and are entirely concerned with the world of the spirit – at a time when European art was solely concerned with the physical world. A watercolour from his later years, *The Simoniac Pope*, reveals at a glance the vast gulf that separated the work of Blake from that of any of his contemporaries. He did, however, have some influence, notably on the imaginative landscapes of Samuel Palmer (1805-81).

In spite of Reynolds, the rise of landscape painting was the greatest achievement of British art in the early 19th century, producing, in Constable and Turner, the two outstanding British painters of the century who – a rare thing for English artists – had considerable international influence. Landscape painting stood outside the

classical tradition altogether; it received no support from the masters of the Renaissance, though it did from the Dutch school of the 17th century. The appeal of a Constable depends on factors excluded by the classical tradition: it demands not our intellectual, but our emotional faculties. To appreciate a picture like David's *Oath of the Horatii*, for example, one needs to understand classical history as well as the principles of classical design; the picture depicts a moment in an episode but depends for part of its effect on the spectator's knowledge of the whole story, and his ability to relate it to current events. None of this is necessary to appreciate a Constable landscape; one needs only a normal acquaintance with nature, common to almost everyone, although of course it helps to know Constable's type of

landscape in particular and to have something of his passion for it. Thus the rise of landscape painting signifies a dramatic shift of artistic interests and demands a different attitude on the part of the spectator. It brought art down from its élitist pedestal, making it available to a much wider audience and at the same time offering the artist greater freedom than he would have in figurative or narrative painting. Gainsborough and one or two others had prepared the way in England, where landscape painters were never confronted with the academic opposition that they encountered in France.

John Constable (1776-1837) was himself a countryman with a special relationship to his native county of Suffolk. A slow developer (he was thirty-five before he made his first

Above:
CONSTABLE, *Barges on the Stour*, about 1811. Constable's sketches have an impressionistic immediacy not apparent in his big finished works. Victoria and Albert Museum, London.

Left:
Oil sketch by CONSTABLE of Salisbury Cathedral, from the river, about 1820. National Gallery, London.

Opposite:
TURNER, *Snowstorm – Steamboat off a Harbour's Mouth*, 1842. Tate Gallery, London.

impact with *Dedham Vale*) he sketched direct from nature, taking enormous trouble before producing the finished work in his studio. He largely rejected the traditional scheme of landscape painting – the dark foreground, lighted distance and overall brown tone, and came closer to nature with his areas of sparkling green, broken up by lighter touches. A religious man, he believed, like the Romantic poet Wordsworth, that closeness to nature was closeness to God. The sky, he said, was 'the chief organ of sentiment', and he gave as much attention to it as academic artists devoted to their figure drawing. His skies, and the general freshness of his tones, have led some critics to regard him as the forerunner of Impressionism, an idea perhaps reinforced by his preparatory oil sketches such as his *Barges on the Stour* (opposite); but his interest in the physical character of objects 'willows, old rotten

planks, slimy posts, and brickwork, I love such things' – prevented light dominating over all. Though many of Constable's major paintings, such as *The Haywain*, which made such an impression in Paris when it was exhibited there in 1824, depict typical East Anglian scenery (it has become even more 'typical' since acquaintance with Constable's view of nature has almost made nature look like Constable rather than vice-versa – a measure of his achievement) he did of course paint in other regions, Salisbury Cathedral (opposite) being perhaps, through several works, his best-known subject. But he did not travel much, and was not inspired by the more spectacular scenery of the Lake District, source of Wordsworth's inspiration. What he did demonstrate, as no artist had done before, was the aesthetic value of ordinary, mundane objects and scenery.

A more obviously Romantic

painter was J. M. W. Turner (1775-1851), who had a most un-Constable-like passion for the heroic. In other ways also the two artists present revealing contrasts. Unlike Constable, Turner was born in the centre of London and had to discover the countryside instead of growing up in it. He was also much more precocious, and more prolific. He first exhibited at the Royal Academy when he was only fifteen, and he produced an unending stream of sketches and paintings throughout his long life during his inveterate travels all over Europe as well as the British Isles. Once, in Yorkshire, he jotted down the details of a spectacular thunderstorm and told his companion, 'In two years you will see this again and call it *Hannibal Crossing the Alps*.' Moreover, he did.

A diligent scholar of art, Turner studied all the masters of the past, sometimes imitating, and indeed

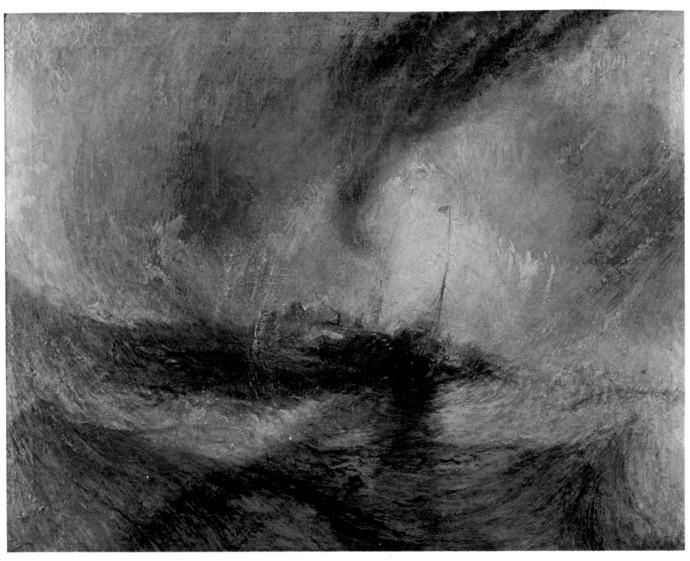

surpassing, his predecessors but, like
many modern artists, ultimately pro-
gressing to a point at which his
carefully acquired early skills could
be jettisoned as redundant. In the
final phase of his art, once regarded as
decadent but nowadays seen as his
most remarkable achievement, he did
not so much anticipate the Impressionists as go beyond them. In these
almost visionary pictures, Turner's
subject was the dramatic effects of
nature, but they were painted with
such freedom that they are close to
being abstract (it is said that Turner
was the first painter to have had one of
his pictures in a gallery hung inad-
vertently upside-down, and to have
said that they should leave it as it
looked better that way). His *Snow-
Storm – Steamboat off a Harbour's Mouth*
belongs to this period. Though he was
then in his late sixties, he had himself
tied to the mast of a boat to observe

this phenomenon. Nevertheless, what
he subsequently painted is not just a
visual record of the scene. Light is the
dominant element (and almost the
only recognizable one), and here
Turner is clearly linked with the
Impressionists; but he was also en-
deavouring to express the drama of
nature in a certain mood in a pictorial
structure, and for that he called upon
emotional, as well as visual resources.

Although Constable and Turner
were the leaders of the landscape
movement (Britain provided a great
number of lesser landscapists, including Samuel Palmer and the water-
colourists of the Norwich School), it
was a continental movement, a reflection of the Romantic reaction against
the ills of industrialism. The painters
of the Barbizon School in France
(named after the village in the forest
of Fontainebleau where they settled)
appear to have been influenced by

274

Constable and resembled him in their loving closeness to nature and poetic feeling. They were brought together by mutual interests and friendship, and poverty, which was not eased by the opposition they had to contend with in France. Despite their close association, they were, of course, entirely individual artists, and though united by their interest in the realistic depiction of landscape, they were in other respects markedly dissimilar. The greatest among them, Millet and Corot, were somewhat loosely associated with the group. Although Jean Francois Millet (1814-75) lived at Barbizon longer than most, his concentration on the life of the peasant in the fields and villages was a commitment not shared by the others. His *Woodsawyers* (opposite) is characteristic in its sombre effect, and suggests

the influence of the Dutch school, an influence that is no less marked in the work of Jean Baptiste Corot (1796-1875). There is more of the classical in Corot, especially in the clarity of such compositions as that of the *Ville d'Avray* (above), and in his later years particularly he compensated for the long years of public neglect, if not outspoken revulsion, by painting more or less conventional classical landscapes for exhibition at the *Salon* in Paris.

Realism, although in fashion in France in the mid 19th century, was mainly of the old-fashioned sort – routine narrative painting of the kind that prosperous burghers delighted to hang in their houses. More up-to-date forms of realism were found shocking: Courbet and Manet both went too far for the conventional taste. Gustave

Above:
Corot, *Ville d'Avray*, about 1837. Though committed to open-air landscape painting and influenced by the Dutch school, Corot also had a deep sense of classical structure, and his work stands somewhere on the road leading from Poussin to Cézanne. Musée du Louvre, Paris.

Courbet (1819-77) came from peasant stock, and his training in Paris consisted of the study of old masters in the Louvre, notably Rembrandt and Velasquez. However, Courbet evolved his own form of realism – 'the representation of real and existing things' – and some of his most notable paintings, such as the famous *Stonebreakers*, had an unmistakeable political content which was found more offensive even than the beards and life-style of the Barbizon painters. Courbet, indeed, was involved in the revolt of the Commune in 1871, served six months in prison and was vindictively hounded by the authorities after he had been released, with the result that he spent his last years in 'voluntary' exile in Switzerland. His famous painting of *The Studio* (above) presents at once most of Courbet's chief interests and many of the reasons why he was so fiercely attacked. In the centre of the picture sits the artist himself, in the process of completing a landscape with a fine flourish. At the left are groups of peasants and beggars, at the right the artist's friends, including the poet (and brilliant art critic) Baudelaire, who is reading a

book. The nude model at the artist's shoulder, depicted with Courbet's characteristic lack of sentimentality towards the female figure, was regarded as particularly shocking, for the same sort of reasons that were to get Manet into hot water a few years later.

Another artist whose work was largely characterized by his sympathy with ordinary people was Honoré Daumier (1808-79). Of humble birth, he was largely self-trained as an artist, and is best known for his satirical lithographs. (In a lithograph, the artist draws the image on stone or a metal plate in a greasy medium (crayon, brush or pen); the plate is moistened with water and an inked roller passed over it, the ink adhering only to the greasy area; a comparatively large number of impressions can be taken from such a plate.) His work for such publications as *La Caricature*, in which he attacked the government, the legal professions and other aspects of bourgeois society, earned Daumier a spell in prison. He used also to make models in clay to assist his drawing, and sculptures markedly different from the rather

dull, classic sculpture of the period. In later life he turned increasingly to painting, such masterpieces as the *Third-Class Railway Carriage* (opposite) displaying his feeling for everyday affairs as well as the startling freedom of his style, which was almost totally unappreciated in his own day.

The outstanding artist of German Romantic landscape painting was Caspar David Friedrich (1774-1840) whose strong, tortured forms of mountain peaks and Gothic ruins, with strange effects of moonlight, often included one or more small, enigmatic human figures. His very subjective art did not make great appeal to the near-contemporary group of landscape painters known as the Nazarenes (originally a sarcastic name, linking them with the early Christians), who were first formed in Vienna about the beginning of the 19th century. They wished to restore a religious spirit to art by returning to the painting of the early Italian Renaissance, and revived the art of fresco.

Another of many more or less derisive names attached to the Nazarenes was 'Pre-Raphaelites', referring

Above:
Third-Class Railway Carriage, DAUMIER (1808-79). Metropolitan Museum of Art, New York. Bequest of Mrs H. O. Havermeyer, 1929. The H. O. Havermeyer Collection.

Opposite:
COURBET, *The Studio*, 1855. Musée du Louvre, Paris.

Right:
A characteristically moody landscape by CASPAR DAVID FRIEDRICH, 1819. Gemäldegalerie, Dresden.

Right:
Holman Hunt, *The Hireling Shepherd*, 1851. The Pre-Raphaelites treated every leaf and twig with meticulous care, and adopted bright tones and brilliant colours. City Art Gallery, Manchester.

Below:
An illustration of the story of Troilus and Cressida by Burne-Jones for an 1896 edition of the works of Chaucer printed by William Morris.

to their devotion to art 'before Raphael', and this name was taken over by the group of English artists who formed the Pre-Raphaelite Brotherhood in 1848. The leading members of the group were Holman Hunt (1827-1910), John Everett Millais (1829-96) and Dante Gabriel Rossetti (1828-82). They revolted against the triviality of academic Victorian art, with its large, rather pompous and unauthentic historical paintings, and were influenced greatly by the art critic John Ruskin, who preached 'truth to nature', as well as by European painting before the High Renaissance. They were 'realists' in a

very precise sense, painting every detail of their uniformly lit and brightly coloured canvases with minute care. They attracted not only a great deal of derision in their own time and later but also a large number of young artists, including Sir Edward Burne-Jones (1833-98) (above) who with Rossetti and William Morris was particularly associated with the second phase of the Pre-Raphaelite movement. This phase witnessed something of a decline in the painting of the original members but was an important influence on the handicraft movement that revolutionized design in the late 19th century.

Many of the paradoxes in which modern artists have found themselves involved are present in the career of the great precursor of Impressionism, Edouard Manet (1832-83). Few great artists have encountered fiercer opposition (a sign of the new gulf opening between art and the public), though by nature Manet, the son of a Parisian magistrate, was far from being a rebel. Few great artists have admired more profoundly or with more open acknowledgment the great masters of the past (in Manet's case, Giorgione and Velasquez particularly), while seeming to confront the traditions of the past more directly. When Manet submitted his *The Absinthe Drinker* to the *Salon* in 1859, it was promptly rejected. That experience was to become a familiar one for this artist, whose minute observation led him into an idiom that, in the eyes of less observant people, appeared thoroughly artificial. A much greater fuss greeted the exhibition of *Le Déjeuner sur l'Herbe* ('Picnic on the Grass') (opposite) in 1863. Essentially, this famous work is a brilliantly updated version of Giorgione's masterpiece, *Concert Champêtre*. The juxtaposition of two artists, fully clothed, with a nude model, was denounced as obscene (it would have been less objectionable if the artists had been wearing Renaissance dress no doubt, as in Giorgione's painting). Still greater fury greeted Manet's *Olympia* (opposite) two years later. This too was an

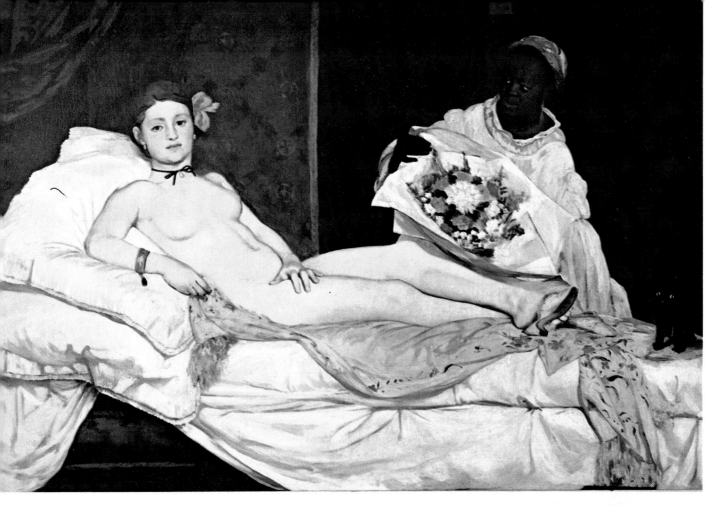

Above:
MANET, *Olympia*, 1863. Few paintings in the history of art have caused more argument, strange though that may seem today. Musée du Louvre, Paris.

Right:
MANET, *Le Déjeuner sur l'Herbe*, 1863. Musée du Louvre, Paris.

imitation of old masters (notably Titian and Goya, who painted similar reclining figures) but painted in an uncompromisingly modern, realistic manner. The critics themselves condemned the picture on paradoxical grounds, objecting both to the 'ugliness' of the figure, its lack of classic sensuality, and equally to the 'obscenity' of the nude. What was really revolutionary about it, the basic cause of offence in academic circles, was its insistence on light tones – the creamy body of the woman depicted with an absolute minimum of modelling (note the merest touch of shadow which delineates the right breast), the illumination squarely frontal, flanked by the dead whiteness of the sheets and the deep darkness of the Negro woman and the background, so that the picture appears as an opposition of balanced areas of dark and light.

It was inevitable that Manet should become the hero of a group of younger artists rebelling against the standards of their time, who became known as the Impressionists. The influence was reciprocated: in his later years Manet became an open-air painter and his works took on a more 'impressionist' appearance, though he never exhibited with the Impressionists.

The main concern of the Impressionists was the depiction of light and colour as they appear in nature, which replaced outline and form as

279

the objective of painting. They thus offered a direct challenge to the academic tradition of high art (in spite of the fact that 'impressionist' tendencies can be found in the work of many earlier artists). Monet, whose painting *Impression, Sunrise* (1874) gave the group their name, once said that he wished he had been born blind and had gained sight later in life so that he could paint things without knowing what they were. This remark sheds much light on the priorities of the group. The Impressionists were generally denounced as rogues and charlatans in their own time, and it was not for many years that Impressionism came to appear as one of the most attractive phases in the whole of European art. Although they shared the dominant interest in light and colour, the Impressionists were of course individuals in temperament, and the styles of the major Impres-

sionist painters are never likely to be confused one with another.

Claude Monet (1840-1926) was the dominant figure of early Impressionism, the first to reject utterly the art of the galleries. His beautiful *Summer* (above) shows his determination to capture the visual qualities of a scene – to create an evocation rather than a description of it. His interest in the effects of light led him to repaint the same water lilies, for example, time and time again, and his work shows most of the main influences that provoked this startling break with the past, including Courbet's inistence on the importance of everyday scenes, the landscapes of Corot, and perhaps of Constable and Turner, the realism of Manet, and the delicate flatness of Japanese prints, which were becoming popular in Europe at this time.

Monet's chief associates, with

whom he painted in the Forest of Fontainebleau and drank at the Café Guerbois, were Renoir, Sisley and Pissarro. Auguste Renoir (1841-1919) was really a painter of a quite different sort, his brushstrokes much softer and his favourite subject not nature but the female nude (page 281). After visiting Italy, where he greatly admired the Italian masters, his work acquired somewhat clearer outlines and he, more directly than the others, linked Impressionism with classical traditions in art. Alfred Sisley (1839-99) on the other hand, remained closer to the primary interests of the movement, confining himself to landscapes. Camille Pissarro (1830-1903)

took up painting comparatively late in life and was older than the rest of the group. His attractive personality made him an important influence on other, younger painters, and he was largely responsible for introducing both Cézanne and Gauguin to Impressionism.

A growing and increasingly disparate group of artists gathered around the Impressionists and exhibited at the Impressionist exhibitions. Edgar Degas (1834-1917) had artistic interests in some ways little related to the concerns of Monet or Pissarro. He found no great inspiration in landscape and was less interested in light for its own sake than as a factor for

conveying movement; drawing was far more important in his paintings. A notably unsentimental artist, Degas liked to depict the female figure in exaggerated poses, and his bathers, prostitutes and dancers are a far cry from the plump and charming young girls of Renoir.

It is generally true to say that the second phase in movements of art manifests some deterioration of standards. This is not true of the Post Impressionists, among whom are included three or four painters of the very highest achievement. Georges Seurat (1859-91) represents in some ways a bridge between the two movements. His subject-matter and use of

Opposite:
SEURAT, *La Baignade*, 1883-84. National Gallery, London.

Below:
GAUGUIN, *Where Do We Come From? What Are We? Where Are We Going?* 1897, perhaps the artist's most rewarding work. Museum of Fine Arts, Boston, Massachusetts.

broken colour were basically Impressionist, but Seurat, an intellectual artist, invented a new technique called pointillism, a 'scientifically' calculated method in which the picture is made up of small, regular dots of colour. Seurat also adopted a highly simplified form which makes some of his paintings approach abstraction. His study of bathers, *La Baignade* (opposite) is a very 'scientific' painting, the result of numerous preparatory studies in sketches made both on the spot and in the studio, and relying on Seurat's profound knowledge of optics, colour, and the expressiveness of form. Its monumental quality is quite foreign to Impressionism.

Paul Gauguin (1848-1903) is an almost legendary figure among modern artists, partly because he gave up family and career (he was a successful stockbroker) to search for

an environment better suited to his art, which he eventually found in Tahiti. The clear air, vivid colours and the silence produced some of his richest works, including *Where Do We Come From?* . . . of 1897 which, the artist believed, 'surpasses in value all my previous [canvases] . . . I have put into it before dying all my energy, a passion so painful in terrible circumstances, and a vision so clear, needing no corrections, that the hastiness disappears [Gauguin believed in painting rapidly] and life surges up.'

Post Impressionism was less of a 'movement' than Impressionism, encompassing the very varied forms of reaction against, or extension of, Impressionist ideas. Gauguin reintroduced a decorative treatment of colour and form. Van Gogh, with whom Gauguin at one point had a short and unrewarding association, then added an intensely emotional

Above:
CÉZANNE, *Grand Baignade*, 1898-1905. As
time goes by Cézanne's concerns as an
artist seem ever more significant.
Philadelphia Museum of Art,
Pennsylvania. Wistach Collection.

Opposite:
VAN GOGH, *Self-Portrait with Bandaged
Ear*, 1889, painted just after his
breakdown when he attacked Gauguin
and slashed off his ear in demented
remorse. Courtauld Institute Galleries,
London.

response to colour. The reputation of
Vincent van Gogh (1853-90) has been
damaged by the notion of him as a
half-crazy primitive, who cut off his
own ear in a distraught moment after
quarrelling with Gauguin, and
eventually committed suicide.
Though ultra-sensitive and passionate, he was a highly trained artist
whose remarkable letters stand as a
monument to his wide culture and
profound thought. His style changed
considerably over the years, but his
greatest work belongs to the period of
a little over two years before his death
at Arles in the south of France. Light

and colour were to him a kind of
divine revelation, as they had been to
the Gothic artists, and by heightening
colour, laid on thickly with fierce
strokes of brush or palette knife, he
turned the objects he painted – always easily recognizable however –
into visions quite unique.

Gauguin's outstanding quality was
his decorative colour, van Gogh's his
intense expressiveness. The contribution of Paul Cézanne (1839-1906) was
structural. In spite of the apparent
closeness to Impressionism of his early
works, Cézanne introduced new
qualities into art of which the Impressionists knew nothing, and which
perhaps justify the title sometimes
bestowed on him of father of modern
painting. He came from a well-to-do
middle-class family and had comparatively little artistic training, failing the entrance exam at the School of
Fine Arts in Paris and narrowly
avoiding the fate of becoming a
lawyer. It was Pissarro who brought
him into the orbit of the Impressionists, and advised him never to use

any but the three primary colours
(red, yellow, blue) and their deriva-
tives (advice, however, that he did not
always follow). His early works were
undisciplined visions of feasts and
orgies, much influenced by Delacroix; later, he painted Impressionist
canvases rather in the manner of
Pissarro. The latter part of his life was
spent largely in peaceful seclusion,
made possible by his family's money
and the passive support of his wife. It
is to this period that his finest paintings belong. Visitors recorded his
vivid comments on art and on his own
goal in art, but these are, characteristically, sometimes contradictory.
What he sought to capture on canvas
was the many-sidedness of reality. 'To
paint', he said, 'is not merely to copy
the subject but to seize a harmony
between numerous relationships.' He
endeavoured to construct a pictorial
image containing the character of his
subject while preserving the reality of
the painting as an object made of
paint. He found portraits difficult
partly because of the complex

287

psychological relationships which had to be incorporated along with the relationships of planes translated into colour. He was a difficult man to sit for, as his wife discovered when he impatiently told her 'Be an apple'. It was, in fact, towards still-lifes that his ideas and methods led him, and some people would regard them as his finest works. He was also interested in the human figure, and his *Grand Baignade* (page 287) is his nearest approach to a great nude composition, in which he submits the human figure to the kind of reconstruction he imposed on landscapes and still-life subjects.

Cézanne represents something of a watershed in art. In some ways he is the direct descendant of both the painterly tradition of Rubens, Watteau and Delacroix and the classical tradition of Poussin and Ingres. His influence on later artists was great and varied; Cubism certainly owed him much and few subsequent painters would have claimed that he had no influence on them at all.

A number of artists in the second half of the 19th century were struggling to get away from the dominant naturalism of the period. 'Remember,' said the painter Maurice Denis in 1890, 'that a picture, before being a battle horse, a nude woman or some anecdote, is essentially a flat surface covered with colours assembled in a certain order.' The Norwegian Edvard Munch (1863-1944) expressed his spiritual unease in 'psychological' paintings like *Jealousy* (above), in which woman appears as a horrifying threat and the atmosphere is one of neurotic terror. Munch spent some time in Berlin and was an important influence on the German Expressionists (see below).

Among artists strongly infected by Impressionism was the American-born but mainly London-based James McNeill Whistler (1834-1903) whose contempt for academic art, witheringly and wittily expressed, led him into a libel action against Ruskin, when the great critic accused him of flinging a pot of paint in the public's face. Whistler was influenced also by Japanese art, but owed little to observation of nature. 'As music is the poetry of sound,' he said, 'so painting is the poetry of sight, and the subject-

Above:
EDVARD MUNCH, *Jealousy*, about 1896. Like others of Munch's eerie 'psychological' paintings, the subject was based on his own experiences. Bergen Billedgalleri.

Opposite:
WHISTLER, *Arrangement in Grey*, a self-portrait, 1871-73. The Detroit Institute of Arts, Michigan.

matter has nothing to do with the harmony of sound or of colour.' He gave many of his pictures musical titles, such as *Harmony*, *Nocturne*. He called his self-portrait (opposite), signed with his device of a butterfly, *Arrangement in Grey*, a favourite colour, as in his best-known work, the portrait of his mother (page 290) now in the Louvre.

Both Munch and Whistler can be associated with a new style sweeping across Europe towards the end of the 19th century known in English-speaking countries as Art Nouveau, which affected all aspects of design as well as the fine arts. It was the first truly international movement in art that owed nothing to the classical

Left:
The Artist's Mother by WHISTLER in a
very famous and much-parodied
painting whose official title is *Arrangement
in Grey and Black No. 1*. About 1870.
Musée du Louvre, Paris.

Below:
The posters of the Czech artist Mucha
(1869-1839) such as this one of Sarah
Bernhardt as Medea, are probably the
most-often reproduced Art Nouveau
prints.

Left:
TOULOUSE-LAUTREC, *Divan Japonais*,
1892. His lithographed posters
advertising various establishments of
Parisian night life brought fine art and
commercial art closer together. Musée
Toulouse-Lautrec, Albi.

tradition since the Middle Ages, and though brief (it had virtually disappeared by the First World War) it had some influence in encouraging painters to trust their own creativity more and conform to generally recognized styles less. Art Nouveau's chief characteristics were a curved and flowing line derived from plant forms, and patches of colour or patterns owing little to the subject-matter. In Germany the style was called *Jugendstil* (the 'style of youth'), and the Vienna of the Secession movement was, after Paris (where

even the Metro stations were designed in a delicious Art Nouveau style) one of the most interesting centres of the style. Two great artists belonging to the Secession movement, though standing a little apart from it, were Gustav Klimt (1862-1918) and Egon Schiele (1890-1918). Klimt's most notable characteristic was his bold use of contrasting areas of brilliantly coloured patterns to give an impression of almost Byzantine splendour (above); Schiele's was his sure clarity of line. They shared a liking for eroticism, in Schiele's case of a some-

Above:
Gustav Klimt, *The Kiss*, about 1910. Klimt is the most famous of the painters whose work can be clearly characterized as Art Nouveau. The heads, hands, feet, etc. of his human subjects emerge from brilliant areas of pattern with little attempt to suggest a human figure. Österreichische Galerie, Vienna.

times startling kind, which was a
feature of Art Nouveau.

For much of the 19th century,
sculpture, though prolific, remained
rather imitative. Auguste Rodin
(1840-1917), the outstanding sculptor
of the century, achieved a new,
creative relationship with the classical
tradition and at the same time opened
the way for future developments.
Rodin was a master of naturalism, so
much so that jealous fellow-sculptors
falsely accused him of trying to pass
off as sculpture a figure cast from a
human body. Though Rodin often
worked in bronze, as in his *Head of
Grief* (opposite), marble was his most
common medium. He achieved light
effects which parallel Impressionism

292

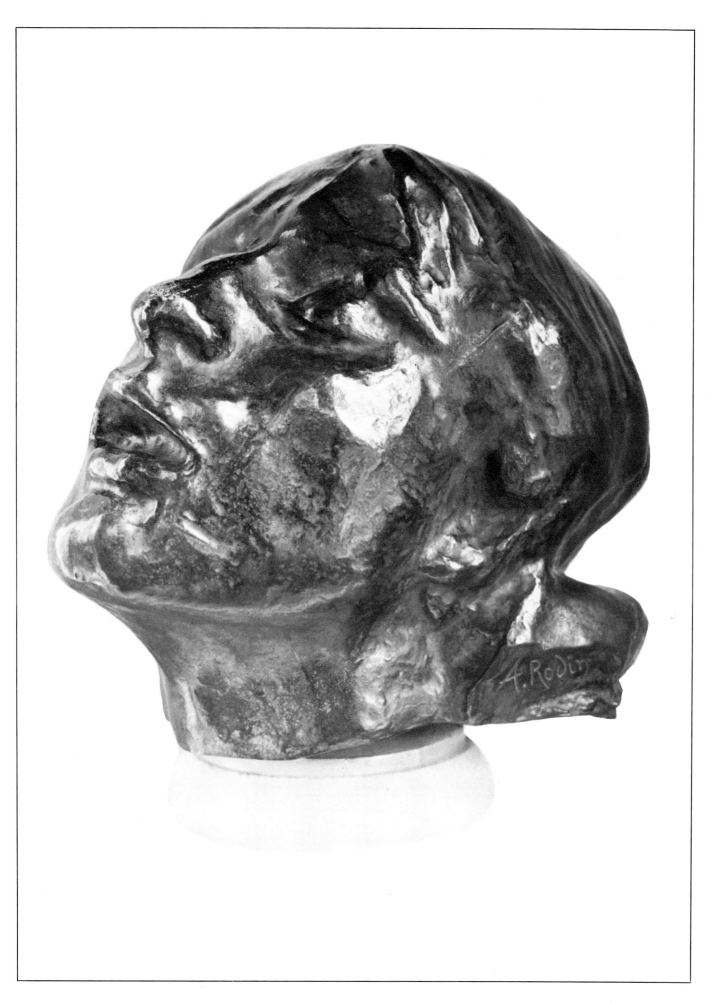

Above:
RODIN, *The Kiss*, 1886, marble, life-size.
Tate Gallery, London.

in painting and emphasized the flesh-
like appearance of such groups as
The Kiss (opposite), an effect further
enhanced by the roughness of the
supporting stone. An admirer of
Michelangelo, Rodin adopted the
trick of leaving his figures half-
emerged from the material in which
they are carved, though in Michelangelo this was more the result of the
work remaining unfinished than a
deliberate dramatic effect, and from
classical ruins Rodin devised the idea
of deliberately truncating limbs or
even heads, having noticed the
effectiveness of such works as the
headless *Winged Victory of Samothrace* in
the Louvre. At the time, many people
found this kind of device offensive and
rather brutal, but the effect was to

point sculpture in the direction of
abstraction, in which the qualities of
mass, line and tension become more
important than representation.
Rodin also liked to capture unusual
poses, first making quick sketches as
his models moved about the room; to
the criticism that this resulted in ugly
figures he made answer that nothing
is ugly if it has character. Like so
many revolutionary influences in art,
Rodin was not by any means a
natural rebel, and some of his work is
not without a trace of that sentimentality and acquiescence with popular
convention that marred the work of so
many of his contemporaries.

Most of the basic premises of art
were questioned by artists in one way
or another during the 19th century,
and this led to a rather bewildering
proliferation of styles and movements
in the early 20th century, a period of
unparalleled creativity and invention. The public gradually grew
accustomed to the idea of art as
something constantly changing, so
that nowadays an artist who exhibits
works of the same kind as those he was

doing ten years earlier is likely to be
told by the critics that he is stagnat-
ing. Of course, it was no new thing for
the style of a good artist to change
quite dramatically in the course of his
artistic development; nevertheless,
the rejection of old standards made of
art in the 20th century a constantly
shifting kaleidoscopic affair with
which ordinary people often felt
increasingly out of touch. For this the
rejection of traditional standards was
largely responsible. Of all the new
ideas that contributed, on the one
hand, to making art so diverse and, on
the other, to its divorce from the
comprehension of the man in the
street, the most important was the
rejection of the old principle that a
picture is based on the visible world.

The first revolutionary movement
in art in the early 20th century to
astonish the public was Fauvism, in
which the outstanding artist was
Henri Matisse (1869-1954). Matisse
and his friends sent a collection of
their pictures to the Paris *Salon*
exhibition in the autumn of 1905, the
effect of which earned them the

295

Above:
PICASSO, *Les Demoiselles d'Avignon*, 1907, one of the most famous paintings of the 20th century, now in the Museum of Modern Art, New York, acquired through the Lillie P. Bliss Bequest.

Opposite:
MATISSE, *Le Luxe II*, 1907-08, a refined version of an earlier painting, *Le Luxe I*. Statens Museum for Kunst, Copenhagen.

nickname *fauves* (wild beasts). A more inappropriate name, however, for the art of Matisse could hardly be imagined; his aim was 'an art of balance, of purity and serenity'. What surprised the critics was the use of broad, flat areas of rather vivid colour, with which Matisse sought to fuse the outer world of his subject with his inner, emotional response to it in a harmonious pictorial composition, as in his *Le Luxe II* (opposite). Despite the strong and unfamiliar colours and the energetic, fluent line, this is a pure and

peaceful picture.

Matisse was experimenting with the nude at about the same time as the Spanish artist Picasso, but he had little sympathy with the – as it first appeared – more objective movement known as Cubism, with which Picasso's name is associated; indeed, Matisse is said to have named the movement, when he contemptuously referred to a painting by Braque as 'cubes'. Cézanne had endeavoured to give painting a solid basis of construction, maintaining that everything in

297

nature is based on geometric figures (he defined them as the sphere, the cone and the cylinder, though he might equally have mentioned the cube). Cubism, quite simply, presented a 'new way of seeing'. It was to be the most influential of all the revolutionary art movements of the early 20th century, and it is no exaggeration to say that it provides the basis for modern movements in Western art ever since.

Pablo Picasso (1881-1973) and Georges Braque (1882-1963), the 'inventors' of Cubism, sought to find a way of representing three-dimensional objects without destroying the two-dimensionality of the picture. They broke up objects into fragments, presenting an analysis of them, seen simultaneously from more than one viewpoint, and sometimes more than one viewpoint in time as well as space. The painting which set Analytical Cubism, as this phase of the movement is known, in motion was Picasso's *Les Demoiselles d'Avignon* (page 297) which was seen by Braque and led to the close association of the two artists from about 1909 to 1912. This picture started off as a more or less conventional scene of sailors and prostitutes, but changed as Picasso

became absorbed with the problems of construction and expression. It was probably inspired by the late figure paintings of Cézanne, while the curious faces on the right are a tribute to the powerful influence on the young Picasso of African art. Possibly in reaction against Fauvism, Picasso and Braque rejected strong colours and adopted a severe monotone, as in Braque's *The Portuguese* of 1911.

Without denying the revolutionary character of Analytical Cubism, it is worth emphasizing that few things in art are entirely novel. Braque's *The Portuguese* is a long way from the art of strict representation, but in some respects it is entirely traditional: the compositional arrangement, focussing on the centre of the canvas and fading towards the corners, is the same as that used by, for example, Leonardo da Vinci. Nor was the depiction of an object or figure from different viewpoints simultaneously entirely new. It was, as we have seen (Chapter Two), a characteristic of Ancient Egyptian art.

The remarkable achievement of Picasso and Braque attracted a whole group of other artists and led to a second phase of Cubism known as 'Synthetic Cubism', which showed a rather different attitude to art and reality. It was more two-dimensional, more decorative, with more colour, and combined different objects in arbitrary ways. One feature of Syn-

thetic Cubism was the use of other media than paint – the beginnings of collage, in which pieces of cloth, paper, or other material are stuck on to the canvas. This technique raises all sorts of interesting questions. Most obviously, it posed a challenge to the tradition of beautiful paint (a feature of Analytical Cubism, incidentally, no less than Impressionism, as Braque's *The Portuguese* demonstrates). The leading figure of Synthetic Cubism, after Picasso and Braque, was another Spaniard, Juan Gris (1887-1927), an intellectual whose paintings were more scientifically ordered, based on fixed patterns of geometrical planes and light, as in his portrait of Picasso (page 301).

Meanwhile another, less important movement had arisen in Italy. This was known as *Futurism* and its leading spokesman was the poet Filippi Tomasso Marinetti, who spoke of the 'midnight fervour of arsenals and shipyards blazing with electric moons, insatiable stations swallowing the smoking serpents of their trains, factories . . .'. It was partly a rather desperate reaction against the artistic heritage which seemed so particularly oppressive in Italy, though its celebration of technology now seems more than a little puerile. It included some fine artists, however, of whom the most remarkable was probably Umberto Boccioni (1882-1916), and made some contribution to the

Above:

MARC CHAGALL, *Self-Portrait with Seven Fingers*, 1911. Chagall was born in Russia but lived most of his life in France. Though influenced by the Cubists, he retained a lyrical expressionism and a fondness for dreams and Russian folk tales which account for the more or less fantastic quality of many of his paintings. Stedelijk Museum, Amsterdam.

development of sculpture especially,
through the Futurist accent on dynamic movement. Boccioni's *Development of a Bottle in Space* (left) in
fact seems closer to Synthetic Cubism
than it does to Futurism, despite the
supposed antipathy of the two movements; the imaginative dissection of a
bottle to display a structure not visible
to the objective eye is similar to the
Cubists' treatment of still-lifes – their
famous guitars and plates of fruit.

The German artists of the Expressionist movement were a less united
group than the Impressionists. Like
Impressionism, Expressionist aspects
can be found in the work of many

Above:
Ernst Ludwig Kirchner, *Reclining Nude with Fan*, 1908, one of the most striking works of the Brücke group. Kunsthalle, Bremen.

Left:
Karl Schmidt-Rottluff, *The Road to Emmaus*, woodcut, 1918. Philadelphia Museum of Art, Pennsylvannia.

Opposite:
Kandinsky, *Light Picture, No. 188*, 1913, one of the earliest of Kandinsky's totally abstract paintings. The Solomon R. Guggenheim Museum, New York.

artists at different times; simply defined, expressionism in art is the attempt to express extreme emotion, usually by means of colour or by some exaggeration of form. El Greco (page 251) might be called an expressionist, but the word is usually reserved for particular groups of artists in northern Europe at the beginning of the 20th century. One of these groups was known as *Die Brücke* ('The Bridge'), a name they adopted to show their hope of uniting the various new movements in art. The leading figures were Ernst Ludwig Kirchner (1880-1938) and Karl Schmidt-Rottluff (1884-1976). Their pure, brash colours and dynamic design resembled the Fauves, but they were not concerned with

such qualities as harmony and rhythm, which had occupied Matisse, only with intense emotional communication. Kirchner's *Nude with Fan* (opposite) took a highly traditional subject and treated it in a very nontraditional way; by such works he hoped to wash away the cobwebs of academic art which throttled freedom. There was a melancholy, pessimistic quality in much Expressionist art, as in Schmidt-Rottluff's spiky woodcut, *The Road to Emmaus*, an example of the new vigour which *Die Brücke* artists brought to the ancient tradition of German graphic art. They lived in troubled times – all were to come under official disapproval under the Nazis – and Kirchner eventually

committed suicide.

Another Expressionist school was the group known as the *Blaue Reiter* ('Blue Rider'), formed in Munich in 1911. Its leading spirits were the Russian Wassily Kandinsky (1866-1944) and Franz Marc (1880-1916). Kandinsky, a man in whom many cultural influences mingled, was obsessed by colour. Before the founding of the *Blaue Reiter* (they took their name from a painting by Marc) he had already begun painting abstracts in watercolours, expressing his emotions of the moment with coloured marks made on paper (below) – the technique of the Abstract Expressionists half a century later (see below). Marc, like so many artists

Above:
FRANZ MARC, *Fighting Forms*, 1914, a late work of this painter of the *Blaue Reiter* school, showing an affinity with Futurism. Bayerische Staatsgemäldesammtungen, Munich.

Left:
FRANZ MARC, *Roedeer among Reeds*. Bayerische Staatsgemäldesammlungen, Munich.

(and others) cut off in his prime during the First World War, is best-remembered for his luridly coloured horses and other animals, but he too had turned towards abstraction before his death (above).

Although associated with the *Blaue Reiter* school, the Swiss Paul Klee (1879-1940), witty, charming, elusive and prolific, was really a law unto himself. He moved easily from representation to abstraction and back again, and worked in numerous different media. Klee searched for the esentials in art, and believed that it grew, or was transformed by the artist's subconscious mind, as the soil is transformed into the leaves of a tree.

In the Netherlands, the movement known as *De Stijl* ('The Style') developed slightly later. Its outstanding member, Piet Mondrian (1872-1944) had begun as a landscape artist, then taken up the Analytical Cubism of Picasso and Braque. He arrived at his familiar style by a process of continual simplification, so that his seascapes were refined down to a minimal arrangement of black lines. Together with Theo van Doesburg (1882-1931) and other artists of the group, he developed his art of dynamic balance

– an arrangement of vertical and horizontal lines with rectangular areas of simple colour (page 306).

Disgust and despair with Western civilization, and with the frightful horror of the First World War in particular, gave rise to the movement known as Dada, a defiant outburst of poets and painters, directed as rudely as possible against all institutions, including art and literature. It began in Zürich, where an international group including Tristan Tzara, Jean Arp, Francis Picabia and others

Above:
An op-art sculpture by TONI COSTA which deceives and intrigues the eye. Galleria Nazionale d'Art, Moderna Arte Contemporanea, Rome.

Above:
MONDRIAN, *Composition with Red, Yellow and Blue*, 1930. Alfred Roth, Zürich.

spent their energies on the mockery of poetry and painting as well as other art forms in eccentric but often liberating ways. They called themselves 'Dada' because that was the meaningless first mumble of a baby, and at an art exhibition in 1920 they provided hatchets for the spectators to hack the works exhibited. Duchamp produced a coloured print of the Mona Lisa, to which he had added a moustache and beard.

Duchamp was to be one of the most influential artists of the century, after Picasso. His *Nude Descending a Staircase* (opposite left), depicting a figure in motion, was exhibited at the sensational Armory Show in New York in 1913, which marked the introduction

of the American public to modern art, and was one of the chief talking points of the show. His even more enigmatic *Bride Stripped Bare by Her Bachelors Even* (opposite), painted on glass, was the fruit of eight years work. It was accidentally broken in 1926, but Duchamp characteristically accepted the cracks as a fortuitous addition by fate. Duchamp also originated the idea of the *objet trouvé* ('found object'), exhibiting a bottle rack or a urinal as an object of art.

In the early 1920s Dada merged into Surrealism. This was an attitude to life rather than just an art movement, though it is perhaps in art that Surrealist ideas have been most influential. Surrealism was greatly influ-

enced by Freud, the founder of psychoanalysis and student of dreams. The Surrealists believed in the importance of the unconscious, and that the most relevant products of the mind were not the product of reasoning but the images that sprang from non-rational sources, including dreams. Surrealist painters like Max Ernst (1891-1976), Salvador Dali (born 1904) and René Magritte (1898-1967) recorded with meticulous accuracy such mysterious, half-familiar images for which there is no rational explanation(see the following page). Picasso, who in one way or another can be linked with almost every new movement in art in the 20th century, had some affinity with the Surrealists, and there is a Surrealist feeling in what is probably his most famous work of art, *Guernica* (page

298), which commemorates the destruction of a Spanish town during the Spanish Civil War. This was a commissioned work, and there was some initial disappointment that the artist had not chosen a more realistic idiom; but Picasso has been proved right, for his painting has become one of the best-known and most powerful indictments of warfare in this century.

When Marcel Duchamp (1887-1968) produced his first 'ready-made' sculpture, he had merely taken to its logical conclusion the movement known as Constructivism, in which the work of sculpture, instead of being carved or modelled, is made up of separate pieces of material, a new idea akin to the collages of Synthetic Cubism which proved a fruitful one for sculptors like David Smith (page 292). Duchamp could also claim to be the originator of mobile sculpture (page 307), since he attached a bicycle wheel to a stool in 1913. The point Duchamp was making with such gestures was that art is not a matter of creating a work of art but of recognizing the aesthetic value of any object. That is not quite the same as saying, as certain later artists said – or implied – that the validity of an object as art lies in the will of the artist: 'It's art if I say it's art.'

The greatest sculptors of the 20th century tended to stand far removed from the exhilarating but often irritating and sometimes time-wasting atmosphere of manifestoes and counter-manifestoes, of dramatic gestures and counter-gestures. Constantin Brancusi (1876-1957) was a Romanian who came to Paris early enough to work in Rodin's studio. Though much influenced by Rodin, his own sculpture was from an early stage primarily concerned with the nature of the material itself rather

Left:
DALI, *Metamorphosis of Narcissus*, 1936-37. This painting is characteristic of the Spanish surrealist's mysterious subject-matter and flamboyant technique. Tate Gallery, London. On loan from the Edward James Foundation.

Opposite:
BRANCUSI, *The White Negress*, marble, 1924. Louise and Walter Arensberg Collection, Philadelphia Museum of Art, Pennsylvania.

than the human figure, seeking some
kind of absolute form. But besides
sculptures of perfect smoothness and
balance, he also produced more
rugged-looking works, usually in
wood, in which he demonstrated the
powerful influence of African carving
on his generation.

The British sculptor Henry Moore
(born 1898) is a less revolutionary but
equally famous artist. He learned
from Brancusi to allow the material to
dominate, but his work was also
shaped by a wide variety of other
influences, including fellow sculptors
like Naum Gabo and Alexander
Archipenko, the first to exploit the
device of a hole in a solid mass. But
the primary source of Moore's art is
his own response to the physical world
and to its qualities of scale, texture
and mass, expressed in monumental
works frequently based on the traditional theme of a reclining female
figure (left).

After the Second World War, the
capital of western art moved from
Paris to New York, where many
notable artists had practised various
forms of mainly non-figurative painting in the 1920s and 1930s, and when
many European artists had arrived as
refugees before the outbreak of the
Second World War.

One aspect of the New York art
world, often pointed out by those with
a cynical view of modern art, was the
increasing importance of dealers;
there was a suspicion that the reputation of some artists was built up
largely by skilful public-relations
work for commercial motives.

The art that emerged from the
United States, and particularly New
York, in the years after the Second
World War, deliberately ignored
European traditions, though it was
inevitably influenced by the recently
arrived European artists, as well as by
Oriental art. The new movement,
called Abstract Expressionism, did
have certain European forebears,
notably Kandinsky, but the Action
Painting of Jackson Pollock (1912-56)

311

was thoroughly American. On his
large canvases, laid on the floor, he
dripped paint direct from the tube to
form swirling patterns; it was the
actual physical act of painting that
was important, and Pollock used to
say he had no idea of how the painting
would look when he started to paint
it. While this method could be, and
was, easily exploited by less creative
artists, there is no doubt that Pollock,
especially when working with restricted colours (above) created something new and interesting.

Willem de Kooning (born 1904)
produced paintings that are more
obviously aggressive – heavy swathes
of paint laid on with a thick brush,
with the paint vigorously asserting its

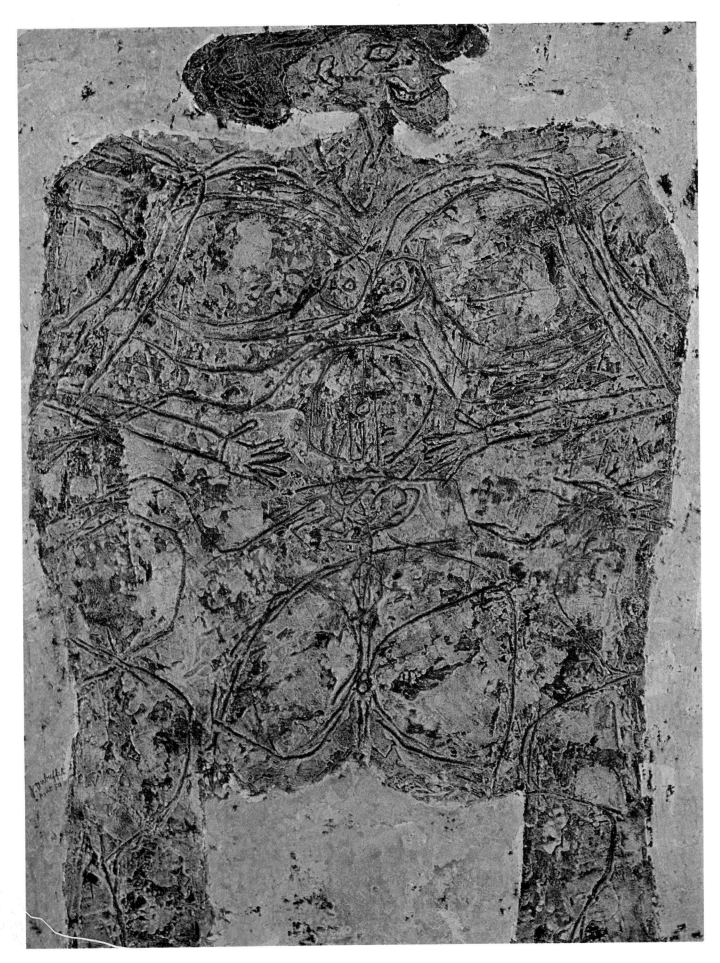

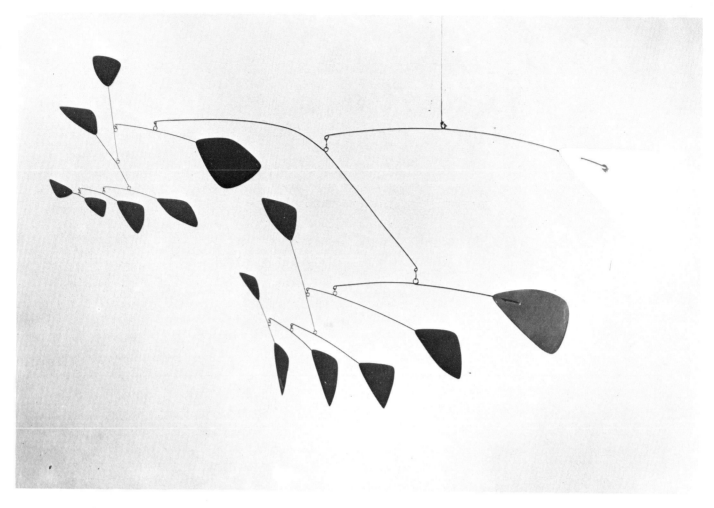

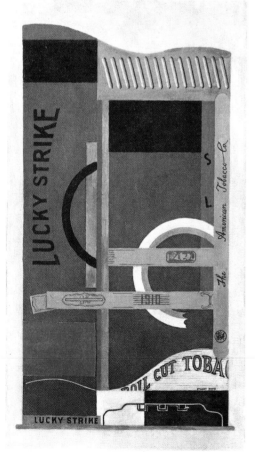

Above:

ALEXANDER CALDER, *Seven Red, Seven Black, One White*, mobile sculpture.

Left:

STUART DAVIS, *Lucky Strike*, 1921, an early example of the interest of American artists in mundane mass-produced objects. Museum of Modern Art, New York. Gift of The American Tobacco Company Inc.

own nature (page 312). His paintings are sometimes figurative, and he devoted much of his time to a long series of *Women*, to whom his attitude seemed traditionally ambiguous, a mixture of fear and desire.

There was a strong tradition of figurative painting in the United States, which had occasionally shown a preoccupation with the mundane objects of modern industrial society. Stuart Davis's *Lucky Strike* was an early example of the tradition which, in the 1960s culminated in what was called Pop Art. This 'New Realism' as it was also called, embraced a great many artists working in markedly different ways, but basically Pop Art was concerned with presenting images from everyday life and the mass media, and typically, though not exclusively, in ways that contradicted fine-art traditions. Roy Lichtenstein produced paintings that looked like blown-up cartoons from the comic strips, complete with captions in bubbles (opposite). Andy Warhol doctored photographs of popular figures, mainly film stars, and

produced casual silk-screen prints of such motifs as tomato-soup cans. The point of this should have been, perhaps, to encourage ordinary people to go out and make their own art from the objects around them, but what – predictably – happened was that people, instead of making their own prints of everyday objects that appealed to them, went out and bought Warhol's soup cans at dizzy prices.

An allied development was Op Art, the creation of striking and bewildering optical effects and illusions, often by highly technical methods (page 305). This, like Pop Art, appeared to be little more than a short-lived fashion, though the echoes of Pop particularly are likely to sound in art for a very long time. On the whole, however, painters tended to return to the painterliness of painting – exploring the potentialities of areas of colour in various forms of composition, their emotional content and other factors arising directly out of the act of placing pigments on a flat surface.

Above:
ROY LICHENSTEIN, *Masterpiece*. Wit and nostalgia were characteristic ingredients of the artist's comic-strip mock-ups. Melvin Hirsch, Los Angeles.

315

Acknowledgements

The illustration on page 240, the lower illustration on page 250 and the illustration on page 258 are reproduced by gracious permission of Her Majesty the Queen.
The illustration on page 106 is reproduced by courtesy of the Board of Trinity College, Dublin.

Photographs

Ägyptisches Museum, Berlin-Charlottenburg 45 right; Fratelli Alinari, Florence 78 top right, 87 bottom, 94 top, 100, 130, 141 bottom, 194 right, 196 right, 200 bottom, 206 bottom, 211 top, 214 left, 247 top; Archaeological Survey of India, New Delhi 165 right, 166, 167 top, 172; Archives Photographiques, Paris 33 left, 115 right, 126 right, 218 bottom, 237, 257 top; Archiv Verkehrsamt, Cologne 112 top; Art Institute of Chicago, Illinois 18, 301 top right; Lala Aufsberg, Sonthofen 46 bottom, 236; Bayerische Staatsbibliothek, Munich 112 bottom left; Bayerische Staatsgemäldesammlungen, Munich 229, 304 top, 304 bottom; Bergen Billedgalleri 288; Biblioteca Nacional, Madrid 269; Bibliotheek der Rijksuniversiteit, Utrecht 104 top; Bibliothèque Nationale, Paris 96, 104 bottom, 122 top, 146, 149; J. Bottin, Paris 54, 61; E. Boudot-Lamotte, Paris 24 bottom, 125 bottom, 138 left, 159; R. Braunmüller, Munich 181; British Library, London 112 bottom right, 153, 154; British Museum, London 13 bottom left, 24 top, 25 top, 25 bottom, 27 top left, 27 bottom, 35, 65 bottom, 66, 109, 117 top, 140 top, 158 top left, 178 left, 250 top, 278 bottom; J. E. Bulloz, Paris 277 top; J. Allan Cash Library, London 47; Chilean Nitrate Photographic Service 14; Courtauld Institute Galleries, London 286; J. E. Dayton, Guernsey 137; Detroit Institute of Arts, Michigan 289; Deutsches Archäologisches Institut, Athens 64 top; Deutsche Fotothek, Dresden 277 bottom; Egyptian Museum, Cairo 39, 41 left, 42 bottom; Egyptian National Library, Cairo 152; Werner Forman Archive, London 37, 40, 43 bottom, 44, 48; Freer Gallery of Art, Smithsonian Institution, Washington, D.C. 144, 145 bottom, 157 bottom, 168 top, 175; Galleria degli Uffizi, Florence 246; Galleria Nazionale d'Arte Moderna, Rome 305; Gemäldegalerie, Berlin-Dahlem 201, 223 bottom; Photographie Giraudon, Paris 72 right, 105, 110, 114, 116, 129 top, 132, 219, 226, 238, 253, 279 bottom, 282 top, 290 right, 229; Glasgow Art Gallery and Museum 214 right; R. Goepper, Cologne 184; Solomon R. Guggenheim Museum, New York 292 right, 303; Frans Halsmuseum, Haarlem 244 top; Hamlyn Group Picture Library 13 top, 13 bottom right, 15 right, 17 bottom, 20, 21, 29, 38, 46 top, 50, 52, 56, 58, 60, 63, 64 bottom, 65 top, 67, 68, 70 top, 70 bottom, 71, 72 left, 73, 74 bottom, 75 top, 75 bottom, 76, 77 left, 77 right, 78 top left, 78 bottom, 81, 82 top, 84 bottom, 86, 92, 93, 94 bottom, 95, 102, 106, 111, 113, 118, 122 bottom, 123, 128 top, 128 bottom, 129 bottom, 133, 145 top, 147, 155, 156, 160, 161, 162, 163, 168 bottom, 169, 173, 174, 180, 183, 185 top, 187 top, 187 bottom, 194 left, 195 right, 198 bottom, 202, 205, 207, 208, 210, 211 bottom, 212 left, 213, 215, 217, 222, 223 top, 224, 225, 227 top, 227 bottom, 228, 232, 233, 235, 239, 241, 242, 244 bottom, 249, 251 bottom, 254 top, 256, 257 bottom, 259, 260, 264 top, 267, 268, 272 top, 273, 274, 275, 276, 278 top, 279 top, 280, 281, 283, 290 bottom, 291, 292 left, 308 top, 310-311, 313, 314 top, 315; Hatay Arkeologii Muzesi, Ankara 33 right; Hessisches Landesmuseum, Darmstadt 230; Hans Hinz, Allschwilz 7, 59; Hirmer Verlag, Munich 23 left, 23 right, 26, 27 top right, 32, 41 right, 43 top, 45 left, 51, 53, 55, 62 right, 85, 89, 90, 101; A. F. Kersting, London 127 bottom; Kunsthalle Bremen 302 top; Kunstmuseum Basel 300; Dr. Andreas Lommel, Munich 17 top; J. Lassus, Paris 84 centre; Bildarchiv Foto Marburg 69 right, 99 bottom, 117 bottom, 125 top left, 125 top right, 126 left; Mas, Barcelona 141 top, 270; F. A. Mella, Milan 88; Metropolitan Museum of Art, New York 57, 139, 212 right, 220; Monumenti, Musei e Gallerie Pontificie, Vatican 74 top, 80; Ann Munchow, Aachen 120; Musée de l'Homme, Paris 15 left, 19; Musée des Augustins, Toulouse 115 left; Musées Nationaux, Paris 11, 34 right, 97, 264 bottom, 265, 290 top; Museum für Islamische Kunst, Berlin-Dahlem 157; Museum für Ostasiatische Kunst, Berlin-Dahlem 179, Museum of Fine Arts, Boston, Massachusetts 157 top right, 284-285; Museum of Islamic Art, Cairo 138 right, 142, 143; Museum of Modern Art, New York 295, 297, 298, 301 bottom, 312 top, 314 bottom; Museum of Primitive Art, New York 12 right; Museum Rietberg, Zurich 176; Museum voor Land-en Volkenkunde, Rotterdam 16; Museu Nacional de Arte Antiga, Lisbon 221; National Gallery, London 251 top, 272 bottom, 284; National Gallery of Art, Washington, D.C. 263; National Museum of India, New Delhi 165 left; National Portrait Gallery, London 261 top, 262 bottom; National Trust, Waddesdon Manor 255; Francis-E. Niffle, Liège 119; Pergamon Museum, Berlin 28; A. Perissonotto, Padua 30; Philadelphia Museum of Art, Pennsylvania 287, 302 bottom, 307 left, 307 right, 309; Pierpont Morgan Library, New York 131, 148; Josephine Powell, Rome 34 left, 36, 98, 170, 171; J. C. S. Priston, Twickenham 12 left; Publifoto, Palermo 62 left; Rijksmuseum, Amsterdam 164, 243, 247 bottom, 248; George Rodger – Magnum 31; A. Roth, Zurich 306; M. Sakamoto, Tokyo 182, 185 bottom; Scala, Antella 42 top, 87 top, 91 top, 91 bottom, 99 top, 103, 124, 127 top, 134, 190, 191, 193, 195 left, 196 left, 197, 198 top, 199, 200 top, 204, 206 top, 209, 216, 218 top, 245; R. W. Schlegelmilch, Frankfurt 121; Raymond V. Schoder, Chicago, Illinois 82 bottom; Skulpturensammlung, Dresden 69 left; Sotheby Parke Bernet, New York 282 bottom; State Hermitage Museum, Leningrad 140 bottom; Statens Museum for Kunst, Copenhagen 296; Tate Gallery, London 262 top, 271, 294, 301 top left, 308 bottom; Tokyo National Museum 178 right, 189; Topkapi Sarayi Muzesi, Istanbul 151 bottom; University of Michigan, Ann Arbor 84 top; Victoria and Albert Museum, London 136, 150, 177, 188, 261 bottom; H. Roger-Viollet, Paris 151 top, 167 bottom; Leonard von Matt, Buochs 79; Wallace Collection, London 254 bottom; Washington University, St Louis 312 bottom; Achille Weider, Zurich 8, 9; J. Ziolo, Paris 192; Zodiaque-Belzeaux 107.

© ADAGP, Paris 1979: 290 right, 299, 300, 301 top right, 303, 307 left, 307 right, 308 bottom, 309, 313, 314 top.

© SPADEM, Paris 1979: 280, 281, 294, 296, 297, 298, 301 top left, 306, 308 top.

© VAGA, New York and SPADEM, Paris 1979: 292.

The illustration on page 289 is from the Detroit Institute of Arts, Michigan, bequest of Henry G. Stevens in memory of Ellen P. and Mary M. Stevens.

Index

319